On the Beat
of Truth

ON THE BEAT OF TRUTH

A Hearing Daughter's Stories of Her Black Deaf Parents

Maxine Childress Brown

Foreword by Scot Brown

Gallaudet University Press
Washington, D.C.

Gallaudet University Press
Washington, DC 20002
http://gupress.gallaudet.edu

Printed in the United States of America

Library of Congress Cataloging-in-Publication Data

Brown, Maxine Childress.
  On the beat of truth : a hearing daughter's stories of her black deaf
parents / Maxine Childress Brown.
     pages cm
  Includes bibliographical references and index.
  ISBN 978-1-56368-552-1 (pbk. : alk. paper) – ISBN 978-1-56368-553-8
(e-book)
     1. Brown, Maxine Childress. 2. Brown, Maxine Childress–Family.
3. Deaf parents–United States–Biography. 4. Children of deaf parents–
United States–Biography. 5.   African Americans with disabilities–
Biography. I. Title.
  HV2534.B75A3 2013
  362.4'23092–dc23
                    2012046554

*My mother, Thomasina Brown Childress
who loved her children unconditionally
and
My father, Herbert Andrew Childress
who struggled all his life*

James Brown, my beloved husband
Our three marvelously talented children:
Scot, Nikki, and Kimberly
My two gifted sisters: Shirley and Khaula
Dear sweet aunt Mary Magdalene Minor (Babe)

Brother Pascal, a Trappist Monk of the Abbey of the
Genesee, who viewed life with a child's innocence
and
Dr. William Talpey, a gifted pediatrician,
who loved flowers as much as my mom
and
Finvola Drury, an extraordinarily dedicated
teacher who insisted I had a story to tell

Contents

Foreword

Scot Brown

Everyone has a story, and is the product of many more stories. The people's historian elevates and exposes the wisdom, wit, humor, and reflections of "Everyday People," or rich lives outside of the perimeter of celebrity. The faces and voices of people encountered daily are, in effect, introductions to stories of lives and communities far too often hidden from social consciousness. The twentieth century saw a dramatic ascension of African American stories in both fiction and nonfiction to a prominent place in literature and historical inquiry. This change continues, with increasingly more complex and nuanced representations of Black lives. Contemporary representations of blackness frequently emphasize the intersection of race with multiple identities and social positions—such as, socioeconomic class, ethnicity, gender, geography, and sexuality.

On the Beat of Truth is the product of my mother's more than twenty-year sojourn into people's history: critically reflecting on her own childhood and adolescent experiences, documenting the memories of Grandma Thomasina, Aunt Mary "Babe" Minor, and other family members. This book provides a glimpse into the cultural world of the Black Deaf community and adds to a growing literature underscoring the intersection of race, deafness, and, by extension, other identities.

Blackness and Deafness were inseparable facets of being for Herbert and Thomasina, and so to, the network of Black Deaf people and institutions that helped sustain them and our family. Grounded in one of the greatest movements of humanity *en masse*—The Great Migration—the family story told here highlights multiple responses to the violence and oppression of American racial apartheid. Just as the Works Progress Administration interviews of those who lived through enslavement were sparked by an awareness of the necessity to record living memories of American slavery, this work answers a kindred and urgent call to document the testimony of folk whose lives were shaped by the quest for community and dignity in the midst of Jim Crow's persistent assault on their humanity—in both the rural south and northern city.

Deafness, Blackness, gender, and poverty all converge as factors that drive migration patterns and hardship faced by the Brown and Childress families as detailed in this account. Some dimensions of this memoir invoke ever-constant themes in the twentieth-century African American experience: flight from impending racial violence, the magnet of economic opportunity, the persistence of racial oppression in the North and the power of Black institution-building in midst of urban segregation. Nevertheless, access to deaf education and employment options (considering their deafness) were also push-and-pull forces affecting Thomasina and Herbert's respective choices and decisions in their movements from the Carolinas and Tennessee, to the metropolitan Washington, D.C., area. In the District, Herbert and Thomasina were heavily involved in clubs and organizations for the Black Deaf community. In some cases these were spaces within institutional pillars of the Black public sphere; such as the deaf worship service of the Shiloh Baptist Church, whereas in other instances they were autonomous social clubs established by and for the Black Deaf community specifically.

Migrations and the rapid growth of Black urban communities in the twentieth century added new dimensions to African American vernacular style and forms of expression, especially in spoken language. In keeping with this trend, the Black American Sign Language (BASL), which shares some operative principles with American Sign Language (ASL) but has its own particular deep structure and syntax, developed. Racially separate neighborhoods along with the segregation of schools for the deaf facilitated the rise of BASL. Both Thomasina and Herbert attended Black deaf institutions and were grounded in both African American communicative form as well as ASL. Furthermore, *On the Beat of Truth* provides a snapshot of processes through which families produced their own signs. Illustrating the workwear of tough agrarian labor, Thomasina's sign for her father, Clarence "Grindaddy" Brown, is synonymous with that of a pair of overalls—characterized by the up and down movements of the thumb and index fingers over the torso, as if detailing a pair of suspenders.

Though a representation of toil was associated with my great-grandfather, Black women in this memoir stand out squarely facing layers of racist, sexist, and economic oppression in both the countryside and city. Many of the day-to-day struggles as remembered by my mother are confrontations with sexism and patriarchy: specifically, in the workplace and, painfully, at home. Indeed, much of the story is driven by my mother's attempt to understand the problematic changes in her father's behavior and treatment of his family. She locates a definitive source of his anger in a specific act of injustice. While this is likely not the sole explanation for his travail, mom's account adds a layer of understanding to the circumstance of being a

Black deaf man determined to be a provider in the midst of poverty, racism, and anti-deaf discrimination.

My grandfather passed away in 1968 at the age of fifty-five. If anger added to his demise, the opposite force sustained Grandma Thomasina. Her consistently loving spirit and disposition left experiences with hardship nearly imperceptible, even to many who knew her well. Living for nearly a century, Thomasina was the Childress family anchor and a special inspiration to her daughters, all three of whom drew strength from her tenacity and sensitivity to the welfare of others. My aunt, Dr. Khaula Murtadha's (known as Barbara in the book) research and scholarship are centered on developing a social justice–oriented pedagogy in education theory and praxis. Aunt Shirley Childress Saxton is a member and sign language interpreter with Sweet Honey in the Rock and has captivated deaf and hearing audiences around the world with innovative sign interpretations of vocal and instrumental sound for more than thirty years. My mom has worked as a community activist in Rochester, New York; taught college courses in African American history and politics; and has been an advocate for the disabled community and human rights, for more than thirty years. *On the Beat of Truth* is her very special addition to the continuum of inspired creativity, drawn from the struggles and sacrifices of those who've come before us.

SELECTED BIBLIOGRAPHY

Jowers-Barber, Sandra. "The Struggle to Educate Black Deaf School-children in Washington, D.C." In *A Fair Chance in the Race of Life: The Role of Gallaudet University in Deaf History*, edited by Brian H. Greenwald and John V. Van Cleve, 113–31. Washington, D.C.: Gallaudet University Press, 2008.

McCaskill, Carolyn. *The Hidden Treasure of Black ASL: Its History and Structure*. Washington, D.C.: Gallaudet University Press, 2011.

Murtadha, Khaula. "Notes from the (Battle)field for Equity in Education," *Leadership and Policy in Schools* 8, no. 3 (2009): 342–54.

Saxton, Shirley Childress. "Shirley Childress Saxton." *Sweet Honey in the Rock* (website). http://www.sweethoney.com/about/Shirley.php.

Wilkerson, Isabel. *The Warmth of Other Suns: The Epic Story of America's Great Migration*. New York: Random House, 2010.

Wright, Mary Herring. *Sounds Like Home: Growing up Black and Deaf in the South*. Washington, D.C.: Gallaudet University Press, 1999.

Prologue

My mother, Thomasina Brown Childress, was a natural storyteller, telling me vivid stories as early as I can remember, from when I was three years old until her death at ninety-six. Stricken with crippling diabetes, renal failure, and ITP (idiopathic thrombocytopenic purpura), Mama would nonetheless reminisce in sign language many of the exceptional episodes in her own life. As the richness of her stories began to unfold, I as a youngster, would seek out further details. Her hands would flow with instant memories, as I asked about the rural South; or the segregated residential school; or about her married life to my father, Herbert Childress. My mother's description of life in the South was so revealing: when segregation was the law of the land; and deaf children attended segregated schools for the 'colored' deaf and blind.

I decided right then and there to write a book documenting all that she divulged—from my mother's birth in South Carolina to my father's in Tennessee. The more stories my mother shared with me, the more I became committed to not only write about my family's life but also to write about significant moments in my own life. I wanted to write about what it was like growing up in a deaf black home where there were voices and words foreign to a young and impressionable hearing child's ear, and where there was a noticeable difference in my parent's reaction and response to white people.

That's when I registered for a memoir writing class taught by an extraordinarily talented instructor, Finvola (Fin) Drury at Writers and Books Literary Center. (Up until that time, all my writing was primarily in academe: writing grants, proposals, and articles.) I benefitted tremendously from Fin's encouragement to write this memoir and her instruction as to how to write it. She provided, not only to me but also to the entire class, inspiration and phenomenal insight into our stories such that we marveled at her capacity to see what we could not see.

So I finally began to write—about growing up during the forties, fifties, and sixties in Washington, D.C., using American Sign Language as my first language in our household. I lived in an all-black community, and attended all-black schools. I am the oldest of three children, all girls (to my father's lasting consternation). This is a story of my early years growing up in a unique family with many contrasts: passionate love of family versus tension and misunderstanding; warmth and love versus confrontation and hostility; poverty versus the struggle to maintain a standard of living slightly above desperation; and courage versus depression. A true profile in courage in the lives of two deaf people during the first half of the twentieth century.

It is also the story of two highly intelligent deaf black parents who struggle against the odds to gain success in their endeavors, with obstacles posed by their deafness and their skin color. This is the story of the lives of my mother and father intertwined with mine, making their story inseparable from my journey throughout my childhood. It covers a span of approximately fifty years, initially concentrating on my parents' experiences from 1913 to the 1940s, when deaf education reflected a wholly different era and approaches to teaching. For example, I gleaned from my parents' stories that speech or speech reading did not exist in instructional form within the segregated deaf schools of the South. And neither was the use of hearing aids or any hearing amplification apparatus. Teletype machines for the deaf did not exist. Relay systems had not been invented yet, and certainly not cochlear implants, a modern day occurrence.

My mother lived with me for twenty years until her death in Rochester, New York, where she often told her history from her remarkable memory: describing details, rendering accurate quotes, and sketching vignettes. I began to document her stories when she was seventy-five years old and often recited these stories back to her, verifying her memory of facts, events, and circumstances. Substantiation of her renditions was most often made through her sister, Mary Magdalene Minor (Aunt Babe), who was seven years younger than my mother. I recorded Mary's verbal sketches until her death at age ninety in December 2010. In the past year, I ascertained and confirmed more facts from my cousin, Della Handy Watters, daughter of my mother's other sister, Della; David Gillis, son of Mary Magdalene Minor; as well as from my father's youngest sister, Marjorie Saxton.

My research was further confirmed by census data and genealogy records, which provided historical information, specifically data regarding the dates of my grandparents' birth, marriage, occupations, number of children, and their names.

Note that Mama and Daddy's words, as well as those of other deaf persons, are written as if they are speaking in American Sign Language (ASL). In other words, I tried to write their words in sentences the way they would normally "sign" them in ASL. All their thoughts and words are printed here in italics. If an English word is usually omitted in ASL, I have added it inside parentheses to clarify the meaning of a sentence. Also, when my parents were young, African Americans were called "colored" and, later, "Negroes." This book attempts to record life as it was then. Please note when I tell stories that have occurred in my own life, rather than in my parents' life, I prefer to use "Black" or "African Americans."

Acknowledgments

There were many individuals who made this book possible as proofreaders, researchers, editors, and photographers as well as religious organizations offering quiet quarters to write. Special recognition is made to Ivey Wallace whose insightful questions shaped the content of this book.

Abbey of the Genesee,
Piffard, New York

About Time magazine: James and Carolyne Blount

Joan Baier

Laura Bambury

James Brown

Scot Brown

Finvola Drury

Sandra Jowers-Barber

Mercy Prayer Center

Joan Lipscomb Solomon

Jared Sabado

Ivey Wallace

Angela Williams-Phillips

Students in Finvola Drury's class

Nancy Cline

Lydia Garrity

Kim Kimball

Carolyn Merrian

Harriet Parmelee

Bobbie Reifsteck

Lucida Sangree

Sue Whan

RELATIVES

Shirley Childress Saxton,
   Reginald Johnson,
   Deon Johnson
Khaula Murtadha, Abdul-Khaliq
   Murtadha, Adam Murtadha,
   Abdul-Haleem Young,
   Yusuf Young, Ahmed Young,
   Usama Young, Thomasina
   Watts
Della and Andrew Handy,
   Andrew (Pat) Handy, Della
   (Babe Sis) Watters, Clarence
   (Brother) Handy
Ruth and Arthur Orether
   Wagoner, Ruth
   (Bonnie) Wagoner Rucker,
   Louise, Wagoner Gross
Loretta Wagoner Warfield,
   Mary Magdalene (Matt)
   Wagoner,
   Arthur Orether (Pep)
   Wagoner, Jr.

Mary Magdalene Minor,
   Joseph Gillis,
   Clarence Gillis, Charles
   Gillis, and David Gillis
Arnell and John Richmond,
   Arnold Richmond
Marjorie Saxton and her
   daughter, Dorothy
Susie and George
   Henderson, and their sons,
   George, Melvin, Irving,
   and Major
Ann Brown, Ernest Brown,
   Beverly Brown,
   William Brown, Carol
   Brown, Carl Brown
Barbara Akers, Michael
   Akers, Michelle
   Akers, Wayne Akers

Nero/Brown Family Tree

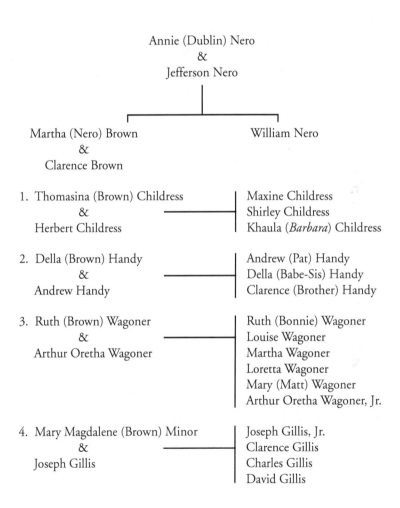

Annie (Dublin) Nero
&
Jefferson Nero

Martha (Nero) Brown
&
Clarence Brown

William Nero

1. Thomasina (Brown) Childress
   &
   Herbert Childress

   Maxine Childress
   Shirley Childress
   Khaula (*Barbara*) Childress

2. Della (Brown) Handy
   &
   Andrew Handy

   Andrew (Pat) Handy
   Della (Babe-Sis) Handy
   Clarence (Brother) Handy

3. Ruth (Brown) Wagoner
   &
   Arthur Oretha Wagoner

   Ruth (Bonnie) Wagoner
   Louise Wagoner
   Martha Wagoner
   Loretta Wagoner
   Mary (Matt) Wagoner
   Arthur Oretha Wagoner, Jr.

4. Mary Magdalene (Brown) Minor
   &
   Joseph Gillis

   Joseph Gillis, Jr.
   Clarence Gillis
   Charles Gillis
   David Gillis

Childress Family Tree

Susie Hicks (Thurman) Childress*
&
Berry Childress**

|

1. Arnell (Childress) Richmond
   &
   John Richmond

2. Odell Childress***

3. Herbert Childress   Maxine Childress
        &   Shirley Childress
   Thomasina (Brown) Childress   Khaula (*Barbara*)
                               Childress

4. Margery Childress Young Saxton
        &   Dorothy Young
   (Unknown) Young

* Susie had children from her first marriage: Major, Mary, Laura, Mattie, Susie, and William.
** Berry claimed all the Thurman children (children from his wife's first marriage) as his own and insisted his stepchildren and his own blood children were equal brothers and sisters.
*** Odell and Arnell were identical twins; Odell died as a child.

On the Beat
of Truth

1

A Policeman Comes A-Knockin'

"My father wants to know what is he going to jail for."

My father was the handsomest man I have ever known. He was deaf. My mother was the prettiest woman I have ever seen. She was deaf. Together they used American Sign Language. And that was the language of my youth.

If sign language could be heard, my mother's voice would be soft and gentle, with her hands making small circular motions connoting her shyness and reservation. Thomasina Brown Childress, born 1914 in Edgefield, South Carolina, was beautiful, with an oval face and large eyes, full lips, a pecan-brown complexion, shoulder-length hair straightened with a hot straightening comb, and a thin willowy figure. She was described as eloquent and poised in the way she walked, dressed, and talked.

My daddy, Herbert Andrew Childress, born 1913 in Nashville, Tennessee, could be described as the exact opposite of my mother. While he too was extremely good-looking, his outstanding features were his light mulatto complexion, his thin lips, his keen nose, and his soft straight hair. His physical stature was stocky, with broad shoulders and muscular arms and thighs. My father's hands were massive, and his signs were powerful, dominating, and forthright, conveying strength and authority.

One of Mama and Daddy's proudest moments was when the cinderblock bungalow at 5901 Clay Street was finally built in 1946, constructed primarily by my mother's daddy, Clarence Brown, a tall lanky dark-complexioned man, who had prided himself on being a master bricklayer. I called my grandfather Grindaddy because that's how Mama pronounced it, and he would lovingly hug me whenever I called out his name.

One spring day in 1945 when I was only two years old, Grindaddy took Herbert to see land blanketed with trees in northeast Washington, D.C., known as the "boondocks" because in those days, it was in the rural part of the District of Columbia.

Grindaddy drove up to the land in his old beat-up, rusty car; he took my father by the arm and waved his massive hand toward a large plot of land. Then, walking to the back of the trunk, Clarence pulled out a thick carpenter pencil and a small notepad, and scrawled in large letters, "You buy land. I build house." My father stared at the note. Clarence pointed to himself and then to Herbert, and mouthed the words "We build you a house." My father responded with a bobbing of his head, showing his ecstatic joy, and together they went to downtown Washington to purchase two lots of land on the corner of Fifty-Ninth and Clay at a price of three hundred dollars.

This was an area long recognized as a segregated area for "Negroes," located a distance from the nation's Capitol, where it was understood that "Negroes" could build homes to live, erect "colored" schools for their children, and buy food from the single-owner grocery stores interspersed throughout the area.

These were "colored" people dedicated to obtaining a better life by working hard, despite having little formal education. Many of them had migrated from the South during and after the Great Depression in search of work. They survived by filling many service jobs, from domestic work, to working

Herbert Childress and his father-in-law, Clarence Brown, before they built our house together. They were called the "D.C. Big Shots."

as dishwashers and janitors in hotels and restaurants. They also found work in the privately owned homes of white people. Many "Negroes" found work in the construction business doing menial grunt work, lifting and toting heavy loads of brick and mortar in the hot, humid air that permeated D.C.

Such was the case with Grindaddy, who had migrated here from Concord, North Carolina. So it was natural for him to gravitate to this part of "Negro" town, D.C.

Building the house was a major task that consumed both my father and grandfather's evenings and weekends for almost a year: clearing the land of the trees, carrying cinderblocks to the area marked off by string, and slathering cement between each piece of cinderblock.

The cherished outcome from their arduous sweaty hard work was a shotgun bungalow with a kitchen, a living room, one bathroom, and two bedrooms. (A shotgun house is one where a shooter could shoot a shotgun at the front door of a

Herbert (left) and Clarence Brown, a bricklayer, began building a home at 5901 Clay St., N.E., in Washington, D.C., in 1947. Herbert was the first Black deaf person to build his own home in D.C.

The partially built house, which when completed was painted white with red trim.

bungalow and the bullet would sail straight through the house and out the back door.) The tiny house was bordered on the south and east sides by a variety of lush green trees: oak, elm, and willow; on the north side of the house, cutting through those trees, was a dirt road leading to a creek some five hundred feet away. Small boulders and darting tadpoles peppered the creek, with slimy goo at its bottom that when disturbed swirled into dark pools of muddy water.

As a kid, I would often step on the boulders, crossing the creek to the other side to climb a steep bank, which led me to acres of flat land covered with vinca vine growing everywhere. I loved to wander through the fields and look among the flowers, especially for four-leaf clovers to bring home for good luck.

When I climbed back down to the creek, I occasionally threw a pebble in the water and watched the tadpoles dart here and there. As I left the creek and skipped down the narrow dirt road, I reached our large backyard, which was strewn with wild Concord grapes hanging from makeshift trellises that seemed to have been there for ages, and as I finally entered the backdoor, deposited the flowers on the kitchen table, and ran straight through the house to climb a wild cherry tree growing right in our front yard. The front of our house faced Clay Street and was met by two other shotgun houses sixty feet apart: a burgundy red house owned by the Fultons and a brick house where the Millses lived. Neither the Fultons nor the Millses had any children, making Clay Street quiet and secluded.

On Fifty-Ninth Street there were two houses on the south side and two houses facing them across the street. We knew only one family, the Ricks family, who moved from Rocky Mount, North Carolina, to settle at 311 Fifty-Ninth Street. In the early days, their house had an outhouse attached to it in the backyard, and only when the city inspectors demanded it, did they build a bathroom inside their home. There were Mr. and Mrs. Ricks and their three children (the two oldest, Slim and Evelyn, were adults, and the youngest, Carol, was three years older than I).

The Rickses were probably the first residents to build in that area, and they were the family who welcomed my mother and father to the neighborhood. Having no telephone in our house, Mama or Daddy would send me to their home to use their telephone. On any given day, I would open the gate of their white picket fence, knock on the door, and usually be greeted by Mrs. Ricks.

I politely asked, "Can I use the telephone please? My mother wants me to call her sister."

"Why you sure 'nuff can, just come on in," said Mrs. Ricks, greeting me with a kindly southern smile and pointing to the black telephone situated on a nearby table in the living room. While going to make the phone call, I basked in the cooking smells floating through the house, savoring the aroma of freshly baked biscuits or pound cake.

"We gonna have dinner. Have some?" asked Mrs. Ricks.

"No. Thank you," I replied, drooling for just one bite, but following Mama's strict instructions to never accept food from anyone.

GROWING up in our community, I saw only Black people. In fact, I thought the entire world consisted mostly of Black people with different shades of beige, brown, and black skins, from the very light, nearly white, complexion to the darkest of the dark.

Rarely did white people ever come to our house. If truth be told, I seldom saw white people in Washington, D.C., proper, unless I went downtown with Mama. Certainly not in our immediate neighborhood in northeast Washington, just six blocks from the Maryland state line separating Seat Pleasant, Maryland, from Washington, D.C. Our neighbors and friends were Black. The postman was Black. My teachers were Black. All the kids I knew were Black. Every once in a while, I would see a white person such as Mr. Don, who owned the grocery store some five blocks away, on the corner of Sixty-First and Dix Streets, where Mama and Daddy bought food on credit. Daddy's boss, Sam the Italian, was white.

Mama and Daddy had a few deaf white friends. My father had a deaf white friend with a crew cut who worked at Fanny Farmer candies, and occasionally they went fishing together. Mama did cleaning in deaf white people's houses in Maryland or faraway Virginia. She took me with her to do the day work: dusting, vacuuming, sweeping, polishing the furniture, or washing the dishes. We traveled on the bus to the white people's homes, transferring from one bus to another three different times, traveling two hours or more. The farther we rode out to Virginia or Maryland, the whiter the complexion of the riders on the bus. By the time we arrived at our destination, Mama and I were the only Black people on the bus.

My mother and I cleaned for Reverend and Mrs. Soulles, white evangelists who occasionally preached at our church, Shiloh Baptist, in Washington, D.C. He could hear, and his wife, who was deaf, spoke in a shrill falsetto voice, so shrill it was barely tolerable to listen to, especially when she stood before our deaf congregation to sing. And sing she would. She signed broad sweeping hand gestures while simultaneously singing full-throated in a variety of notes, most of which did not resemble the tune itself. The Black deaf churchgoers enjoyed Mrs. Soulles' deaf singing and tolerated Reverend Soulles' preaching every four or five weeks. The Soulles were really an anomaly since they were the only white people at Shiloh Baptist Church, a church of at least a thousand hearing and fifty deaf black people. Here was Shiloh Baptist on Ninth and P Streets, N.W., in the midst of a predominantly black neighborhood, and there was Reverend Soulles passionately preaching and signing his soul out to save Black deaf churchgoers from going to hell. Daddy said it was funny that the good reverend's last name was "Soulles" and that they had come to save souls. But it was Mama who was eager to tell me that Reverend Soulles would lose his soul now, since he made love to a young deaf girl. Reverend Soulles had publicly confessed the egregious sin to his wife and to church members in his own white deaf church, a guarantee that the news would spread like wildfire within the deaf communities, black and white, since everyone knew that news traveled faster in the deaf community than in the hearing world. Word-of-mouth gossip can zip like lightning from one deaf household to another, with deaf folk traveling from near and far to spread the word.

As I say, rarely did white people come to our house, and if one did, we assumed that the white person was there in some official capacity. And so it was on this particular day. Daddy, wearing his favorite red flannel plaid shirt and old wrinkled tan slacks, was sitting in his favorite chair in the living room reading the comics in the *Washington Post*, stopping every once in a while to sing:

My bonnie lies over the ocean.

My bonnie lies over the sea.

Bring back, bring back, bring back my bonnie to me.

Dad's voice screeched in a high-pitched wail, *"I am singing, 'My bonnie lies over the ocean,'"* he signed to me with glee. Clearly proud of himself, he continued to make the shrieking noise, grinning all the while.

"Your voice awful," I signed back to him, thinking that he r-e-a-l-l-y can't hear himself because if he could, he would never sing. He looked at me, determined now to sing even louder, and with more resolve. His face was boyish, almost pretty by many women's standards, a sweet cherub face. His mulatto complexion and his long black straight hair, with a slight wave framing his face, gave him a handsome look. His thin lips opened again to let out the loud wail.

Sunday was Daddy's only day off after working six days a week at Sam's Shoe Repair Shop. He took delight and relish in acting childlike, happy he was free for at least a day from the drudgery of repairing heels and soles, free from the occasional stench of people's feet imprinted in old shoes, free from the lingering smell of leather and shoeshine wax.

IT WAS 1953, I was ten years old and in the fifth grade at Richardson Elementary School. I was sitting on the floor, watching our five-year-old television, when the naked lightbulb flashed over the front door in the living room, flicker . . . flicker . . . flicker. Daddy went to the door when he saw the lightbulb flashing, and I followed, a few steps behind him. A big broad-shouldered white man stood there, looking very somber.

Herbert learned his trade as a shoe repairman and cobbler at the Maryland School for the Colored Blind and Deaf at Overlea located outside Baltimore, Maryland. With pride, he was a shoe repairman his entire life and boasted that he repaired the shoes of J. Edgar Hoover, famed head of the FBI.

"Herbert Childress?"

Daddy looked down at me, expecting me to begin interpreting the man's words. I uneasily and shyly moved closer beside Daddy and said, "My father can't hear or talk."

Standing in the doorway, the man looked at me slightly puzzled, then looked at my father, and back at me.

"Tell him he's under arrest." He paused a moment and then gave Daddy a white folded paper, glaring at him. The white man hesitated; he may have thought we didn't understand the gravity of the situation when he stared at my father and then at me saying, "I have to take your father to jail." My signs became excitable as I told Daddy that the man says you are going to jail.

Daddy stared down at the paper, "What? What?" alarm spreading on his face. I didn't know why he was going to jail, so I just repeated my signs, "Man say you jail."

"Jail? Jail? For what?" Flustered, not believing what he was seeing, he said, "Mistake. Wrong. Jail what for?"

I saw the panic on Daddy's face. The confusion and fear. I began to feel a sense of foreboding.

"My daddy wants to know what is he going to jail for."

The man, standing there in the doorway, facing my father and me, did not seem as confrontational as he had been a second or two earlier, and his words became more patient.

"Tell him they say he has done a bad thing. He has to get a lawyer. But first he has to come with me to the police station."

My father was led to the police car, where he slid onto the backseat. At the station, Daddy scribbled on a notepad that he would like them to call his sister, Arnell Richmond. Arnell was his youngest sister and freely used homemade signs, gestures, and an occasional letter in fingerspelling when talking with her brother. When uncertain if he understood her, she would pull out notepaper and pencil and write to him.

In the following days and weeks, the house took on a gray cast of hopelessness and gloom, with seething anger quietly pervading the rooms. Tension, bickering, and a plague of sadness consumed us all. The shadow of fear hovered over us: the fear of the police, the lawyers, and the white people who were going to make Daddy go to jail. Words such as "bail" "summons" and "character witnesses" were thrown about, words I didn't understand, as hearing people came to the house to talk to my father. I was expected to understand, expected to interpret, expected to make certain Daddy understood what was taking place. That's when I realized how smart he was—he understood my signs and fingerspelling even when I did not. I didn't know what I was saying, I was just spelling out the words or using a hand sign that might translate the sentence correctly. I had no idea what it all meant. But Daddy did, as he calmly asked me a question or two and nodded his head to indicate he comprehended it all.

It was my aunt Arnell who made me understand the seriousness of the accusation and of Daddy's situation.

"My lawd, my lawd, she said. "Der's this man runnin' round pullin' out his thing and tryin' to scare all the children. Oh my goodness, what's dis world comin' to? Crazy people everywhere. I know dat's not Herbert. Herbert would n-e-v-e-r do anything like dat."

When I heard the reference to "thing," I thought she meant a gun.

"You mean he's pulling out his gun," I said.

"No, no, chile, the man pulls out his ding-a-ling outda his pants. Oh my God, oh my God." She flopped in Daddy's favorite chair, kicked off her shoes, exposing her swollen feet, and gasped for air as she graphically gave the details as she knew them using homemade invented gestures to talk to my father since she barely knew any formal sign language. Aunt Arnell exaggerated her thin lips and facial expressions so that Daddy could read her lips to understand some of her words. He pulled out pen and paper and wrote to her. And she nodded her round head and looked affectionately at Daddy as he wrote.

Arnell had hazel eyes, a light mulatto complexion, a very stout body, and stringy straight hair that caressed her sloping shoulders. Arnell's most endearing feature was one that all could easily see: she adored my father. "We'll git you oudda dis mess. Lawd have mercy. Lawd have mercy."

Mama was stunned by it all, and as a result, she didn't know what to do. She had no experience with lawyers, jails, or even the police. The only thing she knew how to do was to become virtually invisible and not talk to Daddy or me about the whole mess.

Arnell hired a lawyer, who in turn gave us all the legal particulars, explaining to the family these facts: Daddy was accused by a woman who lived three or four blocks away of indecent exposure. A man had roamed around the neighborhood pulling out his "ding-a-ling" for all to see, and while doing this ghastly thing, he made creepy awkward sounds. The weird man did this at all hours of the morning, day, and afternoon, frightening children going to and from school.

The intervening weeks, although blurry and vague, whizzed by, and the trial was suddenly upon us. The first day I sat in the courtroom audience wearing my Sunday-go-to-church dress Mama made for me. I am awed by the austere mahogany walls, how slick the wood, how smooth, and how rich. There were white men everywhere, dressed in gray or black listless clothes, and not one wearing a smile. Big, unfamiliar legal terms were casually bandied back and forth in the courtroom between the lawyers and the judge. Some of the white men leaned over and talked to other white men. I sat there in the pews, not understanding anything but trying my best to absorb everything, feeling out of place, struggling to be comfortable.

A tall, thin white man walked up to my father and introduced himself as his interpreter. Daddy shook his hand and was genuinely relieved to see him. The interpreter stood by the witness box. The presiding judge, wearing his black robe, entered the courtroom through one of the paneled doors on the left. He was the scariest white man I had ever seen.

Suddenly a booming voice from nowhere yelled, "Hear ye! Hear ye! Please rise." Everyone stood up, and Mama and I jumped to our feet, holding hands!

The prosecutor launched his case by calling on the neighbor who filed the charges, the woman whose child complained that a man showed her his "private thing" while she was on her way to school.

"The man made these weird sounds," said the woman. "My daughter says it was Mr. Childress because she heard him making that kind of sound when she passed by his house one day when he was cutting grass."

"Objection! Objection! That's all hearsay," yelled Daddy's lawyer.

"I'm going to allow the mother to testify to what her daughter told her," said the judge. "I think it would be too hard on the child to recall all that happened. And I am willing to take the word of the child's mother because she is under oath."

I could hear the attorney sigh as my father was sitting next to him. There was no expression of emotion on Daddy's face, which led me to wonder whether he understood the interpreter's description of exactly what had happened.

A short time later, our lawyer explained to Daddy and Aunt Arnell that not all was lost, because we would now have our say. He called person after person to come forward stating that Herbert was a very good person. I heard someone whisper that they were character witnesses. There were Mr. and Mrs. Mills, our neighbors across the street, who said they had known Daddy for many years, and "he is a good family man who is very proud of his children. Why, Herbert Childress even lets us take his daughter to Sunday school at St. Paul's Episcopal Church."

Then Daddy's boss, Sam, a short stubby Italian man, came forward to say that Daddy was a very hard worker and was always on time. "In fact, I don't need to look at the clock in the mornings to tell you what time it is. I just know when Herbert gets to work, it is 8:15 a.m. sharp. Yes sirree, five days a week it's 8:15, and 8:30 on Saturdays. No. No. I don't recollect Herbert ever missed a day from work in all the ten years he has worked for me."

There was the black minister from Shiloh Baptist, who testified that Daddy would come to church on Sunday nights with his family. "Yes, I preach to deaf people on Sunday nights. I don't know sign language myself—I have an interpreter sign for me, Mr. Harry Lee. But I've come to know all the deaf families who attend the services. Well, most of them, once in a while there'd be a new person there from out of town. No. No. I don't preach every Sunday. Every once in a while, especially on the fourth or fifth Sunday, Reverend Soulles would preach there. He's a visiting pastor who knows sign language."

I looked around to see if Reverend Soulles was in the courtroom; he was not. But I did see Mr. Harry Lee, a tall, lanky, very light-complexioned deaf black man who had gained both the trust and affection of the deaf Negro community because he could speak so clearly, and had residual hearing. He often helped his friends by acting as an interpreter or mediator of sorts. His speech was clear and crisp, easily understandable without any slurs. He must have lost his hearing at a much older age than when Daddy lost his. Anyway, Mr. Lee told of Daddy's civic activities, that Daddy was one of the founders of a social club for the deaf for "colored people."

Then "Banana" came forward, too. Because her complexion was a pale, almost yellowish, coloring, I called her Banana. I never learned her real name. She said that Daddy and Mama would stop at her ice cream fountain shop most Sunday nights after church services, just before catching the streetcar home. It really felt good to see Banana, a six-foot-tall, broad-shouldered woman who seemed to be the nicest person I didn't know.

One by one, people were brought in by Daddy's lawyer to give supporting testimony for my father.

Then it was time for my father to testify. The interpreter came forward, too. Daddy was sworn in, and then a rash of questions were thrust at him by lawyers. The interpreter meticulously translated verbatim in Signed English, signing and fingerspelling literally—word for word, everything that was said.

I marveled at how fast his fingers flew. Everything he signed was grammatically correct. There were no gestures, no omissions or changing of signs to make a point clearer. As I listened and watched the interpreter, I saw how his signs were different from those signs Mama and Daddy taught me. He signed the word "what" with an index finger going across the palm of the other hand, while I used both hands palms up and shake them a little, and the word "how" was signed differently, too.

As the interpreter continued his crisp translation, putting the lawyers' questions to my father, Daddy began to frown. His eyes squinted and he shook his head.

"I not understand," said my father.

The interpreter tried to sign the questions again, this time changing a phrase or word in an effort to be understood.

Daddy paused and signed, *"Say again, please."* He squinted his eyes again, longer this time, and slowly shook his head, *"Not understand. Not understand you say. Say again."*

The interpreter obviously frustrated, turned to the judge and said, "It's clear that Mr. Childress does not understand my signs."

Now the lawyers and the judge became agitated, not knowing what to do. Apparently, this was an obstacle they had not anticipated.

The judge then said to the interpreter, "Ask him if he has a preference for an interpreter? Is there someone he d-o-e-s understand?"

Then the interpreter signed slowly, intently, "You know someone who can sign you can understand?"

"Yes, my daughter Maxine sign."

The prosecutor and the interpreter looked in the direction my father was pointing. I sat on the front row, behind the swinging wooden gate, separating the courtroom audience from the legal people.

"Are you Maxine? Can you interpret for your father?"

I meekly nodded and then stood up to walk through the swinging gate. My knees trembled as I walked erectly, thinking to myself, "I can't be scared, so scared I don't know how to sign those big words." The lawyers began to talk in a quiet tone, almost whispering, as they put their questions in simple phrases.

"Ask your father where he works."

"You tell I shoe repairman, Sam's shoe repair." Daddy signed and fingerspelled each word slowly, deliberately, and with extreme measure.

Ask your father what time he goes to work.
"I leave home 7:30. I arrive work sometimes 8:15, 8:30. I buy coffee before work (at) White Castle."
"Ask your father if he has ever been late or missed certain days from work."
"No, I never late. One time bus break down. I late one hour. Most time never late, never miss work."
"Ask your father if he knows that he makes weird sounds when he talks."
"I don't know, I can't hear," said Daddy. There were a few chuckles in the courtroom.
"Ask your father if he drinks alcohol," the lawyer wanted to know.
I quickly had a conversation in my head: "Alcohol? Does he mean alcohol I rub my body with . . . no, no, that can't be. Maybe he's asking about a glass with whiskey in it, or does he mean beer which has alcohol in it—Daddy drinks a lot of beer." My thoughts zigged and zagged in my mind. My fingers were quivering, as I began to fingerspell the word "do," then signed the words "you drink" then my hands visibly trembled, as I spelled out the word "alcohol." Daddy looked at me with a piercing stare.
He had read my mind as he signed, *"Which? Beer or whiskey?"*
I heard my voice; it sounded shrill, as I tried to be loud enough for the prosecutor to hear me. I must get the signing correct . . . just right, but I must help Daddy. I knew he drank cans and cans of beer.
"My father says which one, beer or whiskey?"
"Whiskey," said the prosecutor.
I signed the word "whiskey."
"Yes, I drink whiskey."

Ask your father how much whiskey he drinks.

My hands felt sweaty as I became even more tense. I heard the silence in the room and wondered if everyone was holding their breath to see how Daddy would answer the question.

"I drink this much." Daddy, pulling together his thumb and index finger in one sign, made a gesture signaling the approximate size of a shot glass of whiskey.

"My father says this much." And I imitated the sign my father made.

The lawyer shook his head and laughed. Spectators laughed. The judge snickered. They're all laughing, I thought. That means everything's all right. I looked over at Daddy, who sighed in relief to see others smiling, and he began to smile himself.

Finally, the lawyers made closing statements; afterward the jury plodded out of the courtroom one by one. Then there was the anxious waiting: one, two, three hours later. When the jury returned, a woman appearing very refined in a gray tweed suit announced the jury had reached a verdict. The original interpreter stood in front of my father and began to sign, "We the jury find the defendant, Herbert A. Childress, not guilty."

I sat directly behind Daddy when I heard the verdict and saw his broad arched shoulders suddenly slump down in relief. His lawyer turned to him, shook his hand, and people came from everywhere to congratulate him. But it was obvious Daddy was not happy; he nodded his head and swept Mama, Arnell, and me out the courtroom to the elevators.

The attractively dressed woman walked over to us while we were standing at the elevator with the lawyers. She looked directly at me. "Tell your father I was one of the jurors. I just knew he couldn't have done those things."

Then Daddy's lawyer said, "Aren't you pleased so many people have come to help you. It doesn't mean the woman who brought these charges against you didn't believe this happened. It was just a case of mistaken identity."

I looked at Daddy and signed, "Lawyers say woman make mistake."

He grimaced. His eyes, his face, his breathing, even his stature, all conveyed hatred.

"She make me shame. I pain. I pain my heart. People think bad man me. They think because I deaf, I bad things. I hate woman." He flicked his middle fingers off his thumbs, signing the word "hate" as if it were venom.

As we left the courthouse, we began to go in separate directions. Mama had somewhere to go. Aunt Arnell went in another direction, the lawyer in still another. I planned to go with Daddy to the bus stop, where I would go home, and he to his job. As I walked alongside him, I suddenly heard his teeth grinding, gritting against each other. It was a soft gnawing sound. Grit. Grit. Grit. His upper teeth were grinding against his lower. I looked at him; he was staring directly ahead. His clenched lips were pulled in tightly. His pretty face, pale almost colorless, looked puffy and filled with agony. The fingers on his right hand were moving back and forth as if he were playing the piano. Was he talking to himself? His mind seemed far away. I wanted to say something soothing, but I didn't know what to say to him. We walked beside each other for a few steps. As we crossed the street, he grabbed my hand, looked both ways for approaching cars. I was suddenly conscious of the dampness in the air, the wet autumn-hued leaves on the ground, and the brisk gentle wind blowing in our faces. I clenched his big hand and felt the calluses of hard work. Holding his hand felt so good and secure.

I began to long for things to be as they were. I wanted the old daddy back, the daddy who would smile that wry smile, coyly, when I asked him how did he kiss Mama because his lips were too thin. *"My secret,"* he said. I wanted the daddy back who forgave me for sneaking into his room and trying to steal Fanny Farmer candy given him by his white deaf friend. I wanted the daddy back who would let me comb and plait his hair and would smile when his hair clearly was too straight to be braided and would then unravel. I wanted the daddy back who sang "My bonnie lies over the ocean" with such glee. I'd even forgive him for yelling at us, getting drunk, and insisting that we ate too much and spent all his money. The daddy who drank too much beer and told jokes only he thought were funny. It would be all right if he yelled and screamed at us the way he used to. I just wanted that daddy to come back.

Although he was holding my hand, I felt him slipping, slipping through my fingers, his bitterness, his fury, his anger was slipping, slipping into his world of revenge, of getting even. "I kill her!" "Sheen! Sheen!" "Mong Fong!" "Mong Fong!" his pronunciation of "shit" and "motherfucker."

In the days and weeks following the court trial, Daddy became obsessed with the idea of getting even with the woman, and he continually shrieked obscenities everywhere: when he sat in the living room reading the newspaper, he began to swear, "Sheen, mong fong"; when he ate dinner, he grimaced at the food and said, "Sheen, mong fong"; even when he went to the bathroom, I heard him through our thin walls, "Mong fong." He came home from work reeking of booze and still yelling obscenities. *"I sue her. I take her house. I take everything. I no care she poor. She must pay."* His hands, his face, his body, wanted revenge.

Some weeks later I went with him to see a lawyer. We entered his small office where the well-dressed, chocolate-brown-complexioned lawyer listened carefully as we retold the saga of what had happened to my father. The lawyer responded in measured words, "Well, I certainly believe he has a case. Does she own her own home? Where does she work? We can attach her salary." I sensed my father's momentary optimism that he would at last have sweet vengeance.

We left the lawyer's office to catch the bus and report to Aunt Arnell that we had good news—we were going to sue the woman. We caught the H Street bus and disembarked on Twelfth Street, N.E., at Arnell's row house, only a few miles from Capitol Hill. Daddy traveled this bus route at least once a week to visit his sister, just to eat her home-cooked meals and converse with her by fingerspelling and gesturing a few words. She was the one person he could always depend on to help him. But just as important, she gushed with love for him while bringing him up-to-date news from Tennessee.

This time, when we stepped through her foyer into the living room, our excitement was evident.

"Tell her, tell her what the lawyer said," my father signed. He could hardly contain his glee, but was soon devastated when Arnell became visibly overcome with weariness. Her once-smooth face now showed signs of worry wrinkles on her forehead and dark bags under her eyes as she sat beside Daddy on the purple velvet sofa, struggling to sign that she had had enough. She shook her head and exaggerated the words, "No, No," then pointed to herself and slowly fingerspelled the word "tired."

"Maxine, tell Herbert this case has been a nightmare." Not knowing a sign for the word nightmare, I signed, "This bad dream." Daddy gave her a blank stare, either not understanding me or refusing to acknowledge the possibility of giving up.

Arnell repeated the word "nightmare" several times.

"Oh Lawd, please, please Herbert, let it go. Dis here has been a nightmare. A nightmare, I tell ya, a plain nightmare. Let it go," she pleaded. "She's poor. You'll git nothin'. And it's goin' to cost you a whole lotta money to hire a lawyer, too."

My father told me to tell Arnell that the woman owns her home. And then he asked Arnell, almost as an afterthought, how much a lawyer would cost.

"Well, you tell him, Maxine, that it's gonna cost him hundreds and hundreds of dollars." As I translated this for Daddy, I saw him become devastated as the prospect of justice visited became a piercing disappointment; he knew that his sixty-five-dollar-a-week salary wouldn't allow him to pay for a lawyer.

"I sue her," he repeated it several times.

But Aunt Arnell was just as adamant. "Let it go," she pleaded. "The woman is poor. You'll git nothin'."

I signed, "No money from woman. Woman poor."

My father reminded Arnell for a second time that the woman owned her own home, but Aunt Arnell resorted to a threat: "If you do this, I'm not gonna help you." As I interpreted these words to Daddy, I saw him stare at her, seething, not believing she had the audacity to refuse to help him. He stood up, and without saying good-bye to his sister, he walked out of the room, turned, and beckoned for me to join him.

"Come, we go home."

We put on our coats and walked into the dark night, down Twelfth Street to H Street, where there were many lit shops dotting the bus route where we waited for the X2 Seat Pleasant bus. As we stepped onto the nearly empty bus, I picked a seat near the driver and squeezed my body by the window, allowing

Daddy lots of space next to me near the aisle. I looked over at his face, no longer beige, but now a pasty taupe color. The muscles in his face were tight, his lips rigid. As I stared out the bus window, I couldn't see through the glass since the overhead light inside the bus made the window a glaring reflection of myself. Looking at the window as if it were a mirror, I witnessed Daddy's woeful despair. That's when the image came to my mind of deaf people talking about Daddy, thinking he was guilty, even though he was found not guilty. I could see them now, signing, "*Herbert must go jail. He show children his . . .*" and then they would point to that part of the anatomy between their legs at the crotch of their pants and use the sign of the pointing finger shaking up and down. Some would shake their heads in shock, others would snigger and make fun of him, and still others would say something like "*He like many girls, I not surprised.*"

Yes, I now understood why he felt so humiliated, ashamed. And maybe some of his hearing friends at work believed that he could do such a thing, too.

Then I thought about that woman in court, who was so adamant that my father was the one who exposed himself. I thought to myself, "Daddy! Daddy! If it would make you happy, then you should sue her." But I didn't say anything to him and just kept my hands in my lap.

Several years later I realized the extent of Daddy's determination to seek retaliation against the woman who made the charges against him. He paid a heavy price as a result of her accusation: loss of reputation, personal shame, and a feeling of general humiliation for deaf people on the whole. Perhaps my father minimized the price the woman herself may have paid: the impact of her daughter's frightening experience. In his mind, the prices they each paid were not equal. The woman and her daughter did not pay a heavy enough price since they both could resume their lives, and the mother could encourage her daughter to move beyond the egregious incident. Daddy wanted to level the playing field by suing the woman, so that she would suffer as he had suffered, and would continue to suffer in the years to come.

Yes, Herbert wanted to get his revenge. But he didn't know how. He never sued the woman. But he never was able to let the anger go.

2

Herbert Andrew Childress

"Just as one acquires a possession, Herbert acquired bitterness, confusion, and temper tantrums."

Until Daddy's trial for indecent exposure, one day was much like any other day. Mama would be hunched over the sewing machine, guiding the material with her hands through the metal presser foot, simultaneously moving her own feet up and down on the floor pedal, making the machine miraculously stitch a plain piece of fabric into a garment. When I was a preschooler, I usually sat near her playing with rag dolls or thumbing through children's books Mama bought me. After an hour or two passed, she would stand up, stretch her body to relieve the tension in her back, and begin to reenact for me any recent news she learned: stories from newspapers documenting the crime of the day or stories about what she had learned from gossipy deaf folk. She signed to me slowly, making certain I understood her every word.

Mama always had a wealth of stories to tell me, and the tales flowed with ease as she softly used her voice and lips, along with her hands, to tell a story. She was a marvel to watch as I would ask her about Daddy's early years as well as her own early childhood days.

I became my mother's best friend simply because she loved to reenact for me the stories my father confided to her, sharing his secrets only with her. It was Mama who told me about my Daddy's temper tantrums when he turned about six years old, after a near-death bout of spinal meningitis. She said that from his birth to the time he was a toddler, Herbert was adored, partly because he was his father's only blood son, partly because he was quite simply a beautiful child, certainly the most beautiful of all Susie's ten children. So beautiful was little Herbert, with a light-yellow complexion, straight hair turning a slight curl at the tips, and white features that blacks and even whites, when seeing him for the first time, questioned his race. This often happened, especially in the South, where as a result of slavery just one generation earlier, many "colored" babies were fathered by white masters, and the notion was perpetuated that the more a "colored" person had white features, the more beautiful and acceptable the individual was considered by both black and white society.

Little Herbert certainly benefited from this thinking, as he unknowingly took advantage of having a cherub face with a ready grin, perfectly formed lips, long eyelashes, and soft long hair that invited fingers to run through it. I'm told his good looks came from his father, Berry Childress, who was of Cherokee Indian stock and his mother, the former Susie Hicks Thurman, of mixed black and white blood. Susie, a widow and a bewitching beauty, had six children when she met Berry: Major, Mary, Laura, Mattie, Susie, and William. She captivated Berry's heart, and in order to persuade her to marry him, Berry promised he would treat Susie's children as his own. Was he ever amazed when Susie bore him twin daughters, Odell and Arnell. A year later, Herbert was born, on April 28, 1913. At last, Berry's own blood son. Berry's pride and joy. Then Margery was born, the youngest of the Childress clan.

There was no shortage of children, hubbub, and raucous activity in the Thurman/Childress household. Little Herbert was given free rein to frolic around the house and often cried out "Let's play hide-n-seek" to his brothers and sisters, who

My father's mother, Suzie Hicks (Thurman) Childress bore ten children, six by her first marriage and when she became a widow, she bore four children by my grandfather Berry Childress (twins Arnell and Odell, my father Herbert, and Margery).

happily did whatever he wanted, simply because he was so gleeful, carefree, and fun, and because he brought such delight to their lives. With the older Thurman brothers and sisters, plus the Childress sisters, there was continuous commotion around Herbert, with constant noise and shouting, to which he could easily hear and freely respond.

When little Herbert was six years old, he was moping around the house, listless, when his mother immediately noticed that his bright face had become a blazing pink; his lips were dry and parched. She put her hand on his forehead and, feeling raging fever, made him lie on the davenport in the living room. She hastily applied cold cloths to his forehead, dabbed another cloth on his lips, blanketed him with old coats to stop his shivering, and put her arm under his neck, slightly lifting his head so he could swallow a drop of water. With a hawklike eye, she watched him for more than an hour when she heard him gasping, laboring to breathe.

"Go get Doc quick!" yelled Susie to the kids, who had surrounded the davenport staring at Herbert.

Ole Doc, who lived several miles away, was one of the few "colored" doctors in Nashville. Very familiar with the Thurman kids, he knew that they came to him only for emergencies, and even then it had to be an urgent situation if Mrs. Thurman's homemade remedies failed to cure the ailing family member.

"Mama says you are to come quick. Herbert is so sick. His eyeballs is going back in his head," cried one of the youngsters. Whereupon the doctor grabbed his medical bag, told the kids to come with him, and arrived at their home in the swiftest time ever.

By this time Berry had come in from work and was told that his darling son was very sick and should be brought to the Colored People's Hospital right now! Berry's thoughts flashed to the day before, when he had thrown Herbert in the air after playing mock wrestling with him and, even though they were exhausted, sang songs together. Now in less than twenty-four hours, Herbert's arms and legs swung listlessly in his father's arms as he was being carried to the Colored Hospital. Several days later, while Herbert was in a coma, the doctors declared that he had contracted spinal meningitis and that it was questionable whether he would survive.

"Your brother's mighty, mighty sick," was the message Susie brought back to her older children. Berry stayed with little Herbert, day and night, holding his hand, praying to

God Almighty for this unconscious boy to come back to life. After all, this boy was his only blood son, and even though he repeatedly declared his love and protection for all the other children, it was for Herbert that Berry had such high hopes. He had images of Herbert playing sports as he grew older, maybe even going to high school, and holding down a good job. God knows, it meant so much to him for Herbert to carry on the Childress name; maybe it was a near obsession.

Little Herbert was in a coma for days when he finally began to stir and eventually open his eyes. No one saw his eyes blink and crack open to see his surroundings because at that moment, there were people hovering together as the doctor discussed his prognosis. He recognized his mother and sister, along with two persons he did not know, talking with their backs to him, as if they wanted to shield him from something ominous. It was strangely silent—no talking—not even a whisper from the people standing at the foot of his bed, yet he could see heads nodding, his sister's hands on her hips, and his mother's gestures in the air.

"What's wrong?" He opened his mouth to utter words, and suddenly they all turned around toward him, but he could not hear his own voice. He cried out for Mama. He saw her lips moving, but he could not hear her reply. She rushed to him crying, tears streamed down her face. He could not hear her sobs; he could only feel her heavy breathing as she hugged his frail body in her arms. He, too, began to sob, but the words choked in his throat to tell them why he was in agony, in terror, in shock. It was because he could not hear them.

Weeks later, after Herbert finally was brought home, he often yelled, cried out in frustration, or banged with his arms and feet on the floor to get attention. Initially, his siblings responded to his verbal antics with immediate concern and a determination to soothe his frustrations, but his repeated daily demands caused them to pull away, such that he was often ignored.

His father, who took such joy in just being with him, was not around as much, and when he was, he just stared at the boy and looked away uncomfortably. "How could this happen? The doctors did it, they made my son deaf and dumb," he often said bitterly, with a loathing expression. "It breaks my heart that he can't hear," Berry was often overheard to say to Susie. "I don't know if I can ever get over it."

It was Susie who frequently responded to her son's frantic temper tantrums, holding him in her lap and wrapping her arms around him to quiet his bewildered spirit. And it was his much older sister, Laura, the smartest of the Thurman children, who helped her mother place little Herbert in the Tennessee School for the Colored Deaf and Dumb in Knoxville, Tennessee. Laura and her mother, not knowing how to help Herbert understand he would be attending a school for the deaf, left him standing in the foyer without explanation. He was confused, and then felt abandoned in this strange new place with strange white people all around him, something he had never before experienced in his life. He yelled, screamed, and even fought the attendants as they dragged him, kicking and screaming, to his new room.

"*Where Mama? Where Mama?*" but they didn't comprehend his screeching sounds, and spanked him until his screams eventually became a whimper. Since he no longer had the warmth of his mother's bosom to soothe his hurts, he cried constantly. Almost every day he had a temper tantrum, hitting and fighting other children, the teachers, attendants, and administrators. The superintendent, worn out and weary of Herbert's behavior, wrote Mrs. Childress that Herbert could not remain at the Knoxville School, but they found a location suitable for Herbert at the Maryland School for the Colored Blind and Deaf in Overlea, Maryland, which had gained the reputation of helping youngsters who have emotionally "mixed-up feelings." So Herbert was sent to school in Overlea, but this time, he understood that because he was sent so far away from his whole family, it must have been as punishment for his inability to hear. He understood, and eventually accepted, that his folks clearly did not love him anymore, especially his father. But as Herbert mingled with the other kids at the school, he saw they were just as unhappy as he, and he made friends with them. They playfully teased him, laughed with him, and taught him how to get along with grown-ups, especially those who were extra nice to him. He soon learned the ways of the school.

As HERBERT grew older, he learned a trade as a shoe repairman and became even more handsome. The females flocked around him, giving Herbert a reputation as a ladies' man.

Maryland School for the Colored Blind and Deaf in the early 1930s.

"I can't help it, they force me love them," he laughingly explained to his buddies.

One day the school superintendent and his assistant suddenly appeared at the mock shoe repair station on the school's campus and both grabbed Herbert by his arms. A third assistant appeared who began to viciously beat Herbert with his fists and with a stick. He hurled his fists in Herbert's face, punched him in the stomach, kicked him in the pelvic area, and continued to whip him until the assistant was just too tired to continue. Then the administrators changed places, and the one who was holding Herbert continued where the other had stopped. All three left him on the floor, bloodied, with several of his ribs cracked, his shoulders bruised, and his jaw broken.

Some students found Herbert on the floor and carried him to the nurses, who did not ask questions as to how, when, or why this happened. A few days later, Herbert learned from another student that he was beaten for attacking a young girl and having sex with her. Yes, he had to acknowledge he had been intimate with her, and to acknowledge that he had been intimate with another female friend whom he also liked. Evidently, one found out about the other, became enraged, and informed the superintendent that Herbert had forced himself on her.

When finally released from the school medical unit, Herbert went to his room, packed his bags, and left Overlea school forever. He was twenty-one years old. The year was 1934.

He went to Nashville to stay with his parents to look for work. His father, Berry, had begun drinking hard liquor more and more, especially when seeing his son again, reminding Berry of the devastating illness that had caused his son's deafness. While Berry was pleasant to his son, he remained aloof and distant, occasionally gesturing to him when he had to communicate with him. Berry was heard to repeatedly say to Susie how much it broke his heart that Herbert was deaf and dumb. "He can't hear a word I say, and he can't even talk. Can you understand anything he says?"

Susie responded, "Oh, yes, I understand him, even though I don't know all that sign language. I know what he wants, and if I don't understand, why, I write it down for him to read. You know, Herbert and Margery are real close. Herbert taught her sign language real good. I can always ask her to talk to him for me." (Margery was Herbert's youngest sister.) Thus it was Herbert's mother who showered affection on him and was attentive to his every need. His father, on the other hand, continued to be reserved and standoffish toward his son.

Meanwhile, Herbert became attracted to an extremely pretty hearing girl who lived nearby. He began courting her, brought delicacies from his mother's kitchen, flowers picked from a distant field, and even candy purchased from a local drugstore. He had been visiting her for several weeks when one day her father greeted Herbert at the front door and handed him a note telling him that he did not want Herbert to call on her again.

"Why?" Herbert wrote back on the note.

The father invited Herbert to come in and sit in the living room. Then the father wrote, "I don't want to hurt your feelings, but if my daughter marries a deaf and dumb man, it will be hard for him to get a job and support her. I hope you understand."

Herbert solemnly nodded his head, went home to his bedroom, closed the door, and wept in his pillow.

After days of depression, he decided to pull himself up by his bootstraps and reciprocate the flirtations of a married hearing woman, a nearby neighbor who knew his family very well, and whenever she saw Herbert, she used homemade gestures and exaggerated facial expressions to convey that he was certainly welcome to her bedroom. He began seeing her regularly, partly because he could drown his disappointment about his earlier love and partly because he enjoyed the excitement and thrill of having frequent sex with a married woman.

After several months, he unexpectedly encountered the husband during one of his romantic interludes. That night the husband rushed at Herbert with a butcher knife on his front lawn. The husband swung his arm upward and brought down the knife, intending to thrust it in Herbert's chest. Herbert wrestled with the man and grabbed the butcher knife by the blade. They both fell to the ground. Herbert jumped back up and lunged forward toward him. Gripping the knife, Herbert stabbed the man over and over again in his stomach. The man lay on the ground bleeding profusely.

Blood gushed from a deep gash across the palm of Herbert's hand. He took his other hand to press down on it to staunch the spewing blood. He fled to his house and explained to his mother what happened and that he had to leave Nashville right then. His mother quickly wrapped the wounded hand with clean bandages, helped him to hurriedly pack some clothes, and drove him to a Greyhound bus station in a township many miles from Nashville, lest the police be looking for him. She had to get her son out of the South because she knew that if the county sheriff caught him, Herbert would end up in a prison chain gang, and her beloved son could never survive that.

With tears in both their eyes, Herbert kissed his mother on the forehead, quickly boarded the bus, and took a seat in the rear. As he sat down, he pulled his hat low over his eyes. The bus drove off into the night. His mother stood there watching as the bus's taillights disappeared into the darkness, and with a pained heart, she drove back to Nashville, thinking she might never see her darling Herbert again. He arrived in Washington, D.C., where his older sister, Arnell Richmond, hid him in her home for several months. Herbert never found out whether the woman's husband lived or died, nor did he care.

Eventually, he found work as a shoe repairman and lived a life of routine: working daily and socializing with his deaf buddies. Herbert's deaf friends were folks he knew from Overlea who had given him their Washington, D.C., addresses before he left Overlea, and he was delighted to rekindle their friendships, resuming their carousing days.

Several years passed, and Herbert continued to live with his sister. It was about this time that Herbert's heart was broken again when Arnell told him his beloved mother had died. After returning to Washington from the funeral in Tennessee, he sunk into another depression: barely able to work, barely able to eat, and avoiding his deaf buddies. One faithful and true friend came by to visit with him and insisted that Herbert meet this good-looking lady from North Carolina. Herbert initially was not interested— after all, hadn't women been the cause of most of his troubles, and besides, he was still mourning the death of his mother.

The buddy insisted, picked up Herbert from his house, and brought him to the home where Thomasina Brown lived with her father and sister, Mary. Herbert was instantly dazzled by her stunning good looks and fine figure. She was tall, almost as tall as he, with a slender build. Her poise and fashionable style mesmerized him. He soon learned she was a teacher at the North Carolina School for the Colored Deaf and Blind; he had never met a "colored" hearing teacher of the deaf, let alone a "colored" deaf teacher.

He instantly fell in love with her—he had to have her. Thomasina quickly informed him that she was already engaged to another fellow named Claude, a deaf Mohawk Indian, whom she met when they were both students. Herbert, undaunted, poured on the charm, taking her to restaurants for lunch or dinner practically every day, bringing her candy, and on occasion, bringing her flowers. Slowly, he was making headway. After all, Claude was away with his family in Michigan, and Herbert knew "out of sight, out of mind." Herbert then appealed to her sympathy and compassion when he told her of his mother's death and his subsequent depression and sorrow.

"You make me forget pain," he told her, and "you marry me, I give you all I own, I owe you my life. I take care (of) you and make you happy woman in world. Please marry me."

Then he uttered the words that were the "pièce de résistance": "I will love you like I love my mother."

When Thomasina heard the reference to his mother, she was smitten, and promptly forgot about Claude. She married Herbert in 1938 at the home of a local justice of the peace, with her sister, Mary, as witness to their marriage.

Herbert's initial instincts about Thomasina were correct. She was suave but shy, careful but also carefree and confident. Unlike Herbert, Thomasina, who was born deaf, didn't grow up amid confusion and consternation. She was at ease knowing that all her relatives revered her as far back as she could remember, and they showed their affection by hugging and kissing her all the time from the time she was a youngster. She had the complete love of her family: her mother, Martha Nero Brown; her father, Clarence Brown; her sisters, Della, Ruth, and Mary; and even that of her grandmother, Annie Dublin Nero, an enigmatic figure in Thomasina's past.

3

Annie Dublin Nero and Martha Nero Brown

"Everywhere Mart went, Sina is sure to go."

Mama relished giving me an account of her relatives prior to her own birth. Yes, she enjoyed dramatizing events in Daddy's life before he met her, but she reveled in sharing snatches of her own life, especially about her mother, Martha, a domestic worker; her father, Clarence, a farmer who became a bricklayer; and her grandmother, Annie Dublin, an honest-to-goodness businesswoman who invented ways to earn money, from selling vegetables grown in her backyard to doing domestic work.

"Who was Annie Dublin?" I asked.

"She my mother mother. I don't know when she born, maybe 1875 or 1880," she said, all the while nodding her head while signing to me.

I gave my mother a blank stare, which prompted her to vividly describe my great-grandmother so that I could easily imagine her in my mind.

"She have wavy long brown hair." Mama took one hand and touched the top of her head and brought it down to her waist, shaking her hand slightly so I could see the waves. *"She thin nose,"* then Mama brought her hand to her nose and pinched the nostrils to illustrate how narrow Annie's nose was, and then she pulled in her lips to say, *"Her lips thin like your daddy."*

Next, she launched into her storytelling, shaking her head, left to right, explaining to me that no one knew who Annie Dublin's mother and father were. Clearly, her mother or father had to be white, since she was often described as "near white" or maybe even white passin' as "colored," "but Lord knows why would she do that," is what people would say.

Annie Dublin, with skin complexion described as "high yellow," joined the rodeo as a dancer—skipping, jumping, and twirling ropes and hoops with ease. She proved to be wise with her money, saving it after traveling around the country, and returning to Concord, North Carolina, to buy a home. Her house, they say, was a mansion, costing five hundred dollars, almost three times the cost of an average house in Concord. It was hailed as one of the most beautiful in the area, with flowers continually blooming around it and a massive vegetable garden in the rear. The luscious tomatoes, vibrant green string beans, and leafy collard greens, along with peach and apple trees and sweet watermelons, made her mansion the envy of Concord.

Annie Dublin Nero had two children, Martha and William Nero, by Jefferson Nero, a man few people knew. But what folks did know is that Annie Dublin Nero was smart, efficient, and thrifty, renting spare rooms in her newly acquired house and earning even more money as a laundress by washing, starching, and ironing clothes for white people who could afford to pay her.

If Annie gained renown for owning a magnificent house, she gained even more repute for the lavish care of Martha and William. Both children were well groomed, always wearing meticulously kept clothing; well educated in the basics of reading and writing; and well accomplished in playing the piano. But for all of Annie's devotion to her children, much to her dismay, Martha grew to be unruly and headstrong. Martha, often called Mart, born around 1897, ran off at the age of sixteen with Clarence Brown, a man Annie despised—giving credence to the speculation that Clarence Brown was too dark-complexioned for Annie's taste, but worse yet, he was dirt poor.

"You ain't worth the time of day," Annie said to Clarence, who promptly ignored her. Clarence, tall, with chocolate-brown skin, atypical wavy hair, perfectly aligned ivory teeth, and a ready smile, was quick-witted and charming, and of course, disregarded Annie's infuriating admonition not to marry her daughter. He ran off with Martha to be married by a local Baptist minister, after which they fled to Edgefield, South Carolina, where Clarence had relatives.

The first year, Martha miscarried a baby boy. A year later, she had Thomasina on May 6, 1914. More than two years after that, she bore a second baby, Della, in October 1916; two years later, in 1918, she had a third baby, Ruth; and in two more years she birthed Mary Magdalene (Babe). In six years, she had four babies. Martha endured the agony of labor for each of them and had the assistance of a friend who acted as a midwife.

But it was Thomasina who was treasured from the moment she was born. Even though her mother, Martha, had been in labor for hours on end and endured agonizing pain to birth her, Martha took the baby from the midwife and held her as if she had acquired pure gold. The baby was wrapped in white tattered cloth, with only her face and the top of her head showing a crop of slick black hair. Martha kissed the wet hair, began to nurse her, and as she cuddled the fragile infant, she vowed to love her every morning, noon, and night. The sweet beloved baby was named Thomasina.

As the baby grew from tiny infant to energetic toddler, she crawled in every direction to every nook and cranny. Martha often called out to her before running to catch her, and noticed that when Thomasina was crawling away from her, she never stopped or even turned her head when her name was called. Thomasina was nearly a year old when her mother gradually realized that her baby did not have normal hearing.

"Come here, Sina, come to Mama," Martha cried out with arms outstretched, anticipating and hoping Thomasina would turn around and crawl to her. But all to no avail.

Sometimes the baby even fell asleep when Martha played a lively tune on the piano or loudly sang a peppy song for her family and friends. Adults and children around Martha might look up when she sang, then shake their heads to and fro, tap their toes, and even sing along. But little Thomasina did none of these things, and as she learned to walk with steadiness, she continued to be unaware of any sounds. Mart observed that unless the toddler was facing her, the baby seemed oblivious to any voices or noises except when someone stomped on the floor or had hit the thin walls. Martha finally had to face the truth: her little one could not hear. So Martha told all who would listen, "Da midwife punctured my baby's eardrums with forceps during my hard delivery."

Martha carried her little baby, Thomasina, with her everywhere, calling her Sina (pronounced See-na, the last two syllables in Thomasina's name), and as Sina grew a little older, her mother overheard friend and foe alike paraphrasing the children's nursery rhyme "Mary had a little lamb and everywhere Mart goes, Sina is sure to go." Little Thomasina accompanied her mother to white people's homes and, despite her small hands, tried to help her clean. Sina hung onto her mother's skirt as they visited relatives and friends, went to the market to buy food, and even to farms to pick vegetables or cotton.

All the while, Mart used her ingenuity to invent homemade signs and gestures to communicate with her daughter, making it easy for little Thomasina to understand her mother. Sina understood her mother's gestures for eat, sleep, and potty, all signs requiring her mother to pantomime. The sign for "Daddy" was two hands, one on each side of the chest with two fingers of each hand going up and down illustrating the straps on the overalls worn by her father. The patting of the whole hand on the side of the face meant the person was white. Other signs were commonsense signs, logical in their configuration, such as the hand coming up to the mouth signaling "eat." The head bent over and placed on the top of the hand with the eyes closed meant "sleep" or "bed."

At other times, Mart wanted to show Thomasina how to communicate verbally.

"Come here, Sina, put your hands on my neck," and Thomasina watched her mother mouth words, and felt for vibrations from her mother's throat, and finally learned to speak one and two syllable words, eventually saying the names of her family members. Then, Martha identified different things around the house by exaggerating her mouth to say the word of the nearby object while simultaneously pointing to that object. She pointed to her eye to signify "look" when she wanted Sina's attention. Sina learned to keenly observe nearly every person's facial expressions and lip movements, along with their gestures and body language.

Only on occasion did Thomasina misread what she saw. Once she witnessed her daddy cupping his hand around his mouth, clearly calling out for "something," with an axe in his hand. She quickly hid in the crawl space under the porch, thinking that her father planned to axe her.

"I not understand him. He kill me I can't hear." It was night-time when she finally reappeared from under the house, and she was stunned when her father showed her the chicken he had killed.

DESPITE MARTHA'S pregnancies with three more babies in five years, she treated Sina as the favorite and welcomed Sina's willingness to help care for her younger sisters.

In Martha's mind there was nothing her child could not do except hear. When Thomasina was about four years old, Martha set about showing her how to play the piano.

"I's goin' teach you to play da piano. Just 'cause you deaf, don't mean you can't play." So she and little Thomasina sat on the piano stool, and Martha began guiding her little girl's hands on the black and white keys. Over and over again, Martha showed Sina the order in which keys should be pressed with her fingers until Sina nimbly played a tune with ease. First, she learned to play the scales and then "Three Blind Mice" and other children's songs.

Another time, Martha set about teaching Sina to sew. The two were visiting the town of Concord, when Mart pointed to a dress a lady was wearing.

"See dat dress dere. I'll show you how to make one just like it." They both went to the local market to buy material, with Mart guessing approximating how many yards to buy. When they arrived home, she cut a pattern, using a brown bag for paper, then laid the pattern on top of the material, cutting the cloth along the edges of the pattern, and then bringing the two pieces to the sewing machine. When Mart sat down facing the machine, she slid the material under the metal presser foot, began to move her feet up and down on the pedal underneath the sewing machine itself, sewing the parts together. Thomasina laughed with glee as she saw her mother sewing with such finesse and ease.

"Here, you sew these two pieces together. Dat's da sleeve." Mart pointed to the sleeve of the dress she was wearing, then to the two pieces of material. Sina sat down and began to pedal, up and down; at that moment, Thomasina learned to sew. She wanted to hug the sewing machine, she loved it so.

While Sina delighted in playing different tunes on the piano, she was spellbound by the sewing machine, and as early as five years old, she began putting pieces of material together to sew a dress.

"*I sew dress,*" Thomasina confidently told whoever was present about her sewing, by pointing to herself, then pointing to the dress, and finally pointing to the sewing machine. She was so proud, and her mother was prouder still.

THE YEAR was 1921. Clarence and Martha were still living in Edgefield, South Carolina, with Martha having just birthed baby Mary. Thomasina, age seven, witnessed her mother's writhing and yelling, and actually saw the emerging head of baby Mary at her birth. The midwife handed the baby to Thomasina, who held her as delicately as a ball of cotton.

"*She pretty, same doll . . . black hair, black eyes, little mouth . . . I see baby, I know I love her,*" Thomasina said, while holding the infant.

A few months after giving birth to Mary, Mart made Thomasina watch her as she killed a chicken. She pointed to her eye and then to the chicken and mouthed the words "See him run." As Thomasina's eyes followed her mother's gestures, she saw her mother wring the rooster's neck, and the poor chicken flapped and ran in circles. She and Thomasina watched him drop to the ground, then cleaned out his guts, plucked the feathers, and carried him to the woodstove. They pulled out the heavy black kettle, filled it with lard, and fried a succulent chicken for dinner. Oh, how Sina loved being around her mother.

But life for Sina would radically change once they moved to North Carolina. Up until now, her mother had been her sole teacher.

MAMA NEVER tired of telling me over and over again about witnessing Mary's birth. Not once did Mama vary the details of that story. I saw her face become radiant in the pure joy of recalling such a blissful moment in her life; her smile glowed, and her hands swirled with grace. But her entire expression and mood quickly faded into a dark grimace when she told of what happened to the family in South Carolina and how they had to flee from there. Her hands became almost wild as she described the devastating events occurring to the family.

She began the story by telling me that Clarence Brown, her father, had a hard time. Life for him was cruel, harsh, and brutal as he toiled in the blistering heat and humidity from sunup to sundown as a sharecropper in South Carolina. Long hours and hard work made for a weary and exhausted man who saw no end in sight, picking cotton day in and day out. But despite picking cotton seven days a week with deftness and speed, he barely earned enough to feed his family. My grandfather Clarence knew the white farmers were cheating him, that his earnings barely paid for the use of the shack and food, so he helped himself to greens, corn, or anything that wouldn't be missed, just to feed his family.

Now, it was mid-October, the weather still somewhat muggy. The sweltering heat of the summer had passed, when the farmers hunted Clarence down for the missing crops.

The sun was shining brilliantly in the middle of a clear afternoon, when my grandmother Martha, peeling potatoes on the dilapidated front porch, spotted two white men about a quarter of a mile away marching toward the shack carrying rifles. Fortunately, Clarence was in the back hoeing collard greens and completely out of sight, when Martha yelled to him to hide in the pile of hay.

"They's comin' to git yah." She hissed to Clarence, so that the approaching men could not hear her. They moved toward Martha with rifles pointing at her, demanding Clarence, whereupon Martha adamantly said he wasn't there and encouraged the men to look around the house if they did not believe her.

The men stepped around Martha, who was sitting on a rocking chair on the porch, and marched inside the shack to search for Clarence. Not finding him, they returned to the porch.

"We'll be back!!! You tell that lowdown stealin' dog that his life ain't worth a plugged nickel," one of the men said with hatred in his voice.

My grandfather lay flat on the ground in the haystack for hours on end, until well past midnight, when Martha signaled him to come out. She woke up the sleeping children, hastily dressed them, and whispered in a hushed voice, "Keep quiet, we's got to go, rat now." The still sleepy and drowsy children didn't know what was going on, but they recognized from their mother's face that something very bad was going to happen. Little two-year-old Ruth began to pee on herself. And Della, barely four years old, started to whimper. Martha, turned to Della and said in a low harsh voice, "Hush chile . . . be very quiet . . . hush now." Thomasina, seeing her mother's frantic packing, rushed to help.

In less than an hour, Martha and Clarence Brown and four youngsters crowded almost everything they owned into a wagon: the worn-out couch, the rickety kitchen table with accompanying mismatched chairs, the broken-down piano, the beloved sewing machine, the chipped dishes and drinking jars, the lumpy mattresses, and their meager clothes. In the blackness of night, lit only by dim moonlight, they hurriedly crammed the heavy load onto the wagon pulled by a lone mare. Anything else was left behind.

Martha cradled baby Mary, while Clarence hoisted the other three girls, Thomasina, Della, and Ruth, into the back of the rickety old wagon, putting old clothes over them for protection. Thomasina curled up with her sisters—she had never been so scared. And they escaped—fleeing for their lives.

Clarence whipped the horse at a frenzied pace until they crossed the South Carolina border at sunup, entered North Carolina, and headed on to the town of Concord.

MY GRANDFATHER had a difficult time finding work in North Carolina, hiding out from any suspicious white characters seeking to return him to South Carolina. Once his mother-in-law, Annie Dublin Nero, learned of Clarence's reason for flight from South Carolina, she told the authorities about his thievery, and they promptly put him in jail. He was lucky, though—he was not returned to South Carolina, where a probable lynching was waiting for him. It is not known how long Clarence was in jail, but once he was released, he worked a sundry of jobs, from cleaning and selling fish to learning how to lay bricks, until he eventually became an accomplished bricklayer and house builder.

IT WAS Annie Dublin Nero who insisted that Thomasina enroll in a school. Annie asked a white doctor, "Where do colored children who can't hear go to school?" The answer came quickly enough: the North Carolina School for the Colored Deaf and Blind.

Once Mart learned of her mother's proposal to send Thomasina to school, she rejected the idea outright, as she hated the idea of Thomasina being apart from her. "Lawd, lawd, lawd, what am I to do without Sina? I can teach her whatever she needs to learn."

But pragmatism won out over Martha's emotions. For once, Clarence and Annie agreed on one thing: Sina should go to school because this was, after all, best for Sina herself.

In the latter part of August 1922, Mart and Clarence Brown, along with eight-year-old Thomasina, loaded their horse and buggy with Thomasina's few belongings, and took her to the School for the Deaf. When they arrived at the school grounds, Sina was aghast at the massive brick building, a structure the likes of which she had never seen before, and as she entered the building, she was stunned to see the smooth waxed marble floors.

Then they saw a white teacher approach them, "We're here to bring Thomasina Brown to school," said Clarence somberly.

"Oh, I'll take her to her sleeping quarters," replied the older woman, who grabbed Thomasina's hand. Martha looked at the frightened child and waved her hand down to the floor, meaning Thomasina was to stay. Mart pointed to herself and Clarence and waved her arm away from their bodies toward the door, which meant they were going away. Tears rolled down her face. Thomasina pulled her hand away from the teacher, taking steps to go to her mother.

"No, No. You stay," said Martha, her face wet with tears running down past her nose to her mouth. Sweat accumulated around her forehead. Her mouth became dry as she tried to talk.

"I loves ya, honey," she said as she leaned forward to hug Thomasina, who tugged away from the strange woman, pulling and twisting to go with her mother. Her father waved to his child and looked away as his throat began to ache, and then put his arm around Martha's shoulder to caress her, leading her out of the building. Thomasina began to shout, *"Mama, Mama"*; she stomped her feet and turned away, attempting to wrest herself from the teacher's strong clutches.

The strange woman held fast onto Thomasina and brought her to a large room with eight cots. Thomasina put down her satchel, wept uncontrollably as she lay on the bed, her body shaking.

How could they leave her in this strange place, she thought. Will they ever come back to get her?

Thomasina grieved for several months, weeping and wishing her family would reappear and whisk her away from this ungodly place. But it was not to be. She did not see her mother and father again for ten long arduous months; they never wrote her a letter.

Gradually Thomasina's anxiety dissipated as she was taught the alphabet, numbers, fingerspelling, and sign language. Some of the signs she already knew like *sleep* and *eat*, but she was secretly delighted to learn useful new signs, such as *toilet, toothbrush, toothpowder.*

"I learn many signs: mama, daddy, sister," she longed to tell her family when she saw them. Although she was a quiet, shy girl, she slowly began to express herself after she learned new and different signs. Little by little, she began to understand how some signs for words can form a sentence, and once she learned how to spell, she was able to put the letters together to form words in fingerspelling. All her teachers were white, and they were amazed at her intellect and her eagerness to show them how much she understood and memorized.

"Why, she certainly is very smart!" was the phrase frequently used to describe her. It wasn't long before Thomasina asked for a sewing machine and was directed to the sewing center, set aside for avid seamstresses. Given a bolt of material, she began to copy from memory the styles of fashions in magazines. Then she created and cut patterns from newspapers and made her own clothes, just as she had done when she was home.

MEANWHILE, Martha found work as a domestic, cleaning white people's homes, scrimping for meager earnings of two to three dollars a week. Strong-willed and hardworking, Martha was determined to bring home money for the family because she knew that her husband was not a reliable source for a steady income. But gradually she became exhausted—worn out and close to losing her mind.

"Mart's wore out" was what gossipers said about her. Some said that Clarence was a flirt and had relations with women about town. Martha was too exhausted raising four children, keeping a house, and working as a domestic to fight the young ladies who were mesmerized by Clarence's charms.

"I'm leavin'. I can't take it no mo'. I'se losin' my mind." So Martha planned to walk out, leaving her hungry children, flirting husband, dirty house, and demanding bosses behind. The year was 1928.

Martha Brown packed her clothes in a brown bag and began to head to nowhere.

"I don't have to worry about Sina, since she is in school now and they will clothe and feed her just fine," thought Martha. "But I'se got to tell Baby."

Mary was seven years old at the time, and aptly called Baby because she was the youngest and so very tiny in stature. Martha felt a twinge of guilt leaving everyone and everything behind, especially since Baby was so little, but she decided she could depend on her mother to care for the family, especially Baby.

Mart took Baby for a walk and said, "Here's a little doll for yah honey," and Baby squealed with delight at the ragdoll.

"I'se going away for a while and I'll come back for yah when I can," said Martha, holding the tiny little one's hand, who started to cry and whimper.

"But, Mama, I want to go with y-o-u-u-u-u-u-u," she said as tears streamed down her face. Martha tried to explain again.

"I'se got to go. You'se too young to understand. I'se just got to go." Martha took Baby back to their house, where she left poor little Baby wailing uncontrollably that her Mama had left her.

Martha now left Concord, abandoning her entire family, and told no one where she was going. Days, weeks, months passed. Her mother, Annie, looked for her in nearby small towns. Clarence hunted for her as well, and was accompanied by his girls, who went from house to house with their father, but Martha was nowhere to be found.

Many months passed as Annie Dublin Nero helped feed her daughter's children, but she refused to let them live with her.

"All my rooms are rented. I don't have room for yah." Annie continued to have disdain for Clarence, and the possibility that he might visit her house proved to be such a horrendous thought that she deliberately cut back on her time with her grandchildren.

"I just can't stand to even look at him. And see, I was right about him, look at all the trouble he put my poor daughter through." She blamed him for Martha's departure, and even wondered if Clarence had done harm to her. But she nevertheless sent food to the girls, and especially embraced Thomasina with open arms when she was home from school during the summer. Often, little Mary was invited to her grandmother's house for food and clothing, since she looked pitifully frail and wore grimy tattered clothes. But Della and Ruth were rarely seen at the mansion, and, of course, Clarence was never welcome there.

In the meantime, Clarence Brown worked as a bricklayer and took any extra work that would support his children. With his wife's disappearance, his interest in the women about town waned. After all, he had his children to look after.

After a year had passed, Martha reappeared from God knows where and announced that she had been working in a small town as a domestic for a white couple. She left that job and just recently found work with Mr. Henry, a "colored" man, whom she called Uncle Henry, caring for his invalid wife, and was living with them on a nearby farm in Rockwell, about twenty miles from Concord. Martha believed her children would be ecstatic to see her, but she was soon disillusioned when they appeared icy cool toward her. After all, they had learned to live without her. All this time, they thought she had

A rare photo of Clarence and Martha Brown taken many years after their separation.

died, and here she was, back from the dead. A part of Martha did die this day, knowing her children no longer loved her.

She continued to work for Uncle Henry, even though gossipers said he was her lover. But she nevertheless visited her children and, on occasion, gave them money and brought gifts.

4

Thomasina Brown

*Thomasina Brown—One of the First Deaf African American
Teachers of the Deaf in the State of North Carolina*

Months turned into years while Martha was working on the
farm with Uncle Henry. My mother, who had come to the
Raleigh School with just two dresses so many years ago, now
made blouses, skirts, dresses, suits, and coats. By the time she
turned fifteen years old, she was so adept at sewing that she
soon acquired the skill of knitting and crocheting.

On this particular day, one of the assistant superintendents
approached Thomasina. She signed, "I want you sew a dress."

"What dress?" signed Thomasina with a quizzical expression.

"Make any dress you want."

"What color?"

"Any color you want. You pick material."

"What size?"

"The size you wear," replied the administrator with a smile.

"Okay." Thomasina nodded her head and immediately set
about making a dress and a jacket to match. She completed
making the outfit in less than twenty-four hours and promptly
gave it to the administrator, who thanked her profusely.

This was typical of Thomasina, immediately doing what
was asked of her. The reason she had endeared herself to most
of the staff at the school was because she was so obedient,
completing any task without any questions or reservations.

A week later, a smiling administrator came to Thomasina and signed, "You won. You won. You beat other girls who sewed a dress the same as you. Come with me to auditorium." Thomasina was astounded; she dutifully followed her to the room full of students and spectators and was beckoned by the superintendent himself to come to the stage. Standing beside him was an attractive silver-haired woman who was introduced to the audience as the governor's wife.

"The winner of the sewing contest is Thomasina Brown," exclaimed the superintendent in sign language, "and her prize is a ten-dollar silver coin. Here to present it to her is the wife of the governor of the state of North Carolina." The statuesque woman stepped forward, greeted the young Thomasina with a pleasing grin, and handed her a glistening coin. Thomasina was so astonished, she was practically paralyzed for a moment when she took the coin and signed, *"Thank you."* The superintendent grabbed her hand to lead her offstage.

Later in the afternoon, another administrator asked Thomasina to stitch the governor's wife's name on a pillowcase. She was thrilled to do it and meticulously sewed each letter on the white satin pillowcase. Once again she was asked to present it to the governor's wife. This gracious woman blushed with delight, reached into her purse, and gave coins to Thomasina, who thanked her, then turned and ran to her room. She couldn't wait to go home and show the coins to her family. The year was 1929, the year of the Great Depression.

A few weeks later, the school year ended. Thomasina was given the usual stipend to ride the train home for the summer, and as she disembarked, she saw her father wearing frazzled overalls, looking thin, standing on the embankment to bring her home. She already knew that her mother had left the family, but she did not understand why. When she arrived at the small bungalow, she was greeted by her three sisters: Della, Ruth, and Baby.

"Whoop de doo, Sina's here, Sina's here," they hollered in unison. "She looks wonderful," uttered Della, amazed at how crisp and neat Sina looked in the fashionable attire she had recently made for herself. Della and Ruth had on frayed and faded cotton dresses worn out from so many washings, and Baby looked even more piteous, thin and tiny. Sina looked around the room and saw how things had deteriorated: shabby furniture, peeling paint on the walls, and hardly any food in the old icebox. She knew they were really poor now, and to brighten her sister's spirits, she opened her suitcases and showed the girls her clothes. They gawked at the garments. So excited was Della and Ruth that they grabbed a bundle of clothes, pulling and tugging over pieces of clothing like starving animals grabbing and tussling over pieces of meat. As they tried on each dress, they admired themselves in the mirror and then skipped around the house. Little Baby couldn't wear most of the clothing since she was so petite, but she found a hat and purse Sina had made, along with socks and some underwear.

Then Thomasina gave the ten-dollar silver coin she had won to her father, who began to weep. Later, he bought an armful of food for all to eat. Clarence had been without work for many months, since there wasn't much bricklaying work to be found, nor was he able to do any farming. Many of the nearby farms once owned by affluent farmers had been foreclosed on by the banks. Clarence and his family relied on Annie Dublin to send morsels of food to the girls.

In the succeeding months, Ruth and Della took one garment after another from Sina—so many, that by the end of the summer, Sina did not have clothes to bring back to school. Her suitcase had just one item and a pair of socks in it, leaving

Thomasina trying to think how to explain to her classmates why she had no clothes.

"I tell girls I lost my clothes. No. They see suitcase, it empty. Maybe I hide suitcase, no one look," Thomasina thought to herself. When she entered the dorm room, she saw her schoolmates standing around—some glanced her way, others were talking with each other. That was when she shoved the suitcase under her cot.

The house supervisor suddenly entered the room to do her annual inspection of each girl's batch of clothing to determine what each student needs, from additional underwear, socks and shoes to skirts, blouses, and dresses. When she noticed Thomasina's baggage was not on her bed, the supervisor signed, "You put suitcase under bed. What wrong?"

Thomasina looked away while the supervisor simply stepped beside her, leaned over, and pulled out the suitcase. Thomasina, realizing she was caught, simply opened it and looked over to see several girls eyeing the suitcase devoid of clothes: only a mere nightgown and a pair of socks were there.

"Thomasina no clothes," shouted one of the girls, who had long been jealous of the many dresses Thomasina made and wore. The spiteful girl shoved another girl to grab her attention, and this time, she signed while simultaneously shouting and laughing, *"Thomasina no clothes."* Their signs became a reverberating choir of mockery, giggling, and snickering at Thomasina.

"I shame," she thought as she fled to the bathroom and hid in one of the stalls, weeping. She stopped crying and wiped her face with toilet tissue to find courage to return. When Thomasina came back to the dorm, the girls were still snickering, but she ignored them, then dressed in her lone nightgown and slid into the bed. The next day, she asked for material and began to sew. Putting pieces of fabric together and embellishing each

garment with elaborate embroidery, she made one, two, then three dresses in a matter of a few days. After a short while, she made an entire wardrobe, more beautiful than the garments left behind in Concord.

"Many people say I wonderful seamstress," Thomasina boasted quietly. When she showed folks her clothes, she often snickered at their facial expressions, secretly amused at their amazement that her clothing was not store-bought. Such was the quality of her sewing.

As my mother grew older, in her later teen years she became a stunningly beautiful woman who dressed much like a fashion model. In fact, her outfits were copied from the latest fashion magazines. Thomasina caught the attention of the males at the school, especially Claude, a tall gangly profoundly deaf Mohawk Indian from Detroit, Michigan, who was fascinated by her beauty, her shyness, but most of all, her willingness to give him rapt attention whenever he talked to her. He took her on picnics, to the movies, and to quiet places where they could sit on a favorite park bench, hold hands, and share the silence. To show his affection for her, Claude gave Thomasina candy and sometimes money he had earned by doing odd jobs around the campus. Not having any experience kissing girls, he finally kissed her on the mouth, pressing his dry thin lips against her full rounded lips. They possessed a love that arose from their innocence and goodness.

"You want marry?" he asked.

"Yes," she replied.

"I go Detroit and work . . . cars, earn money, save money, buy house. We marry two, maybe three, years."

The news of their eventual nuptials to take place in a few years was expected, as no one was surprised, since they made such a handsome couple. Thomasina was twenty-one years old.

During this time, Thomasina continued to gain a reputation as meticulous, precise, and neat in everything she did, from keeping her belongings in an orderly fashion to making her penmanship reflect the Palmer method, a long-standing approach for teaching students how to write. She was a hard worker, taking the extra time to do things correctly and properly. But, alas the time had finally come; in a month, she would be graduating from the school. She had been a resident for more than twelve years and at last, had completed her course of study.

It was a bright sunny spring day when Thomasina was walking along the hallway of the school with a bounce in her step, and one of the teachers saw her and said, "The superintendent is looking for you." She promptly went to his office, hoping nothing was wrong. She entered the room, and he greeted her with a smile.

"Would you like work here?" he inquired in sign language.

"What?"

"Yes, will you work here?" he repeated his question.

"Work?"

"Yes, we want you work here." The superintendent became slightly nervous. He had never entertained the possibility she might say no.

"You want me work here?" she repeated the words again slowly. *"Maybe he want me wash toilets and mop floors,"* she thought. After all, she had done that many times in the dorms.

"What I do?"

"You teach here."

"Teach?" she said incredulously.

"Yes, teach. You would teach little children when they first arrive here. You teach children ABC's and signs to children who never knew sign language," he explained.

"Yes. I want work here," she smiled, barely containing her jubilation.

"But I hear you and Claude will marry. We have rule, no married teachers."

"Claude . . . Detroit. Work buy house. Many years save money," she quickly answered.

"Okay. Fine. You work here in Fall."

So began the teaching career of Thomasina Brown. She had no one with whom to share the ecstatic news of her pending assignment, since she usually kept to herself, choosing to isolate from her fellow students, partly because she was shy, and partly because she felt so insecure about her imperfect language.

Well, she decided tell one person, Lilly, a hard of hearing lady who befriended her several years ago, and who often corrected her writing and helped her understand the written directives sent by the administration to students. Lilly had delightful news to tell her as well: *"I am hired, too. I will do cleaning."* When the superintendent saw the extent of the friendship between Lilly and Thomasina, he often arranged for the two to accompany him while he drove his car to complete special jobs: from picking up supplies to bringing back youngsters from the bus or train depot. He was frequently seen going from one place to another, driving the school car with Thomasina sitting in the middle next to him, and Lilly on the right by the door. The three became a familiar sight, much to Thomasina's delight.

Thomasina Brown loved her job so. She waited for each new child in the doorway of the school, greeting them with a hug, knowing how scared they must feel as she herself felt when she first arrived. She gently took their hands as they anxiously surveyed their new surroundings. Many had come from rural areas of North Carolina, as well as other states that did not have a school for colored deaf and blind children.

Thomasina began by teaching each child signs necessary for early survival: *toilet, food* or *eat, bed, sleep, water.* She grouped signs dealing with cleanliness: *bath, water, soap, toothbrush, toothpowder.* Familial signs: *mother, father, brother, sister.* Over and over again, she made the signs for each child to repeat, until she was satisfied they had both understood and memorized the word. She taught them how to care for themselves, from taking a bath to combing and brushing their hair, putting away their clothes, brushing their teeth with toothpowder, and making up their beds. As Thomasina became more familiar with each child's strengths and weaknesses, she grew more fond of them, constantly encouraging them to do their best.

"You can do. You good. I proud you." The children adored her.

IT WAS 1935. Thomasina was twenty-one years old. In the entire time she was at the North Carolina School for the Colored Deaf and Blind, she had never received a letter from her folks, not even from her mother, whom she adored. So when she received a letter from home, she panicked, wondering what could be wrong. It was a letter from her sister, Babe, who informed her that their father had moved to Washington, D.C., to find work. She and Ruth were planning to go there too, and they expected Thomasina to join them at the end of the school year.

In her letter to Thomasina, Babe omitted the details of what happened when she announced to her mother that they were leaving. Babe had made the trip to Rockwell, North Carolina, where Mart was staying with Uncle Henry. She told her mother that their father had heard from a longtime friend who worked as a bricklayer, and this friend told him masonry work could be found in Washington. Of course, Clarence

Ruth, Thomasina, and Mary relocated to Washington, D.C., with their father who left North Carolina to find work as a bricklayer. Della, another sister, was married and stayed in North Carolina.

would take Babe, Ruth, and Thomasina with him. Della, the second-oldest daughter, found refuge with an enterprising young man, Andrew Handy, who worked as a storekeeper, and was determined to own the store someday. She married

Andrew, and true to his word, he became a merchant in the black area of Concord.

Martha was stunned at the news that the family would all be leaving her in North Carolina. She pleaded with Babe to stay.

"Why, you can live with me on da farm," she implored, but Babe would hear none of it.

"You left us when we were just little babies, hungry and with no clothes. Of course, I am going with my Daddy. He took care of us, not you!" Baby uttered these heartless words to her mother, and hoped her mother would suffer, too. But alas, there was no sweet satisfaction. The little girl who had grown up to become a teenager was still tormented by her mother's absence all these years.

As Babe promised in her letter to Thomasina, she and her sisters moved to D.C. Meanwhile, Thomasina came to Rockwell for the summer to visit her mother, but she missed her sisters so much that she, too, wanted to travel to Washington, D.C., to be with the family. She reluctantly told her mother she wanted to spend the balance of the summer in Washington, leaving her mother sobbing, barely able to part with her daughter.

As Thomasina left North Carolina on a train, she waved good-bye to her mother and Uncle Henry; she began to weep because she was afraid. She had never traveled to a destination out of North Carolina, and worse yet, she loathed to leave her mother, who had both loved and worshipped her since birth.

THOMASINA returned to work at the North Carolina School after her respite in Washington, D.C. One thing she loved to do was count her money on payday, as the pay from the state of North Carolina was more money than Thomasina or anyone in her family had ever earned. Her expenses were low since the cost of shelter and food were assumed by the state, and, of course, she made her own clothes.

She knew the entire country had suffered from a crippling depression. Bread lines, while dwindling, could be seen near and far; scarcity continued to prevail throughout the country, especially for "colored" people. The year was 1935, and President Franklin Roosevelt had enacted the WPA as part of the New Deal, creating jobs for those who wanted to work.

During the almost two years that Thomasina had been teaching, much had changed in her family's circumstances: Ruth had married Orether Wagoner and moved from Washington, D.C., to Baltimore, Maryland, where he was able to secure work. Mary, still living with her father, was graduating from Dunbar High School in Washington, D.C., and wanted to attend Barber Scotia College, a college for "colored" youngsters in Concord. Thomasina sent Mary all the money she needed to enroll. Henry, Martha's employer on his farm, died leaving Martha several acres of land in Rockwell, North Carolina. And it was Thomasina who sent her mother three hundred dollars to build a house on the property. Her grateful mother, in turn, put Thomasina's name on the deed as the sole owner.

Life was good for Thomasina. The year was 1937. The school year was coming to a close as she made plans for her summer visit to Washington, D.C. She felt impatient to see her father and Mary, the only sister who signed fluently, using fingerspelling, gestures, and formal signs, and who practiced communicating with Thomasina at every opportunity.

Once back in D.C., Thomasina renewed old deaf acquaintances, letting folks know she was back in town. One of her former schoolmates, Leonard Scott, came by to visit her, accompanied by an old friend, Herbert Childress, a deaf man who attended Maryland School for the Colored Blind and Deaf at Overlea outside of Baltimore. Leonard introduced Herbert to Thomasina.

"He very good-looking," she thought to herself. *"I not sure who best-looking, Herbert or Claude."*

Herbert was of medium build, about five feet nine inches tall, light complexion, a round face, and claimed Nashville, Tennessee, as his home. He was a shoemaker and had a steady job in downtown Washington.

Herbert was immediately smitten by Thomasina's loveliness; she was pretty, as well as poised. He saw she was not impressed with his good looks, the way most women were; in fact, she barely spoke to him at all and appeared genuinely reserved. Her clothes were immaculate, and her shoes matched her outfit. Were they new? He couldn't tell. He began the conversation by asking her about her work.

"What work you do?"

"I teach. North Carolina," she replied.

"You live North Carolina?" he asked.

"Yes."

"Why you here Washington?"

"I live here (with) father."

She saw he asked many questions, but she was most impressed with his language skills; she noticed he spoke better English than she, using signs and fingerspelling and mouthing his words. She didn't know he rarely used his voice, just moving his lips as he signed. He persisted in asking more questions: how old was she, where did she go to school, how many sisters and brothers in her family, and on and on went the questioning. Finally, she abruptly ended his curiosity by going to the kitchen to serve him and Leonard milk and some cake she had baked earlier.

Herbert came back to see Thomasina the very next day. And the next day, and the next day, and the next day. She informed him she planned to marry Claude, but he ignored her engagement and continued to visit her daily; each time he visited her, he brought gifts to surprise her, please her, and win her over. She seemed immensely pleased with the gifts he lavished on her, plus she truly enjoyed his company, especially his sense of humor. His wonderful command of English was better than that of most deaf people she knew, especially Claude's.

Herbert asked Thomasina to be his wife, and when she hesitated, he began to plead with her, telling her he was heart-broken since his mother died. Only Thomasina could fill that empty space in his heart; he desperately needed her.

Thomasina's resolve began to soften. She was seriously thinking about not marrying Claude, since he did not need her as much as Herbert. When Herbert spoke of his mother's death, it pained her so, since she herself was so close to her own mother and couldn't bear the thought that her mother might die, too. So, she told him, *"Yes, I marry you."*

Before she started the fall term that year, Herbert and Thomasina were married in front of a justice of the peace with her sister Mary as a witness. She knew about the cardinal rule that teachers were not allowed to work if they are married, so she cautioned Herbert to tell no one about their marriage.

"Please please, (if) boss know, I lose job."

Thomasina herself never said a word to anyone, not even Lilly, her closest friend.

Thomasina returned to work that fall, and the following four years after that. She met Herbert at the end of each school year in Washington, spending summers with him and counting up their savings for a new home.

It was the 1941–1942 school year, and Thomasina was showing one of her students the signs for fruits: *apple, orange, banana, peach*. A teacher entered her classroom and said, "The superintendent wants to see you right away, right now!"

Thomasina entered his office and saw a crimson red-faced superintendent standing behind his desk with his lips tightly drawn back, making the beginnings of a snarl.

"Are you married?" he asked her point blank.

"*Why you ask?*" Thomasina was shocked by the question.

"I received this letter." He handed her an envelope, once sealed but now opened. Thomasina began to read it. The letter began with the salutation: "*My dear wife,*" and then continued with its message: "*How are you? I miss you very much. Can you send money buy furniture? We can rent apartment. I need $150.00. I will spend money too. I hope hear (from you) soon. Love, your husband, Herbert.*"

Thomasina took her time to read the letter and reread it again. She handed the letter back to the superintendent. She noticed the superintendent put the letter and envelope in a still larger envelope, and she recognized the writing on the larger envelope. Then the superintendent began to query her.

"*Yes, I married,*" she said with her hands trembling slightly.

"And how long have you been married?"

"*Four years.*"

"You've been married for f-o-u-r years," he said incredulously.

"*Yes.*"

"And you told no one?"

"*I never tell.*"

"You know against rules for teachers to be married here."

"*Yes, I know.*" She abruptly turned around, left the office, and went to her room. She packed all of her clothes in two large suitcases, sat on the bed, and waited until nighttime, when she exited the back stairway, lugging suitcases out of the North Carolina School for Colored Deaf and Blind, and walked three miles to the Greyhound bus line to buy a ticket to Washington, D.C. She was too numb to cry. Thomasina had taught at the school for a total of seven years.

Riding back to Washington, recalling the incidents that had occurred during the day, Thomasina was convinced that her best friend, Lilly, told the superintendent. It was Lilly's handwriting on the large envelope, and, after all, Lilly was always trying to curry favor with the superintendent. Thomasina recalled Lilly had confronted her last year with the rumor that Thomasina was married to Herbert Childress. Lilly learned it from deaf friends, who heard it from Herbert himself, who frequently fellowshipped in the deaf community and boasted about being married to a teacher.

"Is it true? Are you married?" Lilly asked long ago. Thomasina never answered her, deliberately changing the subject.

Now traveling on the bus, Thomasina wondered, for the first time and many times afterward, if she had made two major mistakes: to befriend Lilly, and to marry Herbert Childress. That was the beginning of many regrets.

A WEARY Thomasina arrived at early dawn at Arnell's house looking for Herbert, who was asleep in bed. Arnell pushed and shoved Herbert several times to awaken him, since he had drunk a six-pack of beer the night before and was difficult to rouse. When he finally woke up and saw Thomasina, he was devastated by the news that she no longer had a job.

"I not teacher. My boss read letter you send me. You say 'my wife.' He know I married."

He looked at her emotionlessly and with a blank stare. He lamely tried to make the best of a poor situation, since now he no longer could brag about the prestige of having a deaf teacher as his wife.

"That all right. You can work here (in) Washington."

"I don't want live here your sister. I want stay my father," Thomasina said.

"Okay, we move (with) your father. Now you can have baby. No more secret we married." The year was 1942.

5

Maxine

"Ah, Bay, Cee, Day"

The great occasion of Mama's first pregnancy all happened on Ames Street, where she and my father lived with Mary and Grindaddy. The year was 1943.

No one, not her mother, her sisters, or the women at the North Carolina School had ever told my mother what it would be like to be pregnant. Of course, Mama knew she was going to have a baby, but it was so much more than she had imagined, from having swollen feet, an aching back, and weary legs to having an enormously distended stomach as if she were carrying a watermelon in her abdomen. Nine months into her pregnancy, she was so heavy that she waddled when she walked, stopping every few moments to pat the baby who kicked her often and clearly wanted to be born.

She looked down as she put her hands on her hips to stretch her back and saw water streaming down her legs. She did not know what to do. More and more water flowed from between her legs as she struggled to get someone's attention, *"Mary, Mary help. Daddy, Daddy, help."* Waves of pain rippled across her stomach. Mary heard her cries and rushed to determine what was wrong with her sister, and seeing the water on the floor, immediately called an ambulance, which rushed Thomasina to Columbia Women's Hospital. Mary ran to get Herbert, and together they followed the ambulance in Mary's car.

The gripping pain was so agonizing that my mother believed she was going to die. Even though Mary and Herbert were with her at the hospital, she had given up trying to breathe, even trying to live; she could no longer keep up with the torment, the suffering. When she was wheeled into the hospital room, she felt someone placing a mask over her face, and then blackness rescued her from sheer agony. When she awakened, two nurses were standing beside her, one on each side, and then she saw their mouths move and she followed the hand of one nurse as she pointed to Thomasina's knees.

There wrapped in a small hospital blanket was a baby, tucked right between her legs. The nurse picked up the baby and gave it to Thomasina, who had never seen such a beautiful baby. It was a girl. It was me.

"Oh," she thought, *"Herbert wants boy, but . . . he sees beautiful baby, he happy."*

And just as Thomasina predicted, when Herbert saw his own baby through the glass window of the maternity ward, he beamed with joy. Yes, he was momentarily disappointed that the baby was a girl, but he knew there would be a next time, and he wondered if the superstition was true that any event occurring on Friday the thirteenth was doomed. The baby was born on Friday, August 13, 1943. *"No,"* he thought to himself, *"any baby belong (to) me, (this) beautiful, can never have bad luck."* They didn't have a name for the baby, since they thought I would be a boy, to be named Herbert Jr.

Arnell, while standing beside Herbert watching the baby at the hospital, took out pad and pencil to write the news that she had called long-distance to Nashville to announce the baby's birth. That's when Herbert's sister Laura told Arnell that Bill, their brother, had said his wife, Ruth, liked the name Maxine for the new baby. And so they named the baby Maxine.

EVERYONE adored my Daddy when he was born. And they certainly cherished my Mama. But from my very first day, I was idolized.

Thomasina bringing home baby Maxine from the hospital in August 1943. Herbert accepted me as his firstborn, dearly hoping his next child would be a son.

Thomasina was so affected by the miracle of birth, that she held me tightly, intending to never let me go. She began breast-feeding me for hours on end. When we left the hospital, she wrapped me in newly knitted baby clothing she had long ago prepared. She carried me as if I were made of spun gold, a soft delicate treasure to behold. When we arrived home, Mama eased me from her arms to the bed. From that night on, I slept between her and my father every night. After almost a year, a cradle was placed next to her bed so she could watch me intently, day and night. She took me everywhere with her, holding me, rocking me, frequently kissing me on the cheek and neck.

"I not kiss you on mouth because people say I give germs. One day I give up, I put my mouth very soft and kiss your mouth . . . feel you breathe air (in) my air. I love your air."

When I was nine months old, Mama began making hissing sounds almost daily, watching me turn my head toward the sound. She repeated these homemade hissing tests for months and months until I began walking, finally changing the test to calling me, softly saying my name *"m-a-a-s-e-e-n-e,"* which sounded like the word "magazine" without the middle syllable. Only when I responded by running to her or turning my head to see what she wanted did she give me a genuinely pleased expression.

"You hear. Wonderful! Wonderful! God make you hear little sounds. Wonderful!"

Mama took me everywhere with her; rarely did I leave her side, even when traveling on the streetcar throughout the city. One day, when I was about two years old, she held me on her lap in the streetcar and saw people turn their heads, looking at us. She looked down to see my lips moving up and down and wondered if I was uttering nonsense or actually talking. As she looked around, several people standing in the aisle were smiling; two people sitting in the seat ahead of us turned their heads around and grinned. Mama wanted so desperately to know what I was saying, but refrained from writing a note to ask someone. She just smiled back, squeezed me tightly, protecting me, especially from the possibility of *"bad hearing people"* taking me from her.

In those days, a fat baby was considered a cute baby. Mama was barely able to carry me, I was so rotund from breastfeeding

Baby Maxine on the lawn of her parents' first residence on Ames Street. In the background is Herbert's first car, which he loved dearly.

her milk until I was well past three years old. She was given stern advice from a physician telling her I was far too old to be breast-feeding, and that she should stop me. But I was still determined to continue reaching into her blouse for milk. For months and months my little hand cunningly slipped into her blouse to get that abundant supply of nourishment, and Mama abruptly and repeatedly patted my hand until finally I understood there would be no more milk forthcoming from that source.

Maxine, sixteen months, running toward the camera being photographed by Dad.

My face was round with bulging cheeks. My hair soft but woolly, the softness inherited from my father's finely textured hair and the woolliness inherited from my mother's. My nose truly was a round button; my eyes were slanted; and the eyebrows appeared manicured. My round lips stayed open most of the time, if not for eating, then for making baby talk.

By the time I was three, Mama had taught me my ABCs, numbers, colors, and, of course, my name, along with my address, all in sign language—after all, she had the time, since she opted to stay home to care for me rather than go to work. (In those days, most "colored" deaf women were poor and had to work full-time.) But Mama was determined to watch me day and night, rarely letting me out of her sight, except when I was sleeping.

One day she disappeared. Where was my mama? Where was my warmth and protection? Where was she? I was lost in a dark place of abandonment and abruptly thrust in the care of another deaf housewife, Goldie Thomas, who lived one block over on Fifty-Eighth Street. Goldie and her elderly husband were the only deaf folks who lived anywhere near us. My father brought me there in the morning, and every evening he dutifully picked me up after working all day. "Where Mama? Where Mama?" I repeated the question so frequently that finally my daddy said, *"She sick. She come home feel better."*

After several weeks had passed, my father took me and Goldie with him in his car to a hospital boarded by a nine-foot-high black metal fence and a high swinging gate with a huge padlock attached to it. He pulled the car right up to the gate, parked it, and left me sitting beside Goldie in the front seat. I watched him go through the gate, walk along the sidewalk with its massive expanse of lawn on each side, and scramble up the steps to cross the veranda and enter the elegant Victorian building. Moments passed, and then I saw my mother come out of the huge building, walk to the edge of the porch, and wave to me. I was so ecstatic, I scrambled to get out of the car, stood by the gate and waved back and forth with one hand while Goldie held the other.

Daddy returned with a broad grin, *"Mama better. Come home soon."*

After two more months, my mama was finally returned to me. I found out many years later that she had contracted tuberculosis and was in a sanitarium for all those months. At the time, no one explained that to me, and frankly, I don't think I would have understood. I just missed her so.

Once Mama was released, she resumed my care as if she had never been absent. I was determined to never leave her side. If Mama's mother, Martha, was known for little Thomasina following her everywhere, then that entire scenario was replicated with me and Mama because, to paraphrase the old nursery rhyme, "Everywhere Mama went, Maxine was sure to go."

Once Mama wanted to go to the store to purchase meat for Daddy's dinner. It was such a hot rainy humid day that Mama let me lie in the playpen without any clothes on. I had just fallen sound asleep, taking my customary afternoon nap in my playpen. I usually slept for two hours or more. As soon as I fell asleep, Mama slipped out to rush to Don's Grocery, the only grocery store in the area, hoping to be back in twenty minutes if she ran fast. I woke up, instinctively knew that she was not there, somehow squirmed my way over the bars, and pushed past the unlocked screen door to begin walking down Fifty-Ninth Street looking for my Mama. Puddles of water were spread over the entire street since it had rained hours earlier.

Evelyn Ricks, who happened to be in the front yard of her house, began to scream, "There's the deaf mute's baby, she's butt-naked, out in the street all by herself!"

"Go get her," yelled Mrs. Ricks, whereupon Evelyn ran and grabbed me and lifted me in her arms. I had so much mud on me that it looked as if the mud was my skin. "Ugh," said Evelyn as I rubbed the mud all over her too. She spotted my mother entering our house and ran to carry me to her. Mama was horrified at what she saw when Evelyn practically threw me into my mother's arms. Mama hugged me tightly. *"Bad girl, you,"* she said to me as she took me to the bathroom to wash me up. It was a long time before Mama ever left me alone again!

As I said, Mama took me everywhere with her, most especially to Don's Grocery Store. Don's was on the corner of Sixty-First and Dix Streets, exactly three blocks from our house. Not only was Don's the only grocery store in our neighborhood, it was also fully stocked with fresh meats, fruits and vegetables, and fresh baked goods, too. And once entering the store, I would be met with fresh pungent aromas of an assortment of fruits: oranges, tangerines, all sorts of apples. They were stacked on a slanted board propped up against the wall next to the door. Directly in front of the door was a long counter with a cash register on top of it and mouthwatering cakes and cookies behind the glass underneath the counter.

To the left of the baked-goods counter and opposite the fruit stand was a counter six feet high with a variety of meats, ready to be sliced by the butcher. Mama, and sometimes Daddy, would point to the hotdogs, baloney, or occasional sausage meat, and the butcher would promptly wrap it in white paper.

One day Mama took me downtown to see Daddy at the shoe shop to get money to pay a bill. Mama paid the bill and returned to the shoe shop to wait for Daddy to finish work, and then the three of us boarded the streetcar that stopped directly in front of Don's. We disembarked and walked into the store and saw Don standing there. He was a burly short man with thinning black hair and was never seen without his sullied white apron around this thick waist. He greeted us with such affection. He smiled. He waved. He even made homemade gestures to my father and mother, telling my parents he had fresh baked goods that had just come in that morning. I stood by the counter drooling at the sweets when Don, standing behind the counter, reached into it and pulled out a doughnut, "Here you are kid, something good for yah." Gee, I loved that man!

Daddy wrote him a note telling him he wanted to buy food, but did not have enough money to pay for the groceries. Could he pay for it on Saturday, his payday? Don said sure, nodding his head up and down, and grabbed a tablet to write down the name "Herbert Childress" and the amount owed, with the date. Thus began a long-term relationship between Daddy and Don, allowing Daddy to buy things on credit for years and years.

I WAS ONLY four years old when Mama disappeared, once more causing that anxious, frightened feeling inside me. I was given to Goldie to stay during the day, and I remained in a state of confusion and misery. When Daddy picked me up, his face was a little subdued. My instincts told me that this was something new. I was correct. When Mama reappeared, she showed me a baby and told me I had a new baby sister whose name was Shirley. What! Where did that baby come from? Mama never told me a baby was coming to our house, and I expected her to tell me everything. The baby looked so very white; it was bald. They named the baby Shirley, and I didn't know why. This whole situation was very suspicious to me, and I was so apprehensive about this baby thing that I kept my distance from it.

My mother and I (age four) pose for the camera in a studio in 1947.

Mama resumed sewing again after she brought Shirley home. When she was ready to sew, she usually put Shirley on her bed with pillows propped on both sides to prevent her from rolling off the bed. Somehow the tiny thing wiggled from between the pillows and fell to the floor. I heard the baby make a shrill sound and ran to Mama, who leaped from her chair and picked up Shirley, who was wailing, so frightened that she had turned red. Mama rocked her back and forth, holding the baby in her arms.

Mama became frustrated that Shirley refused to drink her breast milk, spitting it out. Somehow Mama managed to feed her from a bottle, telling me the baby didn't like her breast milk. *"(That's) because she fall (on) her head,"* she said.

Eventually, I began to like the strange new thing because it cooed and smiled whenever I was near her.

BY THE TIME I was almost five years old, I could do simple arithmetic, write sentences, and sign words fluently. But then uncertainty and doubt set in. I spoke mimicking the words and sounds the same way my mother spoke, and I realized my mother and father's sounds were different, nothing like the sounds uttered by people who could talk. I began to watch hearing people's lips, their mouth movement, the upper lip parting from the lower lip, going up and down, saying things I didn't understand. Why did Mama say it this way, and they say it that way, because she was always right? I heard Mama say the word *"ta-b-oo"* and heard a hearing person refer to the same thing as "table"; Mama would say *"cha,"* but the hearing person said "chair." Why were these hearing people making mistakes? They were wrong. I really believed that my mother's sounds were correct. Since I was not around hearing people frequently, I couldn't easily compare their speech with that of my parents. Mama shielded me from those *"bad hearing people,"* and in effect became my teacher, my authority, my everything. Whatever voice sounds Mama made around the house I took as gospel that her sounds were correct. I didn't try to understand my father's voice, which screeched and was so garbled no one could possibly understand what he was saying. I sometimes wondered if my confusion would lessen if I were around my relatives, but I didn't see them often—not my aunt Babe or Aunt Arnell. Aunt Arnell rarely came to our home since she didn't own a car, and my father always stopped by to see her after his workday, making her his exclusive confidant. My aunt Babe didn't own a car either; besides, she was working around the clock to earn money to support her family, and rarely had time to visit us.

Maybe I could learn speech from a radio, but Daddy said there was no need for one since he couldn't hear it. Maybe I could pronounce words better if I were around other kids in the neighborhood—except there weren't any kids to play with on Clay Street or even Fifty-Ninth Street. There was Carol Ricks down the street, who was three years older than I, but for whatever the reason, she was a shut-in and did not mingle at all.

The irony is that I never thought of myself as isolated—after all, I had my mother.

IT WAS on one of those visits to Aunt Ruth's, Mama's younger sister, that the truth was revealed. Aunt Ruth lived in Baltimore, Maryland, some forty miles from Washington, D.C. Mama and Daddy and baby Shirley and I hopped in Daddy's green Ford for the long Sunday drive to see Aunt Ruth, her husband Oreather, and my five cousins, all girls.

I was always amazed that their house was full of sounds—chatter and laughter; there was always a busyness, like a house full of bees buzzing hither and thither. On any given Sunday, Mama and Daddy sat with Ruth while she either wrote notes or asked me to sign a few words to tell them the latest fashion, or how to cook a southern delicacy, because Mama was not a good cook.

It was on one of these Sunday trips that I became the focus of all the adults' attention there. We were sitting in the living room, and I was playing with my cousins when Ruth yelled for all to hear, "Lord, the child is talking like them! She doesn't make any sense. Tell Herbert to buy her a television or even a radio. She can't be goin' round talkin' like them. Here let me write to Thomasina." She scribbled:

> **Bring Maxine here on Sundays. She can play with my children and learn to talk right. I want you to buy a television.**

I was five years old when Daddy dutifully bought a television set. It became a perpetual challenge to figure out which sounds were the correct ones: the sounds my mama and daddy made in their attempt to voice a word, or the sounds made by hearing people on the newly purchased television set. Sometimes, just from sheer logic, I figured out that my mother was trying to say the same words that a hearing person was saying. The confusion gradually lessened when I realized that there was another bona fide language out there other than sign language and my parents' sounds.

THE DAY came for me to attend school for the first time. Mama took me to Richardson Elementary School to enroll in kindergarten. The teacher told her she need not stay with me, so my mother left me sitting in a chair in a cold gray room. Already I missed my mother so; I missed the familiar surroundings of home and the feeling of safety and security, and I began to anxiously squirm in the chair, hoping Mama would reappear to take me home.

Three women appeared from nowhere, with one person asking me questions.

"What kind of work does your mother and father do?" asked the teacher, who was clearly the leader of the three.

"My father is a shoemaker. My mother don't work."

"Do you have any sisters or brothers?"

"Yes, I have a sister, Shirley."

"Have you had your vaccinations?"

"I don't know." I hesitated, thinking that was the only answer to give, since I didn't know what "vaccinations" meant.

The teacher began to rifle through papers she was holding in her hand, and talked to the others while looking at the papers. I wasn't sure they understood me, but I noticed they talked to each other as if I were not there.

"The sounds she makes are odd. Do you think she knows the alphabet?"

They don't like me, I think. What should I do? Maybe I should leave and walk home to Mama, but I wasn't sure that I could find my way home, or even whether these teachers would let me leave.

Better to sit here, I thought to myself. I sat motionless in the chair, fearful that if I even budged, some harm would come to me.

"Can you recite the alphabet?" a voice resonated from someone towering over me.

I paused. Did the expression on my face betray that I did not know the meaning of the word "alphabet"?

Then another insistent voice, "The alphabet! You know, your ABCs."

Yes, I understood that! I said the letters as Mama has taught me, pronouncing each letter: "ah," "bay," "cee," "day," "eh," "fff," "geh." The three teachers stood there and stared at me.

"Do you think she knows them?" asked another grown-up.

"I don't know," one teacher replied, and turned to look at me intently. Then she said, "Here, Maxine, here is a pencil and paper. I want you to draw for me. Draw a ball."

I began to feel less tense. "This is easy," I thought and promptly drew a ball.

"Draw a house," the teacher asked.

I did so.

"Draw a girl."

I drew the most perfect girl I could, a girl with a nice face and big eyes, a round nose, a bow for a mouth, black curly hair, and a neck. She wore a pretty dress with lace, had two arms and hands with fingers, long legs, and socks and shoes. Mama always let me draw at home; most of the time, she helped me, as she said the word, made the sign for it, and insisted that I repeat after her.

After drawing a number of objects in response to their commands, the grown-ups took a deep breath, "Now, Maxine, can you write your ABCs?"

"Yes!" Now, I would show them and write as I had for years, just as Mama taught me.

"Well, look at that," one turned to the other, pointing at the paper I had just drawn pictures on. "Yes, she can go on to kindergarten. Maybe she doesn't understand everything because her mother is a deaf mute. I saw her mother when she brought the child here."

Then she turned to me and asked, "Maxine, can your father hear? He's not a deaf-mute too, is he?"

"Yes," I said.

"Well, isn't that something? Both of them are deaf-mutes. Well, well, well." She looked at me as if she was seeing me for the first time. "Come with me, Maxine. I am taking you to your kindergarten room."

The kindergarten teacher took my hand and smiled ever so lovingly that I knew instantly she was the nicest person I had ever met. I was amazed at the desk, the chairs, the blackboard, the chalk; everything was so novel, so different from anything I had ever seen. I couldn't wait to tell Mama about the fun I was having. When she came to the school to pick me up, I was so happy to tell her about the nice teacher. As Mama and I walked toward our house, Mama pointed to the streets and sidewalks, explaining that this was the way I should walk to and from school every day.

"Be careful, you walk only (this) way. Never talk hearing people. Never talk man you don't know. Man take you. I never see you again. You know, 'bad hearing people.'" The thought of never seeing my mother again was so frightening to me that I would dash straight home from school every day. Most of the youngsters who attended Richardson Elementary School lived two or three blocks from the school. I was the only person who lived as far away as eight blocks from the school, and I walked the distance alone.

6

Becoming Aware of Things, Part I

"How Nat King Cole voice sound?"

I always knew Mama couldn't hear me. But I am six years old when I finally realize that she has no notion of what a life with sounds is like. In private, she wants to know the meaning of sound, and she trusts me to explain without embarrassing her around other people. Her hands begin to probe, asking me several questions.

"What mean—the birds sound sweet?" Her face is pensive and questioning.

I wonder why she is asking me and where she has learned that phrase, when I remember the song "I Come to the Garden." There is a line in the song, "The birds sound so sweet, the birds hush their singing." Perhaps she saw an interpreter sign the song, or maybe she read it in a hymnal; I really don't know. I do know I don't have answers for her, only puzzled expressions on my face, as I grope for descriptive words to explain. Persistent, she sees that I am puzzled and unable to explain, so she puts the question in a different guise.

"How Nat King Cole voice sound?"

I feel helpless. How can I answer her? And then it happens. She helps me find the right answers by asking still another question.

"(Is) his voice smooth?"

I know instantly she must have read a description of his voice somewhere.

"Yes, Mama, it is smooth—like your smooth silk material."

She stares at me, giving me a slow understanding smile as if she were now seeing sounds for the very first time.

MAMA'S OVERRIDING objective is to make everything in her life revolve around precision, order, and her ultimate quest for immaculate certainty. Such precision is reflected in Mama and Daddy's work, in my studies, and even in the way we dress.

With extraordinary scrutiny, I am scanned to detect any mismatched, unkempt, ripped, or ruffled appearance of my clothing, which may not meet the rigorous standards of hearing people.

"*Hearing people sly . . . look you up, down, see (if) clothes neat . . . you not right, they laugh you . . . make fun you.*"

Every stitch of Mama's sewing reflects that immaculate attention to detail. And that same penchant for precision is reflected in her mission to become proficient in understanding and writing the English language. She surrounds herself with books, crossword puzzles, word games—anything that will improve her language.

"*My language poor,*" she sighs in frustration. "*I work improve sentences all time.*"

Being able to skillfully express oneself, in Mama's mind, is a true gauge of one's intelligence. Daddy hurriedly comes home one day, after learning that a neighbor, Mr. Ricks, cannot read. My father is stunned. Evidently, Daddy had gone to Mr. Ricks's home nearby on Fifty-Ninth Street seeking his help to make a telephone call. When he arrives at the house, Mr. Ricks answers the front door and looks at the note my father had printed before leaving home. He hands Mr. Ricks the note and is puzzled when Mr. Ricks gives the note to his little girl to read. Daddy knows his own handwriting is very legible and concludes Mr. Ricks is unable to read, even when the writing is neatly printed.

He leaves Mr. Ricks, practically hyperventilating to tell Mama what has happened: *"He can't read. He can't read."*

She responds aghast, *"You sure? He can't read, write? I shock. See, I deaf, I read, write. My language not good, but I read, write."* Gasping, she continues to express her amazement and shame for the neighbor's shocking limitation.

OUR OTHER neighbors, Mr. and Mrs. Mills, who occasionally talk to us, live directly across from us on Clay Street. They have been there for as long as I can remember. Mrs. Mills is memorable for her fair complexion and honey-brown wavy hair, which falls down her back in naturally soft curls. It is her marriage to Mr. Mills, a stout man with a rich dark black complexion that makes me assume that she must be black, too.

It is Sunday morning, the clock over the refrigerator ticks to 8:45 a.m. The doorbell is flashing while Mama and I are sitting in the kitchen. When we go to the door, we're both surprised to see Mrs. Mills. Mama welcomes her to our living room. This is the first time ever that Mrs. Mills has come to our home, and we are really curious about the reason for her visit. She hands Mama a note that says, "Does Maxine go to Sunday school?"

My mother looks over at me and then shakes her head, *"No."*

Mrs. Mills begins to write another note: "Can I take Maxine to Sunday school at my church, St. Paul's Episcopal Church?"

My mother is clearly pleased at Mrs. Mills's request and nods her head, and mouths the words, *"Yes. What time Sunday?"*

"Have her ready next Sunday morning about this time. Okay?"

I then interpret Mrs. Mills' words. My mother signs to me to tell Mrs. Mills that I will be ready on time.

THE MAGICAL Sunday finally arrives when I am preparing to go to Sunday school.

"Hurry, Maxine, hurry. Mrs. Mills take you church."

Mama is pulling a pink pinafore dress over my head and down over my shoulders so my arms can push through the sleeves. She pulls the dress past my waist to my knees, steps back to survey my attire, and bends down to cuff my pink socks in the brightly polished white Mary Jane shoes.

It is time for me to leave for Mrs. Mills's church, and Mama stands on the porch while I cross the street to their house. Both Mr. and Mrs. Mills, who are wearing their Sunday finest, greet me. They lead me to their black car; I slide in the backseat to take the short ride to the yellow Episcopal church about seven or eight blocks away. When we arrive, it is full of children I don't know, who are busily reading their Sunday school books. I feel so awkward and out of place I become tongue-tied and don't attempt to answer any questions posed by the Sunday school teacher. The youngsters all know each other, appearing cozy and relaxed, bantering friendly words, giggling and kidding among themselves. No one asks my name except the Sunday school teacher. I sit on a pew with some space between me and the other kids. It is obvious they are not interested in me, and I feel very much alone. It's a relief to leave and come home to my parents.

"How church?" asks my mother when I first enter the house.

"Fine." I don't tell Mama how uncomfortable I feel at the church.

The next week, when Mrs. Mills asks me to return, I go grudgingly, and do so for several more Sundays.

On one particular Sunday, when she comes for me, I tell her I am not dressed. She tells me she has to leave me and she will pick me up "next Sunday morning." Since now I am expected to dress myself for Sunday school "torment," I figure out that all I need do is take my time every Sunday and tell Mrs. Mills that I am not dressed yet. After this happens for three consecutive Sundays, Mrs. Mills no longer persists in taking me to Sunday school with her. Hallelujah!

I AM IN the second grade now. Mrs. Gibson is my teacher, a petite woman who dresses in flowery prints highlighting her tiny figure. The class is small in comparison to other elementary school classrooms: a total of about twenty students. Every day she dotes on each one of us, calling on each student by his or her first name and asking every child a special question. I sit in the back row of the room and feel particularly special when she finally calls my name to query me.

"And how are you today, Maxine?"

"I'm fine," I say.

"That's very good."

She looks around the room, and asks, "Now, who would like to answer this question? How much is eight plus eight?" I shoot up my hand; she calls my name and I yell, "Sixteen."

"Very good, Maxine. . . . Now, this one is tricky. Remember, class, up until now we have been adding single numbers. Now we will add double numbers. This one is tricky. How much is sixteen plus sixteen?"

I shoot my hand up once again. Mrs. Gibson looks around the room to see if someone else will answer; seeing no volunteers, she sighs and calls on me once again.

"Twenty-six," I answer.

"No, that's not correct."

Two students snicker. I look down at my desk, ashamed that I could be wrong. I glance over to the student sitting next to me, Howard Murray, who looks down at his paper and appears to be as embarrassed for me as I am.

After school, Howard waits for me. He tells me he lives on Fifty-Sixth Street, and we begin to walk in the same direction as my house on Fifty-Ninth and Clay. We reach his house and see his mother standing at the door, waiting for him.

"Well, who do we have here?"

"Mommy, this is Maxine," replies Howard.

"Well, come in, Maxine. I just baked some chocolate cookies. Would you like to have some?" She opens the screen door, anticipating Howard's answer.

"Yes, Mommy."

She leads us to the kitchen, where I smell the most heavenly aroma in the universe.

"Now, Howard, put your book bag in the chair. Would you two like to watch *Howdy Doody*?"

"Y-e-s," Howard and I say the word in unison.

"Well, okay. I'll bring you cookies and milk, and you two can watch *Howdy Doody* together."

She brings us the cookies, and Howard and I sit on the floor, a few feet from the television and chewing on sumptuous chocolate cookies and drinking cold milk. I give the *Howdy Doody Show* my rapt attention, as well as the *Hopalong Cassidy* cowboy show, which followed *Howdy Doody*.

About two hours later, Mrs. Murray comes into the room and says, "Maxine, it's getting dark outside. Do you think your mother will worry about you?"

"No, she won't." I glance at the clock and see that it is after 5:30. "I better get ready to go now."

"Well, Maxine, Howard and I really enjoyed your company. Come again, won't you?"

"Okay." I hastily put on my coat and leave the cozy house to begin walking on the sidewalk toward my house. It is much darker than I had imagined; in fact, it is almost pitch black outside.

I finally reach Fifty-Eighth and Dix Streets, slowly walking along toward Fifty-Ninth, when I see three policemen all carrying lit flashlights: one is standing beside the Baptist church at Fifty-Ninth and Dix; a second one is climbing down a deep grassy embankment across the street from the church, waving his flashlight left and right; and a third is coming toward me. I wonder why there are so many policemen, and look around to see if there is a nearby car accident.

The policeman heading toward me stops and asks, "Are you Maxine Childress?"

"Yes."

He turns around and yells to the others, "I found her. I found her. Here she is."

The officer standing by the church hollers to the other policeman, "We found her. Tell her mother we got her."

Then the other policeman climbs up from the embankment and begins running down Fifty-Ninth Street toward my house.

The officer standing near me looks down at me, "Well, where have you been, young lady?"

"I was at Howard Murray's house."

He takes a deep breath, sighs, and asks, "Did you tell your mother you were going to be at Howard Murray's house?"

"No."

"Next time, tell your mother." He takes my hand and holds it and we stroll to 5901 Clay Street. When he sees my mother, he says, "Here's your little girl. Have a good night." And he walks away. I don't know if she understands him, because I didn't interpret for him. I am too afraid I'll get the whipping of my life. But lo and behold, just the opposite happens to me. Mama hugs me and hugs me. *"Where you?"* "I visit boy school. We look TV." *"No visit anymore. I worry. Maybe you dead. I don't know. I go Mrs. Ricks, call police, look for you."* She gives me a stern look and insists, *"No visit boy never. Understand?"*

I nod my head. I don't ever visit Howard Murray's house again. I can only dream about eating those delicious chocolate cookies.

7

Silent Herbert

"Thank God I deaf, because you talk, talk, talk."

The year is 1949. I am still six years old. Evening comes later and later since spring has come, and the advent of summer is just around the corner. I've crawled into my bed, which I share with Shirley, exhausted from working with Mama all day. I am so tired, I can't sleep and crack my eyes open to stare at the darkness. As I glance around our bedroom, I feel a gentle wind drifting through the two windows, both of which are wide open to allow the maximum breeze to come through the screens. The whippoorwills are noisy. The crickets are making loud sounds, too, as if they are welcoming the pending night. I finally fall asleep to their noises.

The next day, I go to school as usual. When the school day comes to an end, I trudge the eight blocks home with my heavy book bag crisscrossed over my shoulder. I am tired today, perhaps it is from loading myself down with books, or maybe I'm not getting the rest I need. I don't know. But I do know that as soon as I walk in the door after school, Mama is waiting for me at home to help her with the chores. It is wash day today. At least once a week, we have to do the wash in the old wringer washing machine with its rollers on top of the mechanical tub and the swirling agitator in the middle of it. Mama has pulled the machine from the back of the kitchen and puts it next to the sink so she can hook the hose to the faucet. Water flows through the hose filling the tub with water.

"Come here, Maxine. Put clothes here." She has a batch of dirty clothes to cram into the tub, especially Daddy's shirts and khaki pants stained with greasy shoe paste, leather grime, and black shoe polish. I stuff the clothes in the tub, fill it with soap powder, and watch them swirl around, changing the once-clear water to a dirty gray color. She pulls the hose off the faucet and lets the dirty water rush through the hose, emptying the water out of the tub. She repeats the entire process again, this time to fill the tub with clear water to rinse out the soapy suds. After about thirty minutes, Mama releases the rinse water through the hose again. The water splashes in the sink, leaving the cloths limp at the bottom of the tub. That's when Mama picks up each piece of clothing and gently slips it between the two rollers that squeeze water out of the lifeless material.

"Be careful, Maxine. You put your arm there and rollers break your arm." She insists that I hand her each soaking wet article of clothing, and she, in turn, slides it through the two rollers. All of this work—the washing, rinsing, and wringing of clothes—takes about two hours. It is easy to see why Mama wants my help, since she is clearly tired and breathes heavily, only to sigh that we must now begin cooking dinner.

Mama loves to boil vegetables, whether it is carrots or potatoes or rice. Her favorite is rice, which she boils for almost an hour in lots of water, so much water that the rice has to be strained through a colander to draw off the excess water in the pot. She then fries hamburger or fish for the meat entrée. She uses lard or leftover grease to fry everything. Soon however she discovers that some foods need not be soaked in lard.

"Look Maxine, hamburgers not need grease (for) cook. I see now. I put grease before, now I see not need. Not need put lard (in) pan for cook sausage. Wonderful! Now I cook potato salad." I don't know where Mama gets the recipe for potato salad, but it is

delicious. She chops potatoes, green peppers, and onions, and scoops out mayonnaise with relish, making it all glue together. The crème de la crème is the addition of celery seed to the entire batch of potato salad, making it outright scrumptious. I don't know why she doesn't cook it every day, because it is clearly the best thing she cooks.

It is Grindaddy who helps me understand why Mama is not a good cook. She doesn't even try to prepare the foods that I smell at the Ricks's house or at my Aunt Ruth's house in Baltimore. It is a Saturday morning when Grindaddy visits, "Well, what do you have here for breakfast?"

"Here's grits and sausage," I reply.

"What! You should have eggs and bacon."

I tell this to Mama who says, *"We eat grits, sausage N.C. School. We happy."*

So the mystery is solved as to why Mama prepares only the basic foods. No lasagna or spaghetti and meatballs, or corned beef and rib roast, because it is clear the North Carolina School prepared foods that were low in cost and easily cooked for large numbers of youngsters. We are following the North Carolina School food plan.

MY SISTER, Shirley, has learned to walk now, and while she occasionally has a bobble in her step, she still slides along ever so carefully. She is a quiet little girl and rarely asks for anything or even cries. Mama says she is quiet because *"she fell on head when she baby."*

On Saturday, Mama takes Shirley and me with her when she goes downtown to get money from Daddy. Today is his payday. The smell of leather and shoeshine wax float through the shop; we walk to the back of the shop, where Daddy is swirling shoes on a special shoe brush. He looks up to see us and immediately flags down Sam to ask for money to give to Mama. That's when I see the sign for the first time.

"Silent Herbert." The black letters are scrawled on an unevenly cut piece of brown cardboard about four inches tall by ten inches wide. The board is propped up on a shelf just above the wooden counter designating my father's work area at the rear of the shoe repair shop. Staring at the sign, I conclude it is about Daddy—after all, he is the only person there whose name is Herbert. Are they calling him silent because he doesn't talk? But he *can* talk, with his hands. And he can make sounds; his words just aren't understandable to the ordinary person. Don't they know he's not silent? He's not even quiet. I didn't like those belittling words "Silent Herbert." They ridicule Daddy. I feel indignant, indignant for him and for myself as his daughter.

Then I remember one day the shoeshine man glanced at me and told another man, "That's Silent Herbert's daughter. You know, the man who is deaf and dumb."

The taunting label of "deaf and dumb" races through my mind as I think about my father. Daddy's very smart. He's quick with words, and when he writes, his language is clear. Don't they know my father is brilliant? I know my father is smart because he writes sentences where the verb is neatly tucked after the noun, where it belongs.

Daddy's important. Daddy's brainy. Daddy's a big man. I always think of him as big, so big that his torso consumes the room. In fact, he dominates any space, the way a massive oak tree dominates a playground. How can that be? He and Mama are the same height, practically the same size, too. But he seems bigger somehow, stronger, and overpowering.

"Daddy's home. Daddy's home." I sign to my mother as she sits behind the sewing machine; she has already prepared dinner in anticipation of my father's arrival from work. I hear his key turn in the door, his footsteps heading in the direction of the small bedroom Mama uses as both my bedroom and a sewing room. He enters the room with an air of authority and command, sometimes wearily, but always as the recognized head of the household. *"I smell chicken. You cook chicken,"* he says to my mother. "How you know we cook chicken?" I say. *"I can smell chicken. You cook greens."* "Maybe we cook something else," I tease him. *"I know you cook greens,"* he slowly shakes his head, smiling, wondering how I can even challenge his sense of smell. *"You can't fool my nose,"* he proudly declares. He relishes being in the know, the smart one. He seems to savor being the smarter of the two

Herbert was a member of a shoemaker's union. He is pictured with other union workers, second row, center (sixth from the left).

parents, the one with the most experience, the one knowledgeable in the ways of the world, the one with better language skills.

"Yak! Yak! Yak!" Daddy sighs as he repeatedly flaps the top of his hand to his thumb, making the motion back and forth, his hand imitating a duck's beak. Then he says to anyone who is looking, *"Thank God, I deaf. You tell them I happy I deaf because you talk, talk, talk."* His constant biting complaints about my excessive talking started about a year ago. Daddy would stand nearby and watch me converse with the paperboy, the neighbors, the bus driver, the grocery man, the preacher—anyone who talked. I was too young to know that I should interpret what was being said, so Daddy would have to motion to me with the sign for *"what?"* Responding to the quizzical expression on his face, I would brief him with a one- or two-sentence synopsis of the conversation. Then he would nod his head, as if now he understood, and beckon me to come along.

Now that I am six, I give little credence to the accusation that I really talk too much, brushing aside such frivolous thoughts as one sweeps away minor dust, until there is an incident at Daddy's work that gives the perception of my incessant talking a modicum of validity. Mama and I are visiting Daddy at the shoe shop one evening when I blab to Daddy's boss that Daddy works on Saturdays at a different shoe repair shop. Daddy's boss signs to him in excited gestures that he has to pick one job or the other. Then he writes it down in a note to be certain that Daddy understands what he means. Mama and Daddy deduce that I must have been the culprit who told all. When we arrive home, Daddy puts his pointing finger up to his lip and signs, *"Silence. My work. Saturday secret. You dumb; you keep mouth shut."*

"I not talk much," is a constant refrain I tell my parents whenever they see me talking a long time and I neglect to interpret. I wonder if that is Daddy's reason for not having a telephone in our home.

IT'S TIME now to go to our deaf service at Shiloh Baptist Church. Mama makes me wear a light blue cotton dress she has made for me. Daddy looks splendid in his taupe tan suit and exquisitely shined shoes, and Mama has on a navy blue suit with a pink blouse. She looks extravagantly beautiful. Little Shirley is a toddler, three years old, and we all walk down Fifty-Ninth Street to the streetcar stop.

Mama, Daddy, Shirley, and I catch a streetcar around six in the evening in order to arrive at the church service for the deaf, which starts at seven. The service usually concludes by 8:30. Shiloh is at Ninth and P Streets, N.W., an all-black church with an occasional white person attending the services. The members of the deaf congregation, sometimes as many as forty people with their families, are all black.

Every Sunday in a small room on the first floor, a minister gives a sermon for fifteen or twenty minutes with an interpreter. He expounds about our souls going to hell and burning in fire and damnation. I don't know whom to ask what is a soul, and how can it go to hell if the body is dead. If the body burns in hell, then it would burn up again, I reason. I watch the interpreter as he repeats what the minister says in American Sign Language. Most of the time the interpreter is Mr. Harry Lee, a light-complexioned hard of hearing man, tall and lanky, whose wife has rotten teeth.

At Shiloh in the deaf service, I stand in front of people and sing in voice and sign language. Singing and signing has become customary in our deaf church. Since the deaf services lack for a choir, deaf folk are asked to come up front and sing in front of their peers. One by one, a person comes forward and signs a song

A suntanned Herbert with his longtime close friend, Harry Lee, admiring their batch of sunfish caught from a boat. Harry Lee, hard of hearing and fluent in ASL, was an interpreter for the deaf service at Shiloh Baptist Church. He testified as a character witness for my father during his trial.

to an attentive and polite audience. Many times the deaf audience copies the signs of the deaf singer, resulting in the entire audience singing along in American Sign Language. Some actually voice the words while signing. Some sing the lyrics perfectly with a clear voice, while others vocalize using their shrill voice in complete conflict with the song's melody. A few would sing at a slower tempo than is intended in the tune. It is a cacophony of sounds. Only the lyrics are accurate. Sometimes the deaf singer signs the song awkwardly, from short and choppy signs to just fingerspelling out the lyrics while trying to read the songbook from the podium. Despite the quality of the singer's voice or signs, the audience routinely accepts that person's rendition as perfectly natural and gives the singer admiration and respect.

Many times I follow the others to sing "Jesus Loves Me." Mama first taught me the words to that song long ago, and I learned the tune at St. Paul's Episcopal Church, where Mrs. Mills brought me to Sunday school.

> **Jesus loves me, this I know.**
> **For the Bible tells me so.**
> **Little ones to him belong.**
> **They are weak, but He is strong.**
> **Yes Jesus loves me. Yes Jesus loves me.**
> **Yes Jesus loves me. For the Bible tells me so.**

I leave out the signs for the words *for*, *the*, *are*, and *is*, and substitute the words for "little ones" with the sign for *children*, and "Bible" with the sign for *book*. Everyone signs the song with me and appears satisfied with my signing, and I am extremely happy with my performance.

The second song I routinely sing is one I practice signing at home in front of a mirror. And when arriving at church, I stand up in front of a deaf audience and sing with all the soul I can muster in voice and sign.

> **He lives, He lives.**
> **Christ Jesus lives today.**
> **He walks with me. He talks with me along life's narrow way.**
> **He lives. He lives.**
> **Salvation to impart.**
> **You ask me how I know he lives.**
> **He lives within my heart.**

And so I sing that melody with choppy signs, with determination to voice my song while singing: off-key, flat, softly, sometimes loudly. I do not care about signing the lyrics gracefully, but rather to lovingly serenade a group of people who genuinely accept me. I love them so.

It is a bright Sunday morning. The sun is shining so brilliantly, its rays make the plant life glow: the leaves on the oak tree in our backyard, the blades of grass, and even the stubborn weeds actually glisten. This is the first of many Sunday mornings when Daddy is the first to be dressed and is raring to go. He is animated with excitement as he motions to us to hurry and put on our clothes.

"*Come on, come on,*" he gestures to us with his hand stretching his arm outward in a circular motion and pulling it back toward himself.

"Where we go?" I ask him as I hastily dress myself.

"*We go country,*" Daddy responds proudly.

After we hurriedly dress, Mama, Shirley, and I rush to the car. Daddy jumps in the driver's seat and Mama slides in on the other side of him. Shirley and I sit in the backseat and roll down the windows to allow fresh air in the car.

It is not long before Daddy navigates the car through the streets of Washington, then south to the highway heading to Virginia. We pass several small towns before he slows down to exit to Falls Church. The car leaves a smooth paved highway to begin struggling on a rocky road winding through high brush and thick clusters of trees on both sides of what has become a narrow lane. Finally, Daddy drives up to a rail fence about four feet high that is opened with a latch attached to a stockade gate.

When we unlatch the gate, we see a crisply manicured lush green lawn, more than a half-acre long and several hundred feet wide, forming a perfect rectangle inside the fence. This freshly mowed grass seem to appear out of nowhere, surrounded by tall weeds, overgrown brush, and even more trees.

Freed from the stuffy quarters of the car, Shirley and I start to run eagerly down the lawn to the other end of this long rectangular meadow, only to find an unpainted lonesome shack waiting to greet us. We swirl around, out of breath, only to see Daddy and Mama traipsing along behind us. The shack door is closed shut; when Daddy reaches us, he approaches the shack, steps up on the cinderblock step, and bangs on the door and waits a few seconds, then repeats the banging. A few moments later, a tall honey-brown-skinned man opens the door and is deliriously happy to see my father. They hug each other, and Daddy begins to sign to him that he has brought his wife and children.

"My wife," he says, while pointing to my mother. *"Oldest daughter, Maxine; other daughter, Shirley."* He fingerspells our names to the man who stares at all of us.

"No sons?" asks the man.

"No, no sons," responds Daddy shaking his head grimly.

I am gaping at the man's face, more specifically at the one-inch wormlike growth beside his nose. It dangles from his face much like the growth that hangs from a turkey's face. Dumbfounded, I've never seen anything like it.

Daddy points to the man and says *"This . . ."* and puts his pointing finger and thumb together on the face, in a tweezers-like manner, repeating the sign to indicate the man's name in sign language. I bring my hand up to my face and copy the sign, thinking this is the perfect description of the hanging growth on the man's face.

Daddy is delighted to tell us that he is going to give the man money to buy a goat and a pig, and *"When goat and pig grow fat, we kill meat, bring home. We give man meat exchange keep goat and pig,"* Daddy explains, as he reaches in his back pocket for his wallet to give the man money to buy the animals. I am a little awestruck and can't fathom how the pig and the goat will live on the property, let alone how to kill them.

I hastily turn to the man when he makes a sound calling my name and signs to me, *"Go, pick apples, pears. Here baskets."* His hand motions toward an area far away from the shack, and Shirley and I gleefully run through the brush to the waiting pear and apple trees. We fill the bushel baskets so full we are unable to lift them and must hurry back to retrieve Daddy to help us carry them to the waiting car.

We bid the man farewell, and Daddy promises to come back soon. He looks so happy; I haven't seen him look this happy in a long time. Mama is smiling contentedly.

In Daddy's opinion, the only television programs worthy of his unbridled attention are wrestling programs. On Tuesday and Saturday nights, Daddy sits in the large armchair so engrossed in the televised grappling tug of war that his facial expressions actually mimic the wrestlers. His face begins to twist in a malicious frown, embodying the wrestler's orneriness. Daddy bobs and jerks his head as he watches the wrestlers writhe and contort their bodies, practically inseparable one from the other. All of a sudden one wrestler would pull out a small weapon tucked in his pocket, and maim the other while the television camera records the incident for all viewers to see. I step in front of my father to try to convince him that this is all a hoax.

"This all fake," I say, in my effort to persuade him of the facts as I watch the wrestling match. Even at the age of seven, I know these wrestling matches are fake.

"No, this true. True." He easily dismisses my insistence that the wrestling matches are phony by flipping his hand upward and with a simple wave, he animates the *"go away"* sign.

"True, true," he insists.

I walk away. Trying to convince him that wrestling matches are shams and frauds is a waste of time. When the wrestling matches are over, I turn the channel to *The Milton Berle Show*, which also plays on Tuesday nights, and I notice Daddy enjoys Milton Berle's slapstick comedy: dressing in a woman's clothes or having a pie thrown in his face. Sometimes Mama joins Daddy and me to laugh at the absurdity of Milton's pranks.

But when I watch programs like *I Love Lucy*, Daddy taunts me.

"Yak, Yak, Yak, they talk, talk about nothing."

I begin to take notice of programs having minimal dialogue and a high percentage of action, like westerns, with cowboys and Indians fighting each other. Daddy still does not pay much attention to these high-action programs, but he seems to object less to my watching them.

MY FATHER adores fishing. He loves fishing more than any sport, even wrestling. Lakes, rivers, even the Atlantic Ocean, are where he goes to catch different species of fish, especially sunfish and bass. The site of the fishing location depends on the hearing men, black and white, who own a boat or have access to renting one and invite Daddy to come with them on Sunday mornings, his only day off. Oddly, not many of Daddy's deaf friends accompany him.

I wake up early on a particular Sunday morning roused by the footsteps in the living room; I instinctively know the sounds come from Daddy, since he is the only one who is up that early in the morning. I go to the kitchen to see what time it is, since the only clock in the house is on the kitchen wall over the refrigerator. It is five in the morning. Still groggy, I stumble to the living room, and there he is in his red plaid flannel shirt under a sage-green jacket, thick khaki pants tucked in his boots, and wearing a fishing cap. He is waiting to be picked up by the other fishermen. He is standing by the doorway watching through the rectangular glass in the door for their arrival.

"*I go fishing.*" He grins with delicious anticipation.

"Yes. I hope you catch many fish."

"*I will. Remember, you and Mama clean fish.*"

Daddy's passion was fishing. Here, many years later, Barbara, age eight, admires Daddy's catch.

I frown and shrug my shoulders, and turn to go back to bed so he won't see my disdain at doing such a dreadful chore. When I wake up, it is close to eight. I stick my head in the living room and see Daddy asleep in his armchair, still wearing his jacket and hat. I tap him on his leg,

"What happen?"

"Man not come." He appears so lost, so crushed.

At that moment, I hate the men for disappointing my father, hurting him that way; I don't know what to say, except offer an explanation of sorts.

"Maybe man's car breaks down." I offer that lame excuse because there is always something wrong with Daddy's car. He looks surprised at my explanation, as if that is logical, and nods.

"Yes, maybe." He picks up his fishing poles and fishing gear in his black bag and lumbers back to his bedroom.

Now, the very next weekend, the identical scenario is repeated: Daddy is dressed in his fishing attire and waiting in his armchair for the same men at five in the morning. I conjecture that Daddy must have gone to the house of one of the fishermen who promised to take him fishing this Sunday. I hold my breath, hoping they will show up. And turn up they do at 5:30 a.m. The doorbell flickers the lightbulb on and off. I wander to the living room just as Daddy is opening the door to let one of the men come in. He looks elated, really overjoyed that the hearing men have come for him. And I am happy for him, too.

It is 1950 and I am nine years old, almost ten. Once again it is summertime, and my father takes me to Nashville on his vacation. We travel by bus from Washington, D.C., to Nashville, changing buses in major cities. Traveling through the South, I see filthy bathrooms with signs over the doorway entrance reading "Colored." Next door is a bathroom with a "White Only" sign. I peep in the bathroom with the "White Only" sign over the door too, but this room is immaculate. Daddy sees me looking inside the "White Only" bathroom and yanks me to the sidewalk. *"No, no. You can't go. They hang you."* I am stunned.

"No. I want to go in clean bathroom."

"Do what I say. You hardheaded," he yells at me.

It is easier to do as he has instructed; at that moment I realize that coloreds and whites are treated differently. I reason, "If colored people are required to go only in dirty bathrooms and white people go in clean bathrooms, then that means colored people are dirty. But I am not dirty. Mama always makes me stay clean." I sigh because once again this is something I have to decipher. Whew!

When we arrive in Nashville, several of Daddy's brothers and sisters—Laura, Margery, Uncle Bill, and Major—treat my father as if he is a king. The very first thing Margery and Laura do is to serve their beloved brother homemade southern foods: sweet potato pies, fried chicken, hot biscuits. Daddy tells them he is never served this kind of food at home. Everyone knows, even the folks in Nashville, that Mama isn't a good cook. Why, she hardly ever had to cook for herself, certainly not at the North Carolina School, where everything was prepared by the cooks in the massive kitchen, and certainly not at home during the summers when her mother and sisters delighted in fixing the meals when they had the food.

Margery, Laura, and William are so delighted to see Herbert they sit on dining room chairs to reminisce about their childhood pranks with each other.

"Do you remember one Christmas when you hid under the sofa and we could not find you?" says Margery, to an enthralled

Herbert. Margery is the only sister who can fingerspell fluently. Her nimble fingers spell out each word with just a slight pause between words to distinguish one word from the other. Daddy nods his head cheerfully, so pleased that his sister can sign to him. Then Margery turns to me and asks, "Oh by the way, did you get the items we sent you last Christmas?" I don't know what to say to her, so I begin signing to Daddy, "She wants to know if we get clothes for Christmas."

My father stares at me, hoping I can give an explanation, and I, of course, am reluctant to tell her the items are still in the original packaging sent from Nashville, and would still be under the tree if we had not tossed out the tree long ago. The gifts are usually socks, underwear, and an occasional shirt, things I obviously don't appreciate—so much for their good intentions.

"Yes, we got the gifts. Mama says to tell you thank you very much," I say lamely. Oh well, I think to myself. Thank

Many years earlier, Thomasina wore her fox coat while holding me when I was a baby. Sadly, she eventually sold the fur coat because her in-laws insisted on it.

goodness for Mama and Daddy's sense of fun. They love toys, candy, and Christmas as much as I do.

Just then Aunt Laura asks me, "Did your mother sell that old coat?"

"What coat?" I ask.

"That fur coat she said she bought when she was a teacher."

My brain has to immediately switch gears and think about the wonderful burnt orange fox coat that felt so soft when Mama let me run my fingers through it.

"No, she don't have it no more," I mumble softly.

"Good! We told her to sell it. That coat cost too much money for her to have. She didn't need it anyway, besides you all are too poor for her to have a coat like that."

All of a sudden, I feel sad for Mama and decide I'm ready to leave Nashville and come home to her.

8

Becoming Aware of Things, Part II

"I know the exact moment when I realize life is not always what it appears."

Mama and Daddy want me to interpret almost everything I hear, but they don't share with me anything important to them. It isn't fair, after all I am nine years old now.

For instance, when Daddy is leaving for work, I ask him to kiss Mama on the lips, because he just pecks her on the cheek. But I want to see them kiss, because I figure that since his lips are very thin and Mama's lips are fuller, it must be difficult for them to manage such affection. But Daddy's stock reply, with a grin, is *"That my secret!"*

Just a few weeks ago in school, I overheard two girls giggling and whispering about "tongue kissing." What in the world is that? Maybe if I saw Mama and Daddy kiss on the lips, I would know what tongue kissing looks like. Now I'll never find out!

I KNOW the exact moment when I realize life is not always what it appears. It is Christmas Eve, and I am getting ready for what has become a tedious annual ritual for me. In years past, I have mustered my determination and resolve to stay awake all night to meet that most wondrous man in my world, that symbol of generosity, Santa Claus. But despite every effort to keep my eyes open long enough to actually see Santa, I fall asleep.

Invariably I awaken during the predawn hours to discover that he has visited our house already, left toys and gifts, and is back on his sleigh, riding into the night.

And on this particular Christmas Eve night, I have been waiting with restless anticipation for that magical hour of twelve o'clock midnight to finally arrive. By my calculation, Santa will arrive anytime between 12:01 a.m. and the dawning hours. I wait . . . and wait for him to come. My mind races with the images of this fat jovial man burdened with so many gifts—all just for me. I strain to stay awake. But despite all my longing to see him, I fall asleep.

When I awake, I jump from the bed and bolt to the living room and look in that special spot and see that nothing is there. Could what I am seeing be true? I panick. My heart begins pounding in my chest, throbbing in my neck and shoulders. I whirl around and turn to my parents' bedroom; it is just to the right, adjoining the living room. My hands on the doorknob, sweating, I am frantic to tell them of the impending horror. But they have locked the bedroom door! Flustered, I bang on it. I bang, harder, louder, with my balled up fists. I kick the door. Can't they feel this banging? My mouth dry, my throat hoarse from gasping, and my arms weary now from the beating I give the door, I just want to scream, scream, and scream. No!! That would be useless! Wait. An idea!

I rush to go outside. Opening the front door and entering a pitch-black night, I place my finger on the doorbell, a dime-sized button that, when pressed, magically turns on a lightbulb positioned in the corner, near the ceiling in each room. I push down on the button, urgently . . . flicker, flicker, flicker . . . the lights flash on and off, as my finger presses down, and then up, on the bell. Still no motion from the bedroom. I feel a blast of cold wind as I realize I am standing there in a flannel nightgown and with bare feet, too.

The house is so small, a wood and brick bungalow where one can actually stand outside on the front porch and look through the open window blinds and see the bedroom furniture. Peering into the bedroom window, cupping my hand to my forehead, and squinting my eyes to adjust to the midnight darkness, I see absolutely nothing. Pitch black! I resume my doorbell ringing, pushing long and hard on the little button. From the front porch, I see the entire bedroom become illuminated by the special lightbulb designated to shine only when the doorbell rings. I press on and on and on. I refuse to pull back my finger. The light shines in the room for a steadfast twenty or thirty seconds. Finally, I hear commotion . . . footsteps . . . a door opening. I rush inside the house to their bedroom door.

My father is the first to appear. His long salt-and-pepper hair is disheveled; his light-beige cherub face flushed with worry. His calloused, thick hands swing in a circular motion toward his face. He makes short choppy movements with his hands.

"What wrong?" he asks.

In quick jerky motions, I sign back. My thumb goes directly to my forehead as I call, "Daddy, Daddy." Then I make the sign of the alphabet "C" and place it around my nose. It is a commonly used sign for the word "Christmas," and also used in our household for "Santa Claus."

"Santa not come," I say.

My mother, breathless, fumbling with her own flannel nightgown, joins my father at the bedroom door.

"What wrong? What wrong?" Her face and hands are anxious. My father, frowning, turns to her and signs, *"Santa not come."*

Mama's whole body sighs. Her trim body, her pecan-brown face, her strong hands, all seems to exude empathy for my grief.

Her head begins to bob up and down as she signs convincingly, all to no avail, *"Santa come. Santa come. He tired. He work all night bring things (for) children. He come here soon. Come (with) me."*

With her arms around my shoulder, pulling my body snugly close to hers, she leads me to my bedroom and shuts the door while I sob uncontrollably. I look up at her, "You not understand. Santa not come here. He not like me." My body heaves with waves of tears. How could she possibly understand that Santa was not coming? My energy is sapped with consuming worry that I have not been good enough to be given gifts. It is true! He does not bring a toy to anyone who has been naughty or bad. Mama and Daddy have never heard the words to that song. How could they possibly know?

Just then, my father appears in the doorway. His hands waving in broad circular signs, he says, *"Santa come. Santa come."* He motions for me to go in the living room to witness the evidence of Santa's brief presence in our home.

Just then, my mind, my body, my thoughts, even my breathing become paralyzed for a second or two as I am struck by my parents' attempt to fool me. It is impossible for Santa to enter the house, because I did not hear him. Did Mama and Daddy forget that I am their ears? During all my tender years, they had taught me to listen, even when I was not paying attention.

I sign to my father incredulously and suspiciously, "Santa not come. I not hear."

"Come! Come!" My father orders me to follow him to the living room. *"See yourself."*

Under the evergreen Christmas tree—decorated with bright lights, ornaments, and silver tinsel—are festively wrapped gifts; articles of clothing sent by our beloved relatives from Nashville, Tennessee, and . . . standing there . . . standing there in the corner, at least three feet high, is the most exquisite doll, dressed in a white satin and lace wedding gown. With pearls around her neck, a veil made of fine lace covering her face, and a ring of tiny daisies around her head, she is undoubtedly the most beautiful doll ever created.

I stand there, my mouth open, gaping, trying to take in her beauty, when my mind returns to a piercing state of incipient disbelief. I turn to confront my parents, who are standing there with broad grins on their faces. I look at them accusingly.

"Santa not bring doll here. I not hear. You put doll there."

"*No . . . No . . . Santa bring doll.*" Both sign simultaneously. So simultaneous are their signs, they seem almost rehearsed. Their facial expressions convey surprise that I could even entertain such a thought. Is it my imagination? Did I see a glimmer in Daddy's eye? Is there a hint of a smile?

"You put doll there. You Santa Claus." I sign, less reproachful, and more certain now of reality.

At that very moment the mystery is solved. I had heard some of the kids talking with each other at school, telling each other there is no Santa Claus, but I just didn't believe them. Now I have the answer to a plaguing question put to my parents every Christmas since I could remember. How does Santa enter a locked house without my hearing him? There is not a chimney in the house. Does he come through the window? Through the door?

At last, I know the answer.

I am far older than most children when they discover who Santa really is. I've just learned yet another sad fact of life as it really is.

Now THAT I've received the doll, I consume hours staring at her magnificent beauty. I am captivated by her white perfectly round face, her pink rouge cheeks, eyelids that open and close depending on her posture, her perfectly formed mouth, with the upper lip a tad thinner than the full round lower lip. Combing her hair, I would twirl the locks around my finger to form a perfect arrangement of curls to frame her face.

My disappointment that the doll is not a gift from Santa has quickly diminished, translating to constant delight in my perfect doll. She is all mine. I have accepted the fact that it is from my parents, who show me their love by giving me this gift.

In the basement is an old corroded stroller that is a perfect fit for my treasured doll. Once I have scrubbed off years of accumulated spider webs, dust, dirt, and rust, it becomes the perfect vehicle for my perfect little human being and I take this magnificently beautiful doll for a walk.

Promenading down the street with the blue and white stroller gives me an opportunity to stop anyone, strangers or familiar faces alike, who display an interest in me. Pointing to the doll, I say, "Look what I got for Christmas. My Mama and Daddy got me this doll."

My joy is bubbling over. My delight in the doll shines on my face. I am sure everyone can see my sheer happiness.

Having my parents give me the doll reinforces my feeling that our household is just like anyone else's on Christmas day. Our household is normal in every way, regardless of Mama and Daddy's deafness. In my mind, my parents are just like everyone else's parents; they love their children; they love me. Maybe my parents are better than the average family—after all, how many children receive a doll as exquisite as mine?

I take the doll for a stroll to Ann Kenn's house six blocks away. Ann Kenn is one of the few youngsters who is friendly to me. She is a year older than I, even though she is in the same grade but in a different classroom. Ann has five sisters and brothers. Judging from her clothes, she is neglected and unkempt, since the clothes are wrinkled and occasionally outright dirty. She wears thick braids with bits of lint stuck in her hair. I don't care about her appearance, even though she is often disheveled, but since she apparently likes me and is willing to be my friend, I accept her as she is.

Ann's house, a faded dirty white color with green trim, is situated in the midst of an all-dirt yard with an occasional small patch of green grass. The lack of grass in the yard is the result of a dozen children trampling it, turning the yard to dirt. A gray metal link fence, now rusty and twisted, separates the yard from the sidewalk. The leaning fence seems to sway and stands straight thanks only to the occasional post that props it up. The rotting wooden steps that lead to the house have huge nails sticking out in places. The air is laden with a repugnant aroma thick with Clorox, which has probably been used to scrub the floors reeking of urine where baby after baby has peed. The disgusting aroma smacks me in the face as I enter the main entrance door to make an immediate right turn to enter Ann's flat on the first floor. A stairway leads to the second-floor apartment where Ann's aunt lives with her five children.

Ann is the oldest of six. Her father is a tall, thin-as-a-rail man who grins every time he sees me. Her mom has thick curly hair past her shoulders that is often tied back. Her face is thick with freckles. Her full lips, dark from heavy smoking, are uncharacteristically darker than her molasses-brown skin. She is short but with a nice figure, showing little evidence of mothering six children.

I ask for Ann and am told she will join me on the front porch. I am glad to see my friend, who seems to be the only person at school who'll talk to me. I chat with delight about the doll. Ann is not as enthusiastic about my gift. She sighs when she talks and slowly begins to rattle off the things she had gotten for Christmas. I change the subject and show her my fingernails, which are growing at last.

"See how long they are," I boast.

"Yeah, they'll need to be shaped," she responds.

Disappointed that she is not admiring my fingernails, I try to act as if I know what she means. "Oh, I don't want to cut my fingernails. They've just begun to grow."

"I don't mean you have to cut them," she says. "You have to shape them, you know, with a file."

"Yes, I know." I lie because I don't know what she means by having to "shape my nails with a file." I change the topic.

"Where are you going today? Are you going on a trip? My daddy and mama are going to Virginia to our friend's farm," I quickly add.

"Naw, we ain't going nowhere. My daddy was drunk yesterday and he puked all over the place." She pauses, watching me carefully when she mutters, "And he puts his hands all over me. On my titties, too. He thought I was my mother."

I try to understand what she is saying. Did she not say that her father thought she was her mother? I repeat the words in my mind.

"Did he r-e-a-l-l-y put his hands on your titties?" I ask, trying to conjure an accurate picture.

"Yeah," she says matter-of-factly. "He does it all the time."

"Have you told your mother?" I ask.

"Yeah, but I don't think she believes me."

I begin to shudder. At that moment, a wind blows across the porch that chills me to the core. I pause, a little bit stunned and embarrassed, having nothing to say, except that I should go back to my house and get ready to go with my folks. As I push the baby's buggy back home at a much brisker pace, some primal instinct stirs in me as I begin to feel lucky that our house is clean and safe. And I think of Daddy, too. He always insists that I wear a robe or a dress over my slip or nightgown.

He would always say to me, *"No, No, slip not enough——go, go . . . put (on) clothes."* He is adamant. *"Me father. Show me respect. No, no, wear clothes all time around me."*

It is a year later when I see Ann Kenn again. I stop by her house, when she again is brusque with me. Her daddy is in the hospital from drinking so much.

Later on that year, she tells me her mom and dad are not living together. When I see her again shortly thereafter, her father has died. I sometimes wondered if her mother ever came to believe what her daughter told her.

My daddy drinks a lot too, especially beer, but one thing for sure, he would never do anything that would shame me. He loves me too much.

"Come, Maxine, you and Shirley stay with Mary few days," says Daddy somberly. Our clothes are put in a brown bag. Daddy drives my sister and me in his recently purchased green Ford to Mama's sister's apartment in the projects on Fiftieth Street. I don't know why we have to stay there, but am too excited about the unexpected adventure to ask why. I'll be able to have fun with my cousins: Joe, who is three years older than I; Clarence, two years older; Charles, who is the same age as I; and David, three years younger. I notice Mama is not with us, and I ask Daddy where she is. He shrugs his shoulders and tells me she is visiting friends and will be home soon. Because she has been so tired lately, I believe him.

Daddy reappears after four days and brings us home. Mama embraces us and motions for Shirley and me to go to her bedroom. There on the bed wrapped in a soft beige blanket is the most beautiful baby I have ever seen.

"What is baby's name?" I ask.

"Barbara," says Mama. *"Her sign 'B.'"* She makes the alphabet letter "B" and puts it on the front of her face about an inch from her nose.

I never noticed she was pregnant. In fact, I don't think I knew how babies are created, so it never occurred to me that because Mama has a big stomach, she is pregnant. Here we go again, things happening around here and I don't know about it. It's just not fair.

I look over at Daddy, who looks melancholy. Maybe it's because it's another girl!

AT SCHOOL, I don't have many friends. I believe it is because of the wide distance that most of the kids live from the school.

The Childress family. Left to right: Shirley, Herbert, Thomasina, Barbara, and Maxine.

The area is so spread out that the youngsters live many blocks from one another. I am in the fourth grade, and the teacher is Mrs. Frye, a slender stylish woman with shiny black hair, glistening because of the pomade oil on it. She neither likes nor dislikes me—she is aloof toward me.

The only person I try to talk to is Jerome, who sits next to me. I ask him a question like, "How are you today?" And he usually shrugs and answers with only one word. I persist and ask another question, and again he will just shrug. Jerome is a beige-complexioned boy who looks very poor, as his clothes are tattered and his hair has white specks of dust in it. He looks rather pitiful. He doesn't like me and continues to threaten me. I don't know what I have done to him. He just doesn't like me.

I have to walk by his row house in the projects on the way home from school every day.

In class sometimes he leans over to me and whispers, "You better not come down my street, 'cuz I'll git yah!" So after school, I dash out of the building, down the street, pass Jerome's row house, and look back to see him chasing after me. There he is, running after me. I run out of breath almost afraid to turn around to see if he is still there. Finally, I look back and he has disappeared.

I arrive home, out of breath, and tell Mama, "Bad boy want fight me. He run chases me."

My mother anxiously waits for my father to come home, knowing that he should be the one to handle this. *"You go school. Tell teacher make boy stop chase Maxine. He want fight."*

Daddy dutifully goes with me to school the very next day. He wears his taupe suit and striped tie and looks as if he is going to church. He grabs my hand and walks with me to the classroom. Mrs. Frye seems surprised to see us, and she motions to us to go out in the hallway.

My father begins to sign to her, and looks her directly in the eye, while expecting me to interpret. *"My daughter say boy want fight her. You must tell boy and his mother and father stop bother my daughter."*

"Well, who is the boy, Maxine?"

"Jerome. He won't stop bothering me—and he chases me after school."

"Okay. Tell your father I'll take care of it." She smiles apprehensively at my father.

"Thank you," my father signs and gives her a half smile, confident that the matter is closed. *"Tell her I must go work now."*

"Tell your father I am so glad to meet him, and I certainly appreciate his taking the time to come here. Be rest assured that this entire situation will be taken care of," she tells him.

Herbert poses during happy days with his daughters, Maxine, Shirley, and Barbara in 1951.

I sign to Daddy that the boy is not going to fight me anymore. Daddy thanks her again and turns to leave. The entire meeting in the hallway takes less than five minutes.

Mrs. Frye and I stand in the hallway for a moment watching my father walk down the corridor. As we turn to go inside, she says, "Maxine, your father is s-o-o-o-o good-looking. My! My! That is one handsome man. You are one lucky little girl."

I notice Mrs. Frye is much pleasanter toward me now. Why, she is downright friendly, and even smiles at me during the day. Maybe Daddy needs to come to my school all the time!

9

Social Club and Church

"We 'colored' deaf people in D.C. socialize with each other mostly in three ways: our social club, home visits with each other, and our deaf church. We laugh, dance, and worship."

I am nine years old and in two months, I will be ten. It is 1953. It's that time of year again, when "colored" deaf folks from all over the world flock to Washington, D.C., to their annual dance event—it isn't annual, more like every three years or so, because the event alternates between cities each year: New York City, Philadelphia, and D.C. It doesn't have a name—it is simply called the annual deaf dance party. Oh, once in a while, there will be two affairs in the same year, one in the spring and the other in the fall, or someone will decide that there should be a dance in the summer and the other in the winter. Who knows what the rationale is behind the selection of dates for the big event? The purpose, however, is always the same: to meet and enjoy each other, laugh, and even dance, together. When it comes to dancing, it doesn't matter if they can't hear the music, or jitterbug to a romantic slow song, or even dance slowly to a song with a fast beat. They have pure fun, and they don't care what hearing people think when seeing them dance.

The planning for this affair has been in the works for months, maybe even years. A group of deaf people who loosely call themselves "a club" meet every two or three months at someone's home. It isn't until five or six months before the event is to occur when more intense effort is put forth in the planning and implementation of tasks to complete. Someone puts down the deposit for the hall (the location varies each year, and it depends on whether the place has a bar); someone else is responsible for cold drinks; and another will decide whether they will cater the food or prepare the food themselves. (Usually folks decide to cook the food in individual homes and bring it to the hall because quite simply, the cost is much cheaper and the club is able to make a profit.)

Now there are three ways that "colored" deaf people socialize: a deaf club, house visits, and the deaf church. The first is by having a club, of sorts, which doesn't have a formal name—it doesn't even have a bank account. Each person puts in a five-dollar bill each time they meet, and a designated person, usually the president, keeps the money in an envelope, only to announce at their next meeting how much money they have accumulated. You see, their function is not to make money, rather it is to preserve a way to meet semiregularly to cluck like chickens, gossiping about each other or telling jokes that many hearing persons don't appreciate or find amusing.

Daddy is so proud to be the first president of this deaf club in Washington, D.C. He has been president for a number of years. On one occasion, his pride becomes subdued when he has to borrow some money from the worn-out envelope for personal reasons and hopes to pay it back before the next meeting. But alas! He doesn't have the cash to put back in the kitty.

At the next meeting, he is asked to produce the envelope, and he lamely says he doesn't have it.

"*You steal money!*" one of the attending committee members says to Daddy. He is accused of pilfering dollars from the coffers, when he makes the lame excuse that he brought the wrong envelope to the meeting. No one believes him. He promises to have the exact amount the next time they meet.

Daddy is able to replenish the missing dollars before the very next meeting somehow. But Mama tells me that she is not sure if they will elect him president. And sure enough, he was never elected president again.

IN ALL THE years I have known of the existence of the club, I have seen the membership come to our house only once. I really don't see them until it is time for the annual dance when many stay in each other's homes. Our house is one of the host sites for anyone who wants to bed down over the partying weekend. These are Mama and Daddy's friends, who proclaim their intimate knowledge of each other from years past.

I am summoned to the living room by one of my parents to meet old schoolmates of theirs: *"This my daughter,"* my father or mother proudly proclaims. Their friends scrutinize me with squinting eyes that invariably claim I look just like the parent who introduced me. Then after signing to me about their relationship with my mother or father, they turn to my parents and say, *"She signs wonderful, same deaf person."*

"I go school (with) your mama," is a frequent comment, or *"Your mama my teacher."* And they wear wide proud grins boasting of their enduring friendship. This conversation is repeated so many times, it has become a routine and I am bored by all the fanfare until I meet Claude, Mama's old boyfriend. He is lanky and almost six feet, five inches tall with a crew cut. He is obviously a Mohawk Indian. He brings his young son and daughter, both resembling members of the Mohawk Nation, with his handsome son wearing a similar crew cut and his beautiful daughter sporting two long pigtails down to her waist. I wonder, if Mama had married him, whether I would have looked like his daughter. No. I would not have even been born.

I look over at Daddy to see his reaction to meeting Mama's boyfriend. Is he angry or maybe jealous? A thought flashes through my mind of a television program that tells of an actor who is a master of disguise and like the actor, Daddy masks his thoughts and feelings. His face is calm, but void of any expression. He politely shakes Claude's hand and talks with him as if he and Claude are friends. Go figure!

THE SECOND WAY that my folks keep in touch with other deaf folks is for their friends to occasionally stop by the house. Rarely do we know if Mama and Daddy's buddies are coming to visit, and so they drop by the house unexpectedly to bring each other up-to-date news. There is Mr. Lucky, a deaf friend of Mama's who constantly reminds me that he was Mama's classmate; his wife, Mrs. Lucky, who has an excellent command of language and was a classmate of Daddy's at Overlea; and Willard Shorter, an unattractive short man who has a way with the women. There is Harry Lee, our church interpreter; the Scotts, who have a brilliant daughter about six years older than I; the Early family; and Marvin and Cora (I don't know their last name); the Hills; Mr. Thurston; all of whom went to school with Mama or Daddy. There are many other deaf folks I know, but I identify them only by their name in sign language, like the man with gold teeth whose sign is a letter "T" placed on the top of the hand or the extremely obese woman whose sign is the letter "B" positioned on the thigh.

One particular person is Daddy's best friend, Roy Banks, a master mechanic who can repair anything broken and who visits at least once a week to do small jobs, from fixing a leaking faucet to doing major jobs like repairing the roof. There is always a project for him to do. While yes, he is the best handyman we know, he is also admired because he doesn't charge Daddy very much money. After a job is completed, Roy loves to talk to Mama or hang around until Daddy comes home from work to continue the conversation he has started with Mama.

Roy owns a motorcycle and sometimes sits Herbert or Thomasina behind him on the bike, and they ride around, sometimes to the store. Both Mama and Daddy describe the exhilaration they feel after riding with Roy on his motorcycle. *"Wonderful, wonderful. Air blow my face."* Mama's face radiates a glow.

Another unexpected family friend who stops by often is Mr. Harry Lee. Once he popped in to visit Mama during the day when none of us were home. He said, *"You know Herbert have many women; you should make love me."* Mama stared at him. To make certain he understood her clearly, she slowly fingerspelled the word *"No,"* then she stood up and pointed her finger toward the door. Harry left, embarrassed, and with his head bowed. He never propositioned her again.

MY PARENTS have so many deaf friends, some young, some old. Their bond is their deafness and the residential schools they attended together; their racial and cultural backgrounds give my parents a sense of security. These are the same people who are in the club for the deaf, who also attend the church for the deaf at Shiloh, and congregate, as the third way they all socialize together.

It is a routine now to go to church and sing a song in front of the deaf congregation. I practice my signs more frequently now, having seen an interpreter sign a song so eloquently that it became an exquisite form of artistic expression. She sang and signed a song in such a soft graceful way that she captured the audience the same way a master pianist captures the hearts of listeners.

So I practice making my signs become more graceful—softer, wider, and more circular. When I finally stand before the deaf audience, I make the lyrics take on a sway, a movement akin to a ballerina softly propelling her arms and legs in midair. My hands, my arms, gliding back and forth, make each noun and each verb come alive. When I sign "I Come to the Garden," I want you to see the flowers, one by one, blossoming, blending in with each other. When I sing "they smelled so sweet the birds hushed their singing . . ." I want you to smell the perfume the flowers poured forth and the quiet stillness made by birds no longer chirping, tweeting.

I come to the garden alone . . . while the dew is still on the roses
And the voice I hear . . . falling on my ear
The Son of God discloses
And He walks with me and He talks with me and He tells me I am his own
And the voice I hear . . . falling on my ear
None other has ever known.

In my mind, I am there in that garden, surrounded by glorious, blossoming, fragrant flowers. When I finish singing, I look at their faces to see if my singing and signing was acceptable to them. I always look directly at my parents, who are beaming with pride. After the church service, some approach me to say how much they loved the song.

But the mood is always broken when on the first Sunday of each month, a man suddenly appears at the door of the small room and makes a signal to the hearing minister that we are to end the deaf church service. An usher standing upstairs signals the usher downstairs that the break in the upstairs service is taking place and that we should come upstairs to the large room to share communion with the hearing congregation. This is the point in the service where we form a queue and enter the packed room with about a thousand people. We walk along the side of the room with the white pillars separating the dimly lit aisle from the pews. The throng of people all turn to see us enter the gargantuan room.

There is a raised platform behind the podium, and behind this platform is still another raised platform where the choir sings. Everything is burgundy in color. Everything. The wall-to-wall carpet is a thick, burgundy plush pile that seems to stretch to every corner and dominate the room. The pews have matching burgundy cushions.

I feel tiny when I walk into this ornate enormous sanctuary. Every time I enter, I feel like an outsider encroaching on the place where hearing people worship. It is as if the hearing people are all foreigners. I feel intimidated and out of place when seeing so many strangers, but know I am safe with deaf people all around me. Compared to the tiny room downstairs, the room upstairs makes me feel like a tiny little speck, as if I were swallowed up by the huge hearing congregation.

I try to imagine the sermons of the church pastor, a very tall, yellow-complexioned man who has a thumb missing; his mammoth portrait dominates the wall in the corridor.

We take our places and sit in the area designated for us; momentarily, the usher serves a plate of broken crackers symbolizing the body of Christ. I am confused because I wonder how the crackers can be the body of Christ. They look like broken-up saltines to me. After we eat the body of Christ, a chrome pie plate container of one-inch shot glasses of wine tasting like grape juice is passed along to each of us. This is the blood of Jesus. How can grape juice change to blood? Maybe this is all pretend, I say to myself.

Daddy is sitting next to me and I see that he passes both the crackers and the wine to the person sitting on the other side of him. I have never seen him participate in communion.

"Why you not take?" I ask him.

"No, I not take," he responds.

"Why?" I insist.

"I bad," he answers bleakly.

So I figure that he feels he is not deserving of the wine and crackers. But Mama does, and so do I, even though I haven't been baptized.

After the service, the deaf congregation leaves the church to stand on the sidewalk to socialize and gossip. Sometimes the outside church lights are turned off, but deaf folks continue to talk and talk using the street lights to continue their gossiping, mostly about who is having sex with whom, who lost their job, and who drank too much. They talk primarily about scandalous tidbits, mostly about sex, sex, and sex. Some of the gossip is hilarious, true stories inviting commentary and outright laughter:

"You know he broke arm try to break down door, catch his wife have sex with best friend?"

"No, what happen?"

"Best friend jump out window, get ladder, hide on roof."

"What happen next?"

"Husband break door, follow man out window, climb ladder up roof."

"What happen man on roof?"

"He jump, break his leg. Now boyfriend in hospital."

"Where husband?"

"He in hospital, too. Remember, he broke arm, he try catch wife."

"Now wife visit both same hospital."

Everyone has hysterics laughing at the story. But one deaf person listening to this story about someone jumping off a roof remembers still another story where the outcome is so very tragic:

"You remember Maggie who love William Taller?"
"Yes. Taller marry wife name Ann."
"Taller tell Maggie he not leave wife."
"Maggie cry and cry. Her heart broke. She enter bedroom upstairs; jump out window."
"She in hospital?"
"Yes. She break neck."
"God!"
"She can't move body, neck down. No feeling arms and legs."
I am aghast when I hear the story and can't imagine anyone so devastated by a broken heart that she would jump out a window. Why did she do that, I wonder.

I turn to Mama, who is an onlooker to the two people talking with each other, and ask why Maggie would jump out of a window.

Mama says sorrowfully, *"Because she love Taller, want kill herself."*

These are the kind of stories people in the deaf community often share with one another, whether it is in the club setting, visits to the homes of friends, or after-church gatherings.

LATELY, my family hasn't spent much time together, except to visit the deaf man in Falls Church, Virginia, on Sundays during the day or to go to Shiloh Baptist Church on Sunday nights. Mama focuses almost all of her time and energy on Shirley and Barbara now. She teaches Shirley sign language much as she taught me when I was Shirley's age. And Shirley helps Mama with caring for Barbara, which leaves me free to focus on doing schoolwork. I hardly spend any time with Shirley and Barbara, mostly since I am so much older than they and because Mama dotes on them so. She told me once that she absolutely loves caring for babies and little children, and she can't bear for them to grow up. It didn't occur to me until years later that her primary teaching experience was with little kids at the North Carolina School. This doesn't mean she neglects me in any way, but rather she seems to understand and appreciate the younger children more. In fact, she often treats me as if I am a grown-up—she expects me to talk, think, and act like an adult.

Thomasina walks across the lawn of our home at 5901 Clay Street. In the background is a wild cherry tree that Shirley and I often climbed.

Anyway, school is coming to a close, and Mama has discovered the movies as a form of entertainment for Shirley, Barbara, and me. We board the bus to go about eight blocks to the Strand Movie Theatre, and Mama pays the cost of our admission: twenty cents each for Shirley and me; Barbara is free; and Mama, as the adult, pays fifty cents. I am fascinated by the serial movies that end in a suspenseful cliffhanger intended to entice the moviegoer to return to see the next episode. It doesn't matter to me if the serial is a cowboy picture or a mystery thriller. I can't wait to see how the next serial chapter ends: from the *Perils of Pauline* to *Zorro*, or Gene Autry. I can't get enough. So I plead with Mama to let me go alone on Saturdays. She finally acquiesces, but she cautions me that I must learn the way there because I have to walk to the Strand Theatre. So begin my movie adventures. Almost every Saturday, I find out what happened in the next serial. I am in heaven!

Mama usually gives me fifty cents. I clutch my money as I walk along the railroad tracks to finally reach the theater. Before I enter, I stop at the High's Ice Cream Store next door and buy a pint of ice cream for twenty cents. Then I pay the twenty cents for the movie, find a seat up close to the screen, and savor the ice cream, scooping out small spoonfuls with my little wooden spoon and wonder if life can be any better than this.

After the movie, I sometimes walk another four blocks to my Aunt Babe's apartment to see her and my four cousins. (I absolutely love visiting her, since she and Mama are such good buddies, as well as sisters.) It is a long walk, especially up a steep, almost vertical, hill that is so taxing I am out of breath when I arrive to the government-owned apartments known as the "projects." Whenever I get there, Aunt Babe is always shocked to see me.

"Why, Maxine, how did you get here?"

"I walked," I reply.

"Does your mother know you are here?"

"Umm, I think so. She knows I went to the movies."

"You know you are too young to be coming here by yourself," cautions my aunt. I hang around for a short while, talking with my cousins, then begin the long trek home.

On one Saturday, I make my usual visit to Aunt Babe's, but she is not home. Only Clarence is there, who invites me to sit with him on the floor of the bedroom closet. I sit beside him, and he eases his hand up my legs to feel my pee-pee. I jump up and run out the closet door, grab my coat, and practically run all the way home to tell Mama what has happened. Of course, Mama rushes to tell Babe, and Clarence gets the whipping of his life. I think the skin will fall off his bones.

ANOTHER SUMMER has come and gone. It is the conclusion of a torrid season of high humidity, scorching heat, and blazing sun. Mama is wearing a baby-blue seersucker sheer dress that requires a slip be worn underneath it, lest the dress become a see-through garment. Her hair has frizzed as a result of the sweat streaming down her face, now a toasty brown hue. No doubt her dark tan is from being outside doing a variety of chores: hanging up wet clothes on the clothesline; cleaning fish Daddy has managed to catch; even sawing lumber to construct kitchen cabinets Daddy has put off building. She says she will make the cabinets herself.

Now she seems awfully tired, drained by the heat, humidity, and general exhaustion. Just yesterday, she was asked by a hearing assistant minister to volunteer in the church kitchen washing pots and pans for the annual church dinner, a major fund-raising event. She agrees to help in the kitchen, thinking it will not be a major chore. She doesn't realize how heavy the large trays, black kettles, and steel pots and pans would be. She struggles to lift the dirty cookware from the sudsy water, rinse and dry them, then store them in mammoth kitchen cabinets. She was alone doing all this tedious work and felt faint when she finished, only to have to catch the bus home. After arriving home an hour later, she feels a twinge of pain in her stomach, so she plops on the bed positioning herself on her left side. She is eight months pregnant with her fourth child. This time I know she is pregnant because her belly is so huge.

Feeling refreshed after a night of rest, she summons me to accompany her downtown, giving me a green plaid cotton dress to wear. I can't help but admire her blue nylon dress, knowing that even though it looks cool, the nylon retains heat and is not as cool as my cotton dress. Someone once told me that, and now I really believe it, since Mama is sweating so.

We walk down Fifty-Ninth Street, and I hear men up high on telephone poles yelling down to us. "Hey, you down there, you got knocked up, didn't you? Ha. Ha. Ha. Hey you, hey you."

I look up and tell Mama that the two men up on the telephone pole are calling out to us. Mama looks up and tells me to ignore them, almost as if she can hear their taunts.

"No look, Maxine. Walk. Men talk dirty." She grabs my hand and stares straight ahead.

When we return home from downtown, Mama tells me she is tired and will rest now. I don't see her for the rest of the day and evening. When I awaken the next day, Daddy tells me she has gone to the hospital to have the baby. Days pass. Daddy brings Mama home from the hospital. I open the front door to greet her, looking for the new baby, but I see her face filled with such sorrow and agonizing pain. Standing behind her is my father, looking down at the cement floor.

"Where baby?" I look at her arms, one holding her purse and the other holding a brown bag containing her nightgown.

"Baby dead," she says, crestfallen.

"Baby dead," I repeat it again to make myself believe that what she says is true.

"Yes, baby born dead." She sighs, *"Doctor make baby come out. Doctor spank baby girl. Too late for baby, it dead."* She takes off her jacket, walks into her bedroom, and lies on the bed.

I go into my bedroom, lie on the bed, and gaze at the wall.

Weeks become months, and Mama spends most of her time in bed, appearing run-down and disheartened. Occasionally she puts on street clothes to cook, but most of the time Daddy and I do the lion's share of the cooking. I have even learned how to wash clothes in the wringer washing machine, hooking up the washing machine to the kitchen sink with a hose, draining the machine of dirty water. I then fill it up again, just as Mama showed me, then I put individual pieces through the roller wringer squeezing out the residual water from the clothes.

One day I walk in her room and she says, *"Church kill my baby. People leave me alone wash pots. They very heavy. They know better. I hate church because they kill baby."*

I have nothing to say, so I nod my head in agreement.

"I give baby name. Marguerite."

It is months before Mama becomes the Mama I know: animated, caring, and confident. Her new outlook has grown since she began attending Kingdom Hall on Sunday afternoons, studying the Bible with Aunt Babe who is a Jehovah's Witness. That's when Daddy begins to taunt her: *"J.W. not good."* (His abbreviation for Jehovah's Witness is the letter "J" and "W.")

"You bad. You need go Baptist Church." But this is one of the few times when Mama ignores Daddy; she doesn't care what he says. She makes the resolve to never go back to Shiloh again.

FALL BECOMES winter; winter becomes spring into summer, when I am sent to Grandma's house in North Carolina.

10

Summer with Grandma

*"Be careful of the snakes, they will wrap around your leg
and just squeeze it off."*

It all begins with a letter from Grandma written with a lead
pencil in small legible print. Mama rips open the envelope,
carefully reads the letter, and then gives it to me to read, too.
It begins with a thank-you for the five dollars my mother sent
her. Then she says that it is summertime now and she would
like me to come down there for a visit. After all, she hasn't seen
me since I was a baby. The year is 1954. I am ten years old and
will be eleven, and I excitedly anticipate my visit to Grandma,
my mother's mother, Martha Nero Brown, for the summer.

Mama looks at me, guessing that her mother must be lonesome, and wondering if I would like to go. I instantly recall
that Carol Ricks, who lives down the street, has left for Rocky
Mount, North Carolina, for the summer. I discover this when
I go to her house to use the telephone and ask about Carol's whereabouts. Mrs. Ricks says Carol will not return until
September when school opens. When I express my surprise at
the news, Mrs. Ricks says, "Why, a lot of children go down
South for the summer."

When Mama asks me again if I want to go, I tell her, "yes!"
because I can't wait to experience a brand new adventure in the
South! I imagine that I'll be staying at a magnificent mansion
similar to the one Mama describes when she talks about my
great grandmother, Annie Dublin.

"I visit grandma who live big house," I say to mama.

"No. No. My mother live small house Rockwell, N.C., not big Concord." Mama deliberately spells out the alphabet letters, R-o-c-k-w-e-l-l, so I can see the difference between the small rural town, Rockwell, and the larger town of Concord. She says the sentence again, *"My mother no live big house Concord. Her brother, William Nero, fool her. When their mother, Annie Dublin, die, she give house [to] children, Martha and William. William make my mother sign paper, give mother little money. She poor, not know. Now my mother have no house. That why I give mother money build house Rockwell."*

I nod my head signaling that I understand what she is saying. But, I am too excited to really focus on the distinction between my great grandmother, Annie Dublin in Concord and her daughter, my grandmother, Martha Nero Brown in Rockwell. I run to my room to search for our worn-out suitcase, finally finding it in the back of the closet, then scramble through dirty clothes for Mama to wash and eventually pack for me.

The very next day, Mama buys a round-trip train ticket for Concord, North Carolina, packs my summer clothes, and sends me off with the admonition, *"Be (a) good girl."* I hop in the family car with Daddy, Mama, Shirley, and Barbara. I kiss them all good-bye. Sitting on the train, I wave good-bye to them as the train departs from Union Station.

When I finally arrive at Concord after twelve hours, my aunt Della, Mama's sister, and my cousin, Baby Sis, meet me at the train station and whisk me to their home, where I have visions of how much fun we'll have. The next morning, my cousin, Pat, drives me to Rockwell to finally see Grandma again. I see the ugly dilapidated shack that Grandma calls home, and I wonder if I have made a mistake to come here.

Grandma hugs me and tells me to come on in as she takes my suitcase and says, "My, my. You'se so big now. I can't believe you here. Come on in, chile. Yes, yes you sho' 'nuff have gotten so tall. Are you sure you only ten years old? You look older to me."

I suddenly feel a little self-conscious of my size, wondering if I really am that tall. After all, she is barely five feet tall. She takes me to a room and plops my suitcase on the rickety bed.

"Well, well, well. Here is Sina's chile, Maxine. I'se can't believe it. Well, well, well. I guess you'se mighty tired now. Why don't you unpack your clothes, hang them on dat hook there, and get some rest. I'll see you in the mornin'."

I sit on the bed, wondering if this really will be an adventure for me. I slide in between the cold scratchy sheets and finally fall asleep from exhaustion. Then I abruptly wake up in the middle of blackness, only to hear weird sounds like muffled growls and groans outside the lone window in my bedroom. I begin feeling scared and hug myself in the bed, hoping nothing dangerous will attack me.

The next morning at dawn, she asks me, "Well, how did ya sleep?"

"I slept okay," I lie.

A few moments later, I see a lit kerosene lamp on the table. And ask her, "What's that?"

"Oh, that's my lamp I use to read my Bible by."

That's when I muster up the courage to ask her whether she has another one I can have in the bedroom at night.

"You'se ain't scared of the dark, is yah?"

"No," I lie again. "Maybe I can read the Bible at night, too."

"Well, all right, but I thinks you'se scared, that's what I think." She hands me a rusty kerosene lamp and says, "Be careful with dat thing. Don't spill it or you'll burn da house down."

The lit kerosene lamp sits on the floor. The tiny flame flickers, creating shadowy images on the wall. As I watch them, they seem to come alive. The moving shadows are almost humanlike, forming vertical zigzag shapes that bounce up and down from the middle of the wall to the ceiling.

It is nighttime again, and I am petrified. I lie on the rusty wrought-iron bed alone, my arms clasping my body, watching the shadows move, watching the doorway, wondering if the shadows will become human forms and start talking to me. Finally, my heavy eyelids begin to ease together, surrendering to sleep, despite my determination to stay awake. Stay awake I must, because old dead Uncle Henry's ghost might come and drag me away to ghost land. Grandma says he came to see me the night before.

"Why he came rat in here. He came to see me first. Then he took the lamp, walked cross dah room and came to see you. He took a good look at you, chile, while you sleepin'. Ole Uncle Henry stood rat here," she said, pointing to a spot near the foot of the bed.

I try with all my might to picture this shadowy apparition in my mind as she talks. How could all this happen while I am asleep? After all, I never hear a sound, much less catch a glimpse of the ghost.

"What does he look like?" I ask.

"Why he looks just the same, same as when he was alive."

"How did you know it was him?"

"I know him anywhere, it looked just like him! He had on his nightgown, just like he always wore."

I say nothing, mulling over her description of Uncle Henry.

"What's de mattah, gal? You scared?"

I give her a vacant stare, not uttering a word, simply because I am too ashamed to acknowledge my pure fright—an all-consuming fear to the core of my bones, causing me to remain mute.

"Why, you too big to be scared. Ain't nothin' to be 'fraid of. Uncle Henry wouldn't hurt a fly. He just wanted to see yah."

I want to believe her, but I do not. I have become cautious, anxious, and weary. My nerves are frayed after being there alone with Grandma for just a few days of my vacation, especially after all her talk about Uncle Henry's ghost in the house. I am desperately trying to become adjusted to living in the country in rural Rockwell, North Carolina, ten miles from Concord, and some twenty miles from the big city of Charlotte. (Before coming to see Grandma, I never spent much time thinking about dead people and ghosts.)

Grandma lives in a crudely built, bleached gray, four-room shack without benefit of electricity or running water. The reddish interior walls are made of vertical planks of knotty pine held together by three horizontal planks nailed across the wood. There is no ceiling as such, only the roof. Whenever it rains, Grandma puts tin pots on the floor to catch the drips of water trickling their way through the thinly tar-papered plywood roof.

There is a tiny front room, a space barely able to accommodate three or four ladderback chairs. A worn-out, bent screen door, too small for the door frame, creaks open and shut, allowing an occasional visitor to gain entry to the only doorway in the house. A bare wall divides the front room from the kitchen, a still smaller cubicle. The only items declaring it a kitchen are a wooden table nestled against the back of the room with a chair tucked underneath it; a tin basin hanging on the wall; and the black ashy, one-eyed, potbellied woodstove, too big for the little space, which sticks out from the back of the wall to the middle of the room. There is barely any leeway between the table and the stove for movement of any kind. We maneuver our bodies around the stove to cook and eat. Whenever

Thomasina's mother, Martha Brown, standing beside her house in Rockwell, N.C., sometime in the 1950s.

the weather becomes damp, cold, or dreary, we hover over that ugly little stove to capture the glowing heat from the fire. The most space available in that room is the small area on the side of the table, where occasionally Grandma puts an extra chair, which hides a back door she has nailed permanently shut.

Parallel to the minuscule kitchen and tiny living room are two doorless bedrooms, one in front of the other. A wrought-iron bed occupies my room, with its headboard squeezed between the north and south walls. Two feet of space between the south wall and the foot of the bed allow me to walk in the room. Hooks haphazardly nailed to the wall act as clothes hangers, which face me every morning when I wake up looking at that wall. A screened window on the west side of the room lets in the night sounds of crickets and frogs. This is where I try to sleep and where I dread the coming of each advancing night.

I lie awake trying to stay alert and protect myself from the encroachment of snakes, ghosts, rats, or other wild furry animals into my space. I relive Grandma's stories of her brushes with death, the times when she single-handedly tackled the small wildlife indigenous to the area: snakes, lizards, rabid animals "just gone mad," as she says. Her bouts with snakes are peppered throughout almost all her conversations. Grandma tells me that once a snake got into the potbellied stove and poked its head right up through the round plate hole on the top of the stove. She caught its head between the iron lid and the stove itself, killing it instantly.

"Sometimes they'll crawl through the planks of wood or through the hole in the floor, and be careful," she says seriously, "cause they'll squeeze dah life out of yah. They'll wrap around your leg, and just squeeze it off."

Because the house is plopped on top of cinder blocks, making about one foot of crawl space between the foundation and the wooden floor, it is easy for animals to wiggle their way up through the floor. Once, a snake smelling the aroma of bacon Grandma keeps in the kitchen, made its way to the meat. She caught it by mashing her foot on it, just below its neck; grabbing an axe, she chopped it to pieces. I marvel at her strength, her fearless demeanor, but quake all the more with fright.

There is not an outhouse anywhere nearby.

"The whole earth is the bathroom," she says matter-of-factly.

So I do my business anywhere among the trees where I am undetected and given some semblance of privacy, with newspaper in hand, and just squat. The talk of snakes in the woods always remains in my mind, making the trip to the wide open outdoors such a frightening task that I attempt each trip in record speed. Afraid to go alone, I zip to a nearby tree, and do my business and dash back to the house.

"Be careful when you run outside, don't ever step on snake's bones," she cautions, "cause the bones will crawl up inside your leg, and never go away." I don't know if she is kidding or not; I sure enough believe her.

Except for the two-hundred-foot clearing in the front of the house, separating it from the road, the house is surrounded by trees, mostly pine and elm, bunched together stretching for acres and acres. About two miles down the road lives a black family, whose white bungalow house is modern, with aluminum screened doors and windows. They have electricity for light and a nearby pump for water, and unlike grandma's outdoor earthy bathroom, it has an outhouse.

Attached to grandma's house is a porch, a short one, only about three or four feet deep, and as long as the width of the house. She and I sit on the porch, as she talks of my mother in fond, loving, and vivid language.

"Yes, chile, yo' mama bought me dis house. She is de only one who looks after me. I just loves Sina to death." She continues to abbreviate Mama's name from Thomasina to Sina, pronouncing it as "Seena." It is in these few intimate moments, sitting on the porch, feeling the warm cross breeze, when she shares how much she loves my mother. I scrutinize her facial features, her posture, her words to capture the essence of her.

Grandma is short, about five feet tall, stocky in build, with a rectangular body like a stick figure little children draw. Her complexion is a light yellow, and ever so silky smooth. There is not a pimple, not a bump, not a wrinkle. She always wears a rag around her head, tied so tightly, that when she removes it, her hair looks pasted. Deep creases from the rag are carved in her forehead.

"I'se wearin' dis rag tight so it'll keep out da headaches," she says, frequently complaining of the headaches she has to endure.

I'm always anxious to see her hair, cropped at the neckline, parted on the side and combed over to the other side of her face. I admire its soft wavy texture, and its coal-black coloring.

Her teeth are short, resembling children's teeth that have never matured. An upper side tooth is missing, but she veils it carefully with her thin lips. As a result of taking snuff, her teeth have turned a brownish hue. The tips of her lower teeth are tarnished even browner.

The quarter-size lump just inside her lower lip, above her chin is the only evidence of her pocketing a spoonful of snuff in her mouth. Whenever I ask her questions, she makes a motion by nodding her head, then seals her lips tightly together. It is not until she exits to the porch, and spews out a thin rope of dark brown spit, that I realize she cannot answer.

"How come you'se ask so many questions? I declare!" she says when she finally empties her mouth.

It takes a while for me to become accustomed to her, to her superstitions, her wild stories, her snuff, and even her mutterings, as she often talks to herself. Once in a while, I hear my name, but it is muffled with unpleasant sounds. I must be doing something bad, I think, because I sense she is growing tired of me and all my incessant questions and doesn't want me here anymore. It becomes easier and easier to ignore her and concentrate instead on everyday living in this rural isolated countryside. Day by day, my fear of the surroundings gradually lessens, in part because of the routine grandma creates for the two of us.

Almost every morning, just after sunrise, while the white crystal dew is melting on the grass and weeds, we each carry a pail to haul water for the day. We walk a half-mile on a path through the trees and fields to reach a water well situated near a spring. En route, I pass blackberry bushes or an occasional wild apple or pear tree; I stuff the hard fruit in my pockets. In grandma's case, she wraps the blackberries in a handkerchief and tucks them in her bosom. "Dis here is stealin'," she says, "dis land don't belong to us. Be careful, they'll come and shoot ya if you're caught." I know she is telling me the truth because I recall the story Mama told me about the men with rifles in South Carolina who planned to shoot my grandfather, and how the whole family had to flee in a horse-pulled wagon to North Carolina in the dead of night.

After hauling the cold water back to the house, I fill the light gray metal tub with cold water and bathe myself. Then Grandma cooks, frying sliced country bacon from a slab, and we eat it with our freshly picked blackberries. After breakfast on some days, we use the extra cold water to wash clothes with lye soap, using a scrub board propped inside that gray metal tub. Grandma teaches me to dip my clothes in liquid starch made from water left over from cooking rice, and then iron the clothes with a heavy hot iron heated on the wood stove.

Around noon, sitting on the porch, we wait with great eagerness for the mailman to drive his little white truck up to the gray metal mailbox on the side of the dirt road. The mailbox, propped on top of a single post, is shaped like a breadbox with a little red metal flag on the side of it. And on those days around noon, the mailman would pull up that red flag to signal us that there is mail being deposited there. On those occasions when we have letters for him to pick up, we pull up the small red flag, so the driver can retrieve our letters and mail them.

Waiting for the mailman is so agonizing that I sometimes make two or three trips to the mailbox regardless of whether the red flag is up, thinking perhaps he forgot to raise it. I run the two hundred feet looking for a letter from Mama. And it comes about once a week, a letter addressed to Box 2, Route

92, Rockwell, North Carolina. Mama's handwriting is clearly, carefully, and boldly written on the front of the envelope with a lead pencil. Each letter of each word is perfectly written, typical of a teacher's handwriting. The writing takes most of space on the front of the envelope, and Grandma complains about it. "Why does she write so big? They won't think she's very smart when she writes that big." I ignore her criticisms because I know that Mama's handwriting is perfect.

Her letters arrive with cash money included in it, usually one or two five-dollar bills. It is money to purchase goods from the country store, and once we have the money, we walk about a mile or so, along the dirt road, around the bend, and up one steep hill to finally arrive at the country store, and there we purchase our supplies for the week.

Upon entering the store, I savor the aroma of smoked meats that caress my face. The store appears huge to me, almost three times the size of grandma's house; the floors are made of plank wood, now turned a dirty brown-gray color. Three walls, the west, south, and east walls, are lined with canned goods. The windows are next to the door. Grandma picks out several items we need, mostly canned goods, and allows me to select a candy sucker, or a round hardball piece of candy as a treat. She uses the money that my mother sent her to pay for the goods and then she and I load the food in a black nylon fishnet shopping bag. Together we lug the bag, she carrying a handle on one side and I holding the handle on the other. The bag is always heavy, and my arms ache as I try to shift the weight of the bag to my side. It is a relief to finally get back to the little house, and eat one of the meats grandma buys.

Dinner consists mostly of the canned meats: Vienna sausage or spam, and a piece of bread. That's when I learn just how delicious Vienna sausage tastes, and savor each little link.

Once in a while, grandma is given a live chicken from a farmer she knows. With one hand, she squeezes the chicken's head, and swirls its body around in a fast circular motion, and abruptly stops swinging the chicken, breaking the chicken's neck, which makes an audible cracking sound. Then she grabs it, and with an axe chops its head off. It frantically scurries and flutters around in a headless frenzy in the grass, wildly flapping its wings, until it flops down dead. Then grandma soaks the chicken in scalding water, loosening the feathers for plucking. I queasily pluck the feathers off its lifeless but warm body. She slits the chicken wide open, removing its innards. She rolls the cut-up chicken in a plate of flour, then fries it in a skillet of hot lard. And while I think nothing can taste so scrumptious, she eats each morsel uttering criticisms.

"This here bird is tough; it tastes jus' like a tough tom bird."

Since I don't know what a tom bird tastes like, I continue eating until only the remnants of the bones are left, even chewing on parts of the bone. I ask her, "What's it suppose to taste like?"

"Why, I wants it to be a hen bird, soft and juicy." She shakes her head, still disgusted with the tom bird, while I suck on the delicious chicken bone, wishing I had more.

Alas! The last few weeks of the summer come and go, seeming to pass in a matter of moments. It is time for me to return to my home in Washington, D.C., the week before school opens. I am delirious with excitement to return to my mama and daddy: to our bungalow home with its electricity, indoor plumbing, and running water; to those delicious chocolate candies Daddy brings home as a surprise; and to those wonderful newspaper stories Mama dramatizes for us. But even while I long for home, I begin to feel melancholy. I do not want to leave Grandma alone, because she's finally begun to like me and show me warmth and affection.

Finally, the day comes when I pack my suitcases and wait for the ride to Concord. My aunt Della's son, Pat, drives up next to the mailbox in a gray car. As I carry my suitcase up the slope to the waiting car, I turn around to see Grandma standing on the porch. I wave. She waves back, smiling lovingly at me. Then I get in the car. She is still waving her arms, wide fanlike strokes back and forth. As we drive away, I look back through the rear window and see grandma still waving. I can't tell if she is crying or not.

I board the train in Concord, North Carolina, and ride the twelve hours back to Washington, D.C., where Mama is waiting for me at Union Station. Daddy is waiting outside for me in the green Ford; he seems genuinely glad to see me. *"Hi, happy you home."* he says, with his face beaming.

When we arrive at the house, I walk in the living room and call out for Shirley and Barbara. I can hear the pitter-patter of their feet as they leave the kitchen and run to meet me. Shirley puts her thin arms around my waist, hugging me, and Barbara wraps her arms around one of my legs. I never thought I would be so happy to see my sisters. It will be another four years before they go to North Carolina, too, and experience their own adventure.

Daddy goes into his room and brings out a white bag. I can smell the chocolates before he even opens it. And here he goes again, practicing democratic distribution: he parcels out pieces of candy, the first two to me, then Shirley gets two, which are treasures in her hand, and little Barbara is given two, but her fat tiny hands can't hold two pieces at once, so Daddy puts one in each outstretched palm. I still think I should get more since I am the oldest. Life just isn't fair!

IT'S BEEN at least a month since I've been home from North Carolina. It is already late September, but unlike other fall

The Childress sisters wearing Easter outfits made by their mother in 1952.

months, there is not a gradual acquiescing to the winter months—it is unusually cold. Clearly, Indian summer has decided to skip this year. The trees are bare of leaves. No longer fulfilling their obligation to change their foliage colors from blazing green to a collection of golds, browns, and burgundies, the crumbly decaying leaves all lie on the ground. It feels like winter is here already. It might be that winter has decided to visit us without warning, just as an unexpected visitor drops in out of the blue.

The days are gray and cloudy, with constant cold rain pelting down on us as we bundle up in winter clothes for the unseasonably cold and brisk weather.

Just to stay warm, Mama turns up the thermostat, which sends warm air up from the furnace in the basement, straight to the floor just above, forcing the air through the black six-foot-square grate built in the floor in the hallway. Shirley and I stand on the grate, allowing the warm air to blow directly up our dresses and enjoying the blast of heat, which feels absolutely magnificent.

At night, when Shirley and I go to bed, Mama puts winter coats that double as blankets over us as we shiver and try to get warm. I try to cuddle up to Shirley to benefit from her body heat, but she will have none of it. So I complain to Mama that Shirley hugs the edge of the bed and takes the coats, leaving me cold. Mama gives me a blank stare and says, *"Shirley skinny. She need coat keep bones warm."* I sigh and wonder if I should tell her my bones are so cold I can feel them clattering, clanging around in my arms and legs.

No. I don't think she'll believe me.

On these cold mornings, Mama greets us in the morning with a spoonful of dreadful cod liver oil and whole oranges to eat right on the spot, before going to school.

"This good, keep cold away," she says.

Shirley, Barbara, and I grumble, gagging on the nasty-tasting stuff that I secretly believe will make us sicker than the wintry cold itself. Nothing will take the taste away, not even the oranges.

The cold snap is affecting the animals too, certainly the field mice that scurry around in the field behind our house. Suddenly, we are inundated with mice everywhere, which squeeze through cracks and little gaps in the old cinder blocks. They flood the kitchen, dashing through the inside of the stove and running through the kitchen cabinets looking for anything to eat. Not satisfied, the little rascals begin to seek out morsels in other rooms. Mama and Daddy buy a dozen mousetraps, which, even though efficient, don't discourage the mice from running hither and thither throughout the house.

One late morning, I am fast asleep by myself and only one coat to keep me warm, when I suddenly feel movement in the bed, something crawling on my leg. I pull back the covers and see a gray intruder scrambling to jump out of the bed to find another haven for warmth. I holler, terrified. I run to find my mother, screaming with my hands, "Mama, Mama. Rats everywhere." (In our house there is no distinction between the sign for "rat" and "mouse." They are all unwelcome critters.)

That's it. Mama has had enough! Yes, the mousetraps are catching mice faster than she can reload the trap, but that is not sufficient as she is going to catch them with her bare hands!

Mama stealthily stands by a cabinet, leaving its door ajar, careful not to make a sound. The unwitting mouse sneaks in from the back of the cabinet and begins to nibble on a bag containing corn meal. Like a swift bird of prey, Mama grabs the squealing mouse in her bare hand and chokes it to death.

I know it may be hard to believe, but no more mice come back. Mama has singlehandedly scared them off!

11

From Chocolates to Fresh Goat and Pig Meat

"What if I had been the chocolate candy bandit?"

I love chocolates: chocolate cookies, chocolate candy, chocolate cake with thick chocolate icing. I must have been eleven years old and in the sixth grade when I discover that chocolate just plain makes me feel good and eases the troubles I have at home or school. It is about the same time, I think, when I realize the next best thing to having chocolate twenty-four hours a day is having a father whose good friend works in a chocolate candy factory. And not just any candy store, it is Fanny Farmer Fine Chocolates, if you please. They sell only the finest—the choicest creamy chocolates, mouthwatering candies with luscious nuts, or jellies with creamy filling inside each delectable piece. Fanny Farmer Chocolates are hailed as superior to any other, not just for their exquisite taste, but also because each piece has to satisfy rigid inspection standards. Any candy failing the test, no matter how minor the flaw, is promptly given away to employees, or worse yet, tossed aside to oblivion.

I am ever so grateful for Daddy's loyal and most generous friend, a deaf white man whose name I never learn. He wears a crew cut, a dingy white apron, and a wide welcoming grin whenever he sees Daddy and me in the back rooms of the candy factory.

At home, every three or four days, Daddy stands outside the bedroom door and parcels out two or three measly little pieces for each of the three of us. His hand dips into the white paper bag, and up come three pieces. "Maxine, come here. Here are three for you. Shirley, come here, you have three. And even Barbara, just a tiny tot, gets three."

I cherish each piece, taking little bites, savoring the taste, wishing it would last forever. Somehow I reason that I should get more because I am the oldest. Oh well, I'll never be able to convince Daddy of that. If I can just get some more candy, then I will never want any more after that.

On this particular day, I yearn for chocolate candy. I can taste it melting in my mouth, the light chocolate squares with chewy caramel on the inside. Or the dark chocolate ones with syrupy cherries waiting to be crunched and savored. Maybe I'll get one with raisins or almonds, or perhaps some with creamy fillings: vanilla, strawberry, or mint. They are not my favorites—I eat those only as a last resort. Sometimes I guess what the fillings will be, especially the candies with the different nuts. Oh, if I could just have some candy.

It is a Sunday afternoon, Daddy's only day off. He is sitting in an armchair, his head nodding, asleep. Did I hear a purring sound? Is he really sound asleep? The chair is in front of a large double window, some ten to twelve feet directly opposite the door to his bedroom. I stand there, watching the up and down movement of his breathing. I conclude he's sound asleep, and that I can go in his room and get some candy.

Tiptoe . . . tiptoe . . . I have to be careful. He can feel my walking vibrations on the floor. I open the door ever so carefully, so slowly. S-c-r-e-e-c-h. He'll never hear that. Better be careful, he might feel the air draft from the door opening. I ease it open and slip inside. I see the white bag containing the chocolate crown jewels on top of the dresser. Two steps, I grab the bag and stop to breathe in that magnificent chocolate smell, when I hear something. No! No! It can't be. It's Daddy. He's coming. Alarmed, I look around, thinking that perhaps I should jump out the window, but I don't have time to try to open it. What to do? What to do? He'll have a tirade. Would he beat me? Would he mock me to all his relatives and friends, *"I caught Maxine stealing,"* with his hands signing the word "steal" as if in slow motion.

I toss the bag back on top of the dresser and dash under his bed, squeezing my body as close to the wall as possible. For some absurd reason, I hold my breath, thinking he won't find me if he doesn't feel me breathing. The door creaks open. I hear one, two, three footsteps . . . slow ones, sure-footed. The steps walk to the bed. They stop short of it.

Oh, he'll be going to bed. Good! When he falls asleep, I'll be able to crawl out.

One second, two seconds, three seconds, he is still standing there. And then . . . suddenly he pulls up the cover, bends over, and lowers his head. His face, only inches away, is looking squarely at me. *"Hi!"* he says, and beckons his pointing finger for me to come out.

I squirm out from under the bed, expecting the pits of hell to open up and swallow me. He smiles, a rather knowing chuckle, reaches over to the white bag, and gives me three more pieces of candy.

As far as I know, Daddy never mentions this incident to anyone, not even to Mama.

"YOU EAT CANDY?" Standing in the kitchen with her hands on her hips, Mama is the interrogator determined to track down

the culprit who lifted the chocolates from her dresser. She must have reached for the candy while concentrating on her favorite pastime, the newspaper crossword game called "Pruzzle," and realized the candy bag was empty.

"No." I shake my head so furiously that my brain feels as if it is bouncing around in my skull. Many months have passed since the incident with my father catching me in his room looking for candy, but this time I am pleading "not guilty."

"Candy in drawer, gone," signs Mama, looking first at me, then at Shirley. *"Who take candy?"* she asks.

"Not me," I exclaim.

"You sure?" Mama's hands are persistent and emphatic, *"You tell truth!"* She has to be certain. She has no recourse but to invoke the "Swear-to-God" sign on us. That's when she makes the sign and we are required to imitate it, putting the letter "B" up to her lips and then bringing her hand and arm straight up, as straight up as she can, with the palm now flatly facing the ceiling as if it will stretch toward the heavens. It is as if the letter "B" means the word "beat," and bringing the hand and arm straight up in the air is a signal that whatever one is swearing has to be "on the beat of truth."

Reproducing my mother's sign, I now swing my hand and arm up, swearing I am honest on the beat of truth, knowing that the penalty of deception will require God to invoke my immediate death or, worse yet, send me to hell for all eternity if I even remotely consider lying.

"Not me," I repeat my signs to my mother while shaking my head, thinking she suspects me because she knows how much I love chocolates. For some reason, I don't believe my father told my mother of my attempt to swipe the candy from their bedroom.

She looks a little surprised and turns to Shirley, *"You eat candy?"*

"Yes," says Shirley, who dispenses any effort to deny taking the candy, looking at Mama with a spunky expression.

Mama is taken aback by Shirley's outright candor and says, *"No do again,"* shaking her pointing finger at Shirley. I can't believe it. Shirley doesn't even get a punishment or anything. I wonder what my mother would have done if I had been the chocolate candy bandit.

I HAVE AN immense craving for something sweet, but no money to purchase any goodies. Daddy's supply of chocolate candy has long ago dried up. I'm not sure if the same deaf white man with a crew cut has disappeared and no longer works at Fanny Farmer. For whatever reason, candy doesn't seem to be available to us anymore.

All I know is there surely must be a way for me to get candy, ice cream, cake, or something sweet. How am I going to do it? Whatever I do, I must do it soon, especially since my parents and Barbara have gone to visit another deaf couple who live in southeast Washington and I don't expect them home for a few hours.

Suddenly, a brilliant idea! I remember that Mama and Daddy buy food on credit at Don's Grocery. Suppose I write a note from Mama asking for Oreo cookies and vanilla ice cream. I take pencil in hand and write the note:

> **Please give my daughter one box of Oreo cookies and one pint of vanilla ice cream. Please put on credit.**
> **Thank you,**
> **Mrs. Childress**

I write the note with devilish ease, since I am so accustomed to rewriting Mama's notes to my teachers, sometimes explaining my absence from school due to illness, or writing to inform the

A photo taken much earlier of Maxine, age eight, and Shirley, age three.

school that my parents will not be at the PTA meeting. Since Mama taught me how to write cursive, my handwriting and hers are almost identical. Hardly anyone can tell the difference.

Then I plan to walk up to Don's and give them the note, when a pang of cowardice grips me. What if the grocer asks if my mother really wrote this note? What if either my mother or my father catches me? What will they do to me? Then I remember that Shirley is barely given a reprimand for taking Mama's candy, so I decide to ask her to bring the note.

"Shirley, come here. Bring this note to Don's," I say to Shirley.

"You want me to take this note to the store?" she asks, repeating my sentence.

"Yes, the man will give you cookies and vanilla ice cream."

Shirley pauses and actually thinks about what I am asking her to do, and she looks at me suspiciously. She is only six years old, but I've long ago realized she is far more mature than her age, plus she doesn't talk as much as I do and will surely keep this escapade a secret.

"Okay, I'll take the note. But you better give me some cookies and ice cream," she threatens.

"Sure, sure. You'll see," I say convincingly.

Shirley heads out to get the ill-gotten treats, and it seems to take forever for her to return. I begin to have dark thoughts that she has somehow been caught and will tell all to the police for bringing a forged note. And horror-of-horrors, they will, of course, tell Daddy. And Daddy will be beside himself with fury.

All of a sudden, she walks in the house with a brown bag.

"Did you get it?" I ask breathlessly.

"Sure," she says confidently, with a big conspiratorial grin.

"Wow," I say with sheer admiration for Shirley's daring accomplishment. I grab two bowls from the kitchen cabinet and begin to scoop out extra large spoonfuls of vanilla ice cream and divide the package of cookies between us. Nothing in the world tastes so delicious.

Saturday is Daddy's payday, and I know he will stop at Don's to pay our grocery bill. I become apprehensive and outright nervous that my father will discover my sinful act, and this time he will not excuse me. He'll tell the world I am a thief.

But alas! In the coming weeks, my father and mother never mention it. I can only surmise they didn't see a detailed bill and just paid the total amount due. Whatever the reason, I never repeat that experience again! Not ever. The goodies are not worth it.

SEVERAL MONTHS pass, and still neither Daddy nor Mama has said one word to me about cookies and ice cream. Now it's Sunday morning, and Daddy is preparing to go to Falls Church, Virginia, to see his deaf farmer friend with the one-inch growth on his face. My father usually insists that we go with him at least once a month: to pick fruit and vegetables, sometimes pears, apples, or cabbage and corn; to check on the goat and pig that are being raised for the slaughter; and to ensure that our newly acquired pet, a cocker spaniel named Blackie, is doing fine. Mama, Shirley, Barbara, and I aren't excited about going, but Daddy insists we should go because he has a surprise for us. We ask repeatedly what he has planned. He grins, *"Surprise. Surprise."*

There is excitement in the air when we finally arrive in Falls Church, and Shirley, Barbara, and I rush to the gray cabin, only to see a mature goat tied to a tree. Daddy and Mama stroll ever so slowly behind us, and when Daddy sees us standing by the goat, he lets us know the animal is going to die soon. *"We kill goat for meat,"* he says proudly.

The farmer and my father bind the goat's two front hoofs together and tie his back hoofs to hoist the poor struggling animal up on a sturdy limb. It thrashes about, straining to kick

I help butcher a goat.

them. They take a baseball bat, knocking it unconscious. The farmer gets a rifle, stands back from the goat, and shoots it right between the eyes, and then pulls back its head and slices its throat with a sharp butcher knife. The goat jerks about, and then it abruptly stops moving. The animal is pronounced dead. The farmer smoothly slashes the animal's throat, cutting it in a straight vertical line from the throat to the animal's stomach.

Blood is everywhere. Daddy and the farmer ignore the blood and begin to carve out its intestines, which reek of a revolting odor.

Shirley, Barbara, and I can't stand the stink any longer, as it is making us sick. Even Mama, who is watching from afar, says she wants us to go and pick pears, and by the way, she will join us, too. When we return from pulling pears from nearby trees, we see that the goat has been soaking in a tub of boiling-hot water, ready for Daddy to scrape its hide, and next, to cut it up in large pieces, from the shoulder to its shank.

Daddy is exhilarated. I've never seen him so happy. *"Now we eat meat long time. Save me much money."* He brings the butchered meat to a deaf friend's house to place in their freezer. *"I give man (some) meat. I not need pay (him) freeze meat."*

It's about a month later when Daddy announces we all need to go to Falls Church to kill a pig this time. Just as I am about to protest going with him, I see Mama sign to him, *"You go yourself. Children need go church!"*

Whew! Mama is quick to save the day.

12

Crossword Pruzzles and Pearl Bailey

"Television steal your time."

Newspaper clippings are scattered all over the bed. A small pocket dictionary of synonyms lies in their midst. Nearby are still other dictionaries: a three-inch-thick *Webster's Dictionary,* a thesaurus, a crossword puzzle reference book, two more pocket dictionaries, and countless other student dictionaries. My mother loves getting the daily *Washington Post* newspaper, which she avidly pores through every day: first, to read the news of the day, second, to pick out sensational news to dramatize for me, and third, to play the weekly "Pruzzle" game, which resembles the daily crossword puzzle.

Mama, wearing a faded cotton pastel dress, sits on the edge of her bed, in a hunched-over position, with a yellow pencil in her hand. Her lips are taut; her just-washed face has a soft glow from using Ivory Soap; her forehead contains tight wrinkles of tension. The scarf wrapped several times around her head is tied in a knot at the back of her neck.

Mama is staring intently at the neatly cutout squares of crossword "Pruzzles" on the bed; one is in her hand. She has purchased five newspapers, cutting a Pruzzle from each as neatly as she cuts pieces of fabric.

A Pruzzle is a special game, similar to a crossword puzzle, except that some letters of the alphabet are already printed in the Pruzzle. The letters printed for one word, for instance, may be "F_N." The space between the letter *F* and the letter *N* could be filled with the letter *I*, spelling the word "fin," or it could be filled with the letter *A*, spelling the word "fan," or still yet, it could be filled with the letter *U*, which spells the word "fun."

She writes a letter in the square, stares at what she has written, then erases it, and puts in still another letter.

This is a typical day for her. She discovers that she is not the winner of last week's Pruzzle contest sponsored by the local newspapers. Every week she waits for the newspapers to come, hoping her name is listed as the winner. Every week she is disappointed, but not daunted. She resolves to try harder; after all, she reasons, *"This help better my English."*

It is her weekly routine, to clip out, ever so straight, perfectly along the dotted lines and ever so neatly, the prized Pruzzle.

The answers to the last week's Pruzzle are listed in a column next to a fresh new one for this week. Some of the clues are deliberately misleading and construed to mislead the poor hopeful reader in believing they have a chance of winning. Weeks go by, three, four, five weeks without a winner, with the subsequent pot of winnings increasing by hundreds of dollars. Actually, the chances are slim. But Mama is convinced she has a chance and buys several newspapers just to clip out the Pruzzle and fill in as many of the potential answers as she can conjure. Mama insists I help her complete the Pruzzle, and proclaims with exasperation, *"We win money!"*

I am tired of the games, because our chances of winning seem so remote, despite her determined efforts. I tell her, "We'll never win."

"Yes, we win, you . . . see! People read newspaper. Surprise deaf woman win." Other times, she genuinely asks for my assistance.

The clues are always elusive and slightly deceptive. The paper gives the clue, such as "something a mother treasures, and the letters in the Pruzzle are "S_N," with a blank space between the two letters. The temptation is to put in a letter *O* to form the word "son," but the newspaper gives a ludicrous explanation for the answer, which is "sun." A mother loves to plant, they say. It is beyond me how they can justify the word "sun" rather than "son," but Mama, disappointed once again, says that she is not just hopeful of winning, but that she is hopeful of "improving her English." *"See my English improve . . . my English better (and) better."* She refuses to believe this game is rigged.

My mother's signs for "improve" and for "better" are one and the same. We know which word Mama means by watching her lips as she mouths the words and makes the sounds for "better," and then the word for "improve." Week after week, she pursues these crossword games. Week after week, she swings her hand, clicking her thumb against the ring finger, showing that she just missed being the winner by one or two wrong answers. "Doggone it" is the literal translation of the sign. She makes the one sign, then pulls in her lips to show her disappointment. *"I miss win . . . wrong word,"* she says.

Her fervent hope is to win money, to get a piece of luck to make life a little better for us. *"I pay man build two rooms, I rent rooms, I make money,"* she reasons. She never tires of her dreams: to improve the house, to pay her bills. She claps her hands together with a swish.

One day, however, she reads in the *Washington Post* that the United States Supreme Court has ruled on a case that has been covered frequently in the newspaper, deciding that segregated schools are unconstitutional. The case is *Brown vs. Board of Education of Topeka, Kansas.* Mama is both excited and worried at the same time. She reads it repeatedly and then brings the newspaper to her sister, Babe, to ascertain whether this new law will affect the North Carolina School for the Colored Deaf and Blind.

"Yes! Yes! All the schools have to make 'colored' and white students go to school together," Babe explains patiently.

"You sure?" Mama asks, hardly able to fathom how the two races of children could be in the same school together.

She reflects on the news and comments pensively, *"It good if 'colored' children go with white children, but I not believe North Carolina bosses let happen. Bosses sometimes mean. They stop 'colored' children go school."* (Mama's prediction proves to be wise and accurate, since the recent headlines document the staunch segregationists' efforts to block Negro children from integrating schools.)

She brings the newspaper back home with her and continues reading other articles. Then notices an advertisement from Beneficial Finance Company. She recalls having received a letter from the loan company informing her that she is eligible to borrow money from them again. *"I finish pay loan company. Ha, Ha. They no more take my money. No more make big profit. Loan company eat my money."* The sign for "eat" is made very slowly for dramatic effect. *"They write me, bother me many time I late pay. Now I finish, (all) paid. Now want me borrow money. No! They think I dumb. I borrow money, they make big interest. Ha. Ha. No more. I tear letters."* She rips the advertisement into tiny pieces.

IF SEWING is Mama's first passion, then decorating the house is her second. She loves to make each room beautiful, from framing windows with lacy curtains to painting walls with bright colors. Many times I see Mama using paint or varnish to liven up the place. I remember seeing her slather the kitchen floor with thick varnish, hoping she can change it from a dull linoleum to a bright and shiny surface. Sometimes it is useless to even try, the cracks in the floor are in need of desperate repair. But that doesn't stop Mama. She frequents Salvation Army and Goodwill stores to buy household items: rugs, lamps, table cloths, bedspreads—anything to embellish a sad room. Such was her determination to make all things wonderful and lovely.

On this day, it is chilly, the sun will be setting soon and dusk will become night. I curl up on the couch struggling to analyze an arithmetic problem, doodling on a notepad, and ignoring the constant humming of the sewing machine in the bedroom. The lightbulb flickers on and off. I look through the door glass and see two white men wearing gray uniforms; then I see a white truck parked at the curb with the words "Oriental Rugs" marked on the side of it.

As soon as I open the door, a man says, "Is this 5901 Clay Street?"

"Yes," I say.

"Does Thomasina Childress live here?"

"Yes."

"Well, I have a rug here to deliver."

"Are you sure? Wait a minute. I'll get my mother." I look for Mama in the bedroom and say to her, "Man say he has rug."

"Yes, Yes. Tell man bring here." She wears a broad grin as she goes to the living room. Chuckling, she waves to the men to come in.

Two men enter toting a rolled up rug wrapped in brown paper and drop it down on the living room floor. "O.K. sign here," he says to Mama, as he hands her a yellow tablet.

Mama signs the tablet, and is beaming brightly. She turns to me and explains what she has done, *"I go fancy rug store*

downtown. I see rug. Write paper ask how much. Man say worth
$1,000, sell $500.00. I say, sorry, can no buy."

Mama continues her tale by describing how the man stares
at the note, then stares at her; he takes her pencil and writes he
will sell for $200.00.

"I look man long time. Man see I deaf woman, know I honest;
sell rug cheap. I write man, 'I give you $10.00 layaway.'"

Then Mama describes the man sighing, shaking his head,
and staring at her. *"Man look my eyes long time. Man write O.K."*

Mama tells me it took her two years to pay for the rug.
"Sometimes I give man $10.00, sometimes $20.00, sometimes pay
Fridays, sometimes two weeks. I finish pay last week."

She is positively ecstatic. *"I keep secret. Surprise! Surprise!"*

I look at Mama, stunned with disbelief.

Mama and I tear off the brown paper and roll the rug out
on the living room floor. It is magnificent! The size is nine feet
by twelve; the primary color is a deep green with red and yellow
flowers trimming the border; the medallion in the center has
red flowers with unique designs around it.

Mama shows me the contract she signed with the rug man.
It says the handmade carpet is made in Tabriz, Iran. It is made
of lambs wool with silk added as highlights and cotton as the
foundation.

Shirley and Barbara come running into the living room in
response to the commotion. "Look at the rug, look at the new
rug," they yell. "Daddy will be so surprised when he comes
home."

Mama glows with pride; I've never seen her so exuberant.
She is deliriously happy to be our hero.

MAMA'S FATIGUE and weariness soon replaces that brief and
precious moment of happiness in our house. Mama is always

tired. She doesn't make my clothes anymore, since she must work at a laundry to earn a regular paycheck. My clothes are no longer stylish. There isn't time for her to devote to my needs; I come home when no one is home, take the house key hidden under the mat on the porch, and begin doing homework. Shirley comes home a little after I arrive. I am eleven years old. I have a relatively simple agenda: to please my teachers and get good grades, and to try with all my wits to be liked by the other students in my class. That isn't so easy, because I instinctively know something is wrong. I am ill at ease at school, and I don't fit in.

It is about this time that I learn for the first time, that when I was around three years old, Mama had suffered from tuberculosis, had to stay for several months in a sanitarium. She also has sickle-cell trait, which means she has a certain amount of anemia, causing her fatigue.

Now I understand why Mama is always tired. Things aren't as well kept as they used to be and she doesn't seem to laugh as much. *"Your daddy wants me (go) work,"* she says. She isn't one to disagree or argue with him. She keeps her thoughts to herself, nods her head, and listens to him as he vacillates from one mood to another from day to day.

Some days, he is loquacious and unusually attentive, telling her about all the gossip among the deaf. And such juicy gossip it is: *"Marvin beat his wife . . . beat, beat, and beat. Pow! He hit jaw. Pow! He hit eye. Pow! He hit and hit. . . . she leave Marvin. She move. Now she lives with Marvin's friend."* And so Daddy would give vivid descriptions of the gossip he acquired.

On many days, when Mama feels spry and fit, she becomes animated and wants to perform just for me. She becomes even more demonstrative than Daddy in telling stories she has read in the *Washington Post. "Maxine, Maxine, come here.*

See newspaper, man kill woman." She stands there in the living room reenacting the murder. She stalks across the room, stealthily tiptoeing, sneaking up to the poor imaginary victim. She grabs the imaginary victim's neck from behind, and then pretending to be the criminal, she squeezes the victim's neck. Pull! Choke!

Mama paints this scene in gestures and signs, her face alive in the animation, *"Her legs kick, kick."* I could see the victim's legs thrashing.

"Woman pull man's hands." I could see the woman gasping, trying to break the stranglehold on her.

"He hold tight, tight, tight. She can't talk." I see the woman gasping, trying desperately to mouth a word, trying desperately to yell for help.

Then mama reverts from being the victim to the role of the killer. *"He squeeze neck. She die."* Mama's body droops, indicating all life had exited the poor victim.

"Man pull body, bury it." But Mama doesn't just say these words, she actually takes her hands and begins pulling and tugging the body. I can sense the weight of the body as the killer struggles with the corpse to bury it.

Mama begins digging the dirt with an imaginary shovel. She looks coyly around, makes a hissing sound, and pulls her lips tightly together, indicating the killer has to be very quiet, he can't say a word, not even a sigh. She looks over her shoulders, to the left and the right, to make sure no one is coming, and continues to dig. Then the killer drags the body to the mound of dirt next to the freshly dug hole, one ankle in each hand, rolling it into the grave, and shoveling the dirt over the poor dead woman's body until the grave is completely filled. That corpse could never be found.

"How the policemen find the body?" I ask her.

"*I don't know,*" she says. "*Maybe someone see killer (and) tell police. Police find, and now man jail. Go electric chair.*"

That's how storytelling began in our house. Mama finds juicy tidbits from *Jet* magazine, the *Afro-American* newspaper, or from the *Washington Post* and just relives them. She often performs her reenactments when I come home after school. She especially enjoys my expressions of astonishment to all the criminal activity taking place in the entire country, and it doesn't take long for me to deduce that on occasion she takes delight in describing any horrendous illegal act. She never fails to tell me the race of the criminal, especially if he is "colored." "*They show picture 'colored' man, never show picture white man,*" she says sadly.

Occasionally, I cut her off with a question or a sigh, which tells her that I am weary of her stories. That's when Mama abruptly changes roles from being a criminal to mimicking a singer. There she is, standing with an imagined microphone, holding it, swaying her hips, moving her lips, making the song of love come alive. Her mouth hardly makes a sound, but you can easily see from her lips that she is singing, "*I love you. You so beautiful.*" She usually makes the words up as she goes along, arching her shoulders, a lovesick expression on her face, puckering her lips and singing. It is amazing. She has captured the essence of a singer performing on an imaginary stage, smacking her lips, throwing her head back in laughter, putting her hands on her hips, moving her mouth to act as if she is talking to the audience, and then pointing to her feet, "*My feet hurt,*" just as the black singer-comedienne Pearl Bailey would say, "Lordy, chile, my feet hurt."

Mama recalls that once I interpreted a TV show of Pearlie's routine of her feet hurting. So Mama licks her lips, points down to her feet, and says once again, "*Hurt! hurt! Feet hurt!*"

Mama stands there for a brief moment, indicating that she is watching the imaginary audience roar with laughter. Sometimes she becomes the audience and reenacts their laughter.

"People laugh (and) laugh," she signs, rocking back and forth, with one hand over her stomach and the other on her chest, indicating that the people can hardly breathe. She keels over, then brings her head back with her mouth open, signaling that a person is laughing and laughing. Mama's hands go to her face, showing that the person is so hysterical from laughter, they are crying. Her hands would wipe away the tears; she sighs, exhausted from the agony of such intense laughter. Then she mimes singing again, beckoning the audience to join her. She is exactly like Pearl Bailey. It is such a wonderful re-enactment. I can't believe it.

And my mother does not limit her singing to women: she switches sometimes from Frank Sinatra to Nat King Cole or Sammy Davis Jr. It is easy to recognize which one she's imitating. She mimics Frank Sinatra by snapping her fingers, pulling down the brim to an imaginary hat, and swaying her shoulders in an up-and-down movement.

For Nat King Cole, she holds the microphone close to her mouth and imitates Nat by standing straight, hardly moving her body, raising her eyebrows and mouthing a few words emoting love.

Sammy Davis Jr. is easy for her—she merely puts her hand over one eye since Sammy wore an eye patch and sings into the microphone.

After each performance, she beams with sheer delight as I clap my hands with pure pleasure. Then something very sad happens.

It's the middle of the week, late in the afternoon, and I take a nap only to be awakened by sounds of weeping in the living room. When I enter the room, there is Mama with Aunt Babe, both crying with Kleenex in their hands to wipe away their tears.

"What wrong?" I look over at Mama and then to Aunt Babe.

Mary's voice trembles as she says, "Ruth is dead."

"What? You mean Aunt Ruth in Baltimore?" I'm hoping I have the wrong person.

"Yes, your aunt in Baltimore," replies Mary, sobbing. "She died having a baby. Lord. Lord. We all knew she shouldn't have a baby. It killed her."

I try to fathom Aunt Ruth as dead, the aunt who had such life in her voice, spirit in her eyes, who tried to teach Mama how to cook, and insisted Daddy buy a television so I could learn how to talk.

Daddy comes home from work and Mama tells him the bad news. He is devastated, his coloring becomes pale, an ashy white. But he doesn't shed tears, instead he pulls in his lips, tightens his jaws, and spews out fury. *It all Orether fault. He know doctor say she no more babies. He know better. It all his fault.*

My mother and father adored Ruth's wit, her matter-of-fact joshing, particularly about me. (I found out later that she frequently teased my daddy saying he "didn't do it" with my mother since it took Mama four years to become pregnant with me. Ha. Ha. Ha.)

Yes, my mother and father miss Ruth terribly and they mourn her death with such agony. Just as my father holds Orether responsible for Ruth's death, so do the others in the Brown family: my grandmother, Martha; my grindaddy, Clarence, my aunts, Della and Babe, and of course, my mother. They all put on zombie masks, hiding their animosity toward

Orether, especially at the funeral. After the funeral services, when we head back to Washington, Daddy vows to never visit Baltimore again.

I SIT ON the floor with one leg tucked underneath the other, Indian-style, watching *Howdy Doody* on television. I sit close to the set when I hear Mama's feet approaching me; then I hear her voice calling me, *"Maseene."* I turned to see her with a stern expression, *"You clean room and study homework. Television steal your time."* I repeat that phrase "steal your time" to myself several times and realize at that moment how much I underestimate how smart and observant Mama is; I have underestimated her simply because she doesn't have superior language skills. It occurs to me that I had always thought of Mama as deaf first, then an individual second. It's the other way around: she is first a person with her own identity, and second, she is deaf.

I begrudgingly go to the bedroom, straighten the covers on the bed, and plop down on it to read my favorite fairy tale; the worn-out pages of *Rose Red and Snow White.* I frequently take out that book, along with *The Ugly Duckling,* from the traveling bookmobile parked near the main entrance of our school.

I read the story over and over again and fantasize about being in the skin of Rose Red or Snow White:

> The girls had run away, but the bear called after them: "Snow-White and Rose-Red, do not be afraid. Wait, I will come along with you."

> Then they recognized his voice and stayed where they were, and when the bear was beside them suddenly his bearskin fell from him, and he stood there as a handsome man, all dressed in gold. "I am a king's son," he said, "and

was bewitched by the godless dwarf." Snow-White
was married to him and Rose-Red to his brother, and
they shared with one another the great treasures.

Once again, my mind floats to never-never land, where I wish
I could go and never again feel afraid, and where if anyone were
to hurt me, I could depend on a king, even a prince, to protect
me. My fantasy is interrupted when Mama comes in the room,
stares at the book. When I tell her the book is about a girl who
marries a king. She declares, *"That not homework. You do school
work!"* shaking her head.

I don't tell her that reading fairy tales is an outlet from the
drudgery of school. Daydreaming is my only respite.

13

The Bench

"The thought occurs to me to just pray."

The year is 1955. I am twelve years old. Some days I find school outright exhausting. As I trudge along Fifty-Ninth Street approaching my house, I pass Mrs. Johnson's home.

Mrs. Johnson's two-story house on Fifty-Ninth Street is less than eight hundred yards from our house. It has dull gray shingles and is sandwiched between two other houses of similar architecture—two-story single-lot houses designed to accommodate the average family with three or four children. Mrs. Johnson's house slopes downward into an embankment some three or four feet from the street.

Every day since starting the seventh grade, I am in pure misery. I am so miserable I want to cry, but no tears come; each step I take feels like a heavy weight on my legs; I imagine my bones aching. Nobody likes me, at least none of the kids at school, and I don't know why. The kids shun me. Whenever I approach any of the other students, they step back or turn to someone else nearby to start a conversation. Why? It is as if I have a chronic infectious disease, leprosy maybe. Clearly, I still am not fitting in with the youngsters in my first year of junior high school, the seventh grade.

No longer in elementary school, I now have six classes, each with a different teacher: Algebra, French, American History, English, Gymnastics, and Music Appreciation. My homeroom class is comprised of all girls, young ladies who are considered academically advanced; I am in grade classification 7-8. The first number, seven, means I am in the seventh grade, the second number, eight, just means that I am in the top grouping for gifted or talented girls. But I don't think the other girls are that clever, since they treat me so poorly. Smart people just aren't that mean. My clothes are not stylish; maybe that's the reason. Feeling alone and rejected, my only friends seem to be an occasional teacher who acknowledges that I am a hard worker, and therefore an above-average student. But even academic excellence does not draw friends to me. Alas, getting good grades is not a cure-all for the pain of the other students' blatant rejection. Why? Why? Why don't they like me?

Yes, it has to be the clothes I wear. I don't know what else it can be. Most of them represent the black bourgeois, and they wear the latest modern fashions. They come from the working and middle-class "Negroes" (the word "colored" is no longer fashionable or acceptable), whose parents are government employees, postal workers, or teachers in Washington, D.C. Most of their mothers remain at home, while the fathers plod off to work. There are precious few people working in industry or assembly lines simply because Washington, D.C., possesses few manufacturing plants. Negroes who do not have a college degree or technical skills may be among the lucky few who land janitorial or mailroom government jobs in federal offices and nearby military bases in Virginia. Some have jobs in the service industry: hotel cleaning, laundry cleaning, and, of course, shoe repair or domestic work.

Every school morning I hike long city blocks to reach Kelly Miller Junior High School, designated to serve our neighborhoods and named for a mathematician who was the first Negro to complete graduate school in the 1880s. I walk past single bungalow homes, up a wooded hill and down and around blocks of attached row houses. I cross a nearby bridge and circle housing projects, cut through treed lots, cross another bridge to finally arrive a half hour from the time I left home. And at the end of the day, I weave through city blocks to pass Mrs. Johnson's home and then finally reach my house.

My shoulders slope with the load of heavy books whenever I walk, especially after school hours when the tedious weight of trying to please other people weighs me down. I am also exhausted since I started taking naps shortly after arriving home and waking up after midnight to do my homework for the next day. That means I often get less than four or five hours sleep.

As I pass Mrs. Johnson's house, exhausted and weary, I see her sitting on the porch, and her presence promptly cheers me. She sits on a black wrought-iron chair, with pads behind her back and underneath her. I never knew Mrs. Johnson's first name, how many children she has or even how old she was. Just that she is up in age, seventy or eighty, and that she sits there on that wrought-iron chair on most sunny days and greets me as I walk past her house. Day in and day out, she sits there on her wrought-iron chair.

Her once-black hair seems to be giving up, submitting to the dominance of strands of white and gray. Her complexion is a dullish pecan brown. Her skin is beginning to sag—drooping in places under her chin. Her thin arms, betraying a skin that once wrapped around her plumpness, flap as she waves when I pass by. Her hands seem too large for the thin arms holding them; the wormlike purple veins on the tops of her hands and the long knuckled fingers make her hands look massive. Those hands are meant, it seems, to help lift her from the chair and navigate her as she grips the wooden stick, a tree limb, now used as a cane to pull her upward from the chair. She slowly, so s-l-o-w-l-y, eases herself from the clutches of the wrought-iron chair, and takes the three or four steps to open the front door. I have seen Mrs. Johnson struggling to walk to the door on only two occasions. For the most part, she is sitting on the porch.

On this day, as on most other sunny warm days, there she is, only a few feet away from the screen door. She wears a drab calico dress, faded from its many washings. Her shoes are plain black orthopedic tie-ups, with a space between the sides of her shoes and her feet, telling me that each shoe is a bit too wide.

I am so glad to see her.

"Hi, Mrs. Johnson."

"Well, hello, Maxine. And how are you today?"

"Just fine, Mrs. Johnson."

"You just now coming home from school?"

"Yes, Mrs. Johnson."

"And how did you do today in school?"

Day after day the conversation repeats itself.

On this particular day, the conversation takes an unanticipated twist. It is a crisp, warm, bright sunny day with the sun's rays softly glittering on the street.

"Hello, Mrs. Johnson."

"Well, hello, there, Maxine. Say, Maxine, come here a minute."

Her request is so out of the ordinary. What does she want? She has never asked me to join her in any conversation other than the customary "Hello" and "How are you?" Surprised, I step down the three or four steps to the short sidewalk, step up the single step to the porch, and sit in the wrought-iron chair beside her.

"Listen, Maxine, I see you got a new bench on your porch. Where did you get that bench?"

My eyes peer over to our house sitting there on the corner, with the trees surrounding it. There in the middle of the porch is a glistening white wooden bench, simple in design: four legs with a wooden plank as its back.

"Yes, my daddy made it. He just made it last Saturday."

"Why, I need a bench like that one."

"You do?"

"Why, yes, I do. You see this old chair? It's so hard for me to get up from the chair once I sit down in it. I need a bench like the one you got. Why, say there, Maxine, do you think your father could make me a bench like that one?

"Why, sure, Mrs. Johnson." I don't hesitate.

"You do, huh? When do you think he could make it for me?"

"I don't know. But I'm sure he will do it very soon. I'll ask him."

"I'd be happy to pay him. How much do you think he'd charge?"

"I don't know, Mrs. Johnson. I don't think he'd want very much."

"Well, how much?" she insists.

My mind begins to search for an answer to her persistent question. "Well, I don't know. Maybe five dollars."

"You think so?" she said, surprised. "Okay, tell him I'll pay him five dollars to make me a bench. And ask him if he would be kind enough to paint it green."

"Okay, Mrs. Johnson, I'll ask my daddy."

Excitedly, I dash home to await my daddy's arrival from work; I listen for his footsteps at the magic seven o'clock evening hour. Finally, the door creaks open, signaling to me that he is home at last.

"Daddy! Daddy!" my hands swinging in wild circuitous motion, "Mrs. Johnson wants you to make her bench. She wants same bench you made." I was positive my father would be proud—proud that a neighbor, a respected elderly hearing woman, wanted his services. I had pictured in my mind, somehow, that he would rush to make her the bench.

Beer stank on his breath. He is coming home more frequently now after having drunk many cans of beer at work. His drinking seems to have intensified since that terrible court case that he can't seem to forget.

I ask him again if he will help Mrs. Johnson. His hands lazily, but firmly, say he doesn't want to be bothered.

"I no have time make bench. I tired."

Flabbergasted, I have to make him see that Mrs. Johnson is depending on him to make her a bench. After all, it isn't a frivolous request. She had said she needed it because her back would hurt if she continued to sit in that old dilapidated wrought-iron chair.

"Daddy, you must make Mrs. Johnson's bench. She needs it."

His face crimson red, he explodes. Fury replaces his initial reaction of impatience and annoyance.

"No! No! I tired. I not make bench (for) old woman."

Desperately, I signed, "She'll pay you."

"How much?"

"Five dollars."

"S-h-e-e-n!" His way of pronouncing the hearing word for "shit." He flipped his hand downward at me to signal his dismissal of such a low price, how ridiculous it would be to even consider five dollars as payment.

I feel my excitement fleeting, my enthusiasm and delight beginning to wane. Was I going to lose the battle with my father? If money doesn't motivate him, then all is lost, and so I decide to just beg.

"Daddy, please, please make bench for Mrs. Johnson. She needs very bad."

"No," his answer is so firm.

Crestfallen, I feel utterly defeated since my efforts to persuade him seem futile. The feeling of hope just oozes out of my body like a balloon whose air is slowly seeping out, fizzling to nothing

Her words reverberate in my mind as I imagine the desperation in her voice, pleading for the bench. I picture the comfort a new bench would bring her. I finally succumb to sleep that night despite my agony—how am I to tell her that my daddy refuses to make her a bench?

Oh my God. What am I to do? Sleep comes slowly. When my eyes open that next morning, I awake to a birds-singing-sun-is-shining day. The feeling of last night's dread clutches at my throat—how am I to tell Mrs. Johnson?

No. Maybe I won't have to tell her. It is Saturday. Daddy has gone to work. Maybe he'll change his mind about making her a bench when he comes home tonight. Usually when he comes home from work on Saturday, he's relieved that the week has come to an end; he looks forward to his one day off on Sunday.

Alas! Saturday night is just a replay of the night before. He seems all the more steadfast in his determination not to construct anything, let alone a bench.

"No! No! I not work (for) old woman. I not make bench. I work hard pay bills. I not time make bench."

It was final. I would have to tell Mrs. Johnson that Daddy refuses to do it. How am I to tell her? What am I to tell her? I imagine a woman who will be devastated, crushed, disappointed.

The next day is Sunday, but I don't go to Sunday school or church. I am consumed with thoughts of what to tell Mrs. Johnson and I spend the day walking around the house agonizing over this seemingly impossible dilemma. Suddenly, the thought occurs to me to just pray on it. After all, Harry Lee, the interpreter for the deaf congregation at church, says it often enough: pray, pray, pray. So I go down to our unfinished basement, with its gray cinderblock walls and dirt mud floor, and kneel down on my knees. I put my praying hands together, and utter pleas to Jesus.

"Please, Jesus, make my daddy make a bench for Mrs. Johnson." Tears begin to well in my eyes, and trickle down my face. "Oh please, please, Lord Jesus, Mrs. Johnson needs a bench because it will help her back. Please, please tell Daddy to make it for her." My voice is hoarse—raspy, as I implore the Son of God to help me.

I feel nothing. I hear nothing. No deep resonating heavenly voice speaking to me. I realize there is no hope and no help will be forthcoming. I stiffly, slowly, pull my body up from kneeling on the floor. Silence is all around me; only the sounds of an occasional bird chirping bring me to the reality that I have to deal with the pain of not being able to help Mrs. Johnson. I think the old woman's heart will be broken. Tears stain my cheeks as I hobble my way back to the upper world, back up to the one-floor bungalow and open the front door to sit on the porch. It is warmer now, hardly a breeze. The air becomes still as I sit on our cherished bench with my back facing the closed screen door.

I hear the screen door open behind me, and I turn to see Daddy, looking fresh, clean, and crisp. He steps out on the porch and faces me. His rough calloused hands swing gracefully in the air, *"Maxine, I make old woman bench. I want (my) five dollars."*

Did I thank Jesus for telling Daddy to make Mrs. Johnson a bench? I don't remember.

14

Becoming Aware of Things, Part III

"All humiliation has done for me is bring hurt and shame."

I am still a despondent twelve-year-old. I worry daily about doing my homework and getting A's in my classes; I am anxious too about buying new clothes and where I'll get the money to pay for them.

Okay, I say to myself, I'll worry about buying new clothes later, right now I've got to do this English assignment to write a comparison-and-contrast story. I curl up on the sofa in the living room and begin writing a story in pencil, with the intention of writing it over in ink. (Mama says always write in pencil, so I can erase mistakes as many times as I want.)

The next day, I go to school and give the completed assignment to my English teacher, who reads it, and gives it back to me. "Maxine, I want you to read this story to the class." I take the paper back and read it aloud from my desk:

> **I compare my mother to a swan who glides in the water gracefully because she is soft and gentle. My mother can dress up like a queen. She can wear a pretty dress she has made and look so beautiful.**
>
> **In contrast, she is as strong as a man. She can chop wood with an axe. She built cabinets in our kitchen. She bought wood from the lumber store. She cut it with a saw.**

**She painted two cabinets with white paint. She nailed
one cabinet on one side of the window and nailed the
other cabinet to the wall on the other side of the window.**

This is comparison and contrast.

No one says a word. There is a noticeable silence after I read my
two paragraphs when the teacher says, "Thank you, Maxine.
You wrote a good example of comparison and contrast. Class,
you heard the story, that's how you should write it."

One of the girls utters, "Ugh!" in the back of the room. I
am not surprised, since I've noticed that most of the girls don't
talk to me or even like me. Oh well, at least the teacher likes
me, and that's the important thing.

A TEACHER stops me in the hall and tells me she is planning a
program.

"Would you like to be the mistress of ceremonies, Maxine?"

"Mistress of ceremonies, what's that?" I ask.

"Oh, that is the person who begins the program and intro-
duces each of the speakers by saying a few words about them
before the speaker appears. Do you think you can do that?"

"Yes, I think so."

"Fine. Come to my room and I will give you a script that
you should memorize by next week. Okay?"

"Thank you."

I rush home. I can't wait to tell Mama I will be in a program where I will give a speech. I decide it is easier to say to
her that I will be talking on a stage in front of many students
than to use the phrase "mistress of ceremonies," a phrase even I
didn't clearly understand.

For the next few days, I am almost constantly in the bathroom, practicing my lines. Shirley and Barbara complain to

Mama that they can't use the bathroom because I've locked the door and won't let them in. Mama pleads with me to share the bathroom, to no avail. I must learn the script and I don't have time to indulge my two sisters.

While practicing one evening, the thought comes to me I must find something to wear. That's when I panic, because I realize I don't have anything nice to wear. I don't want to ask Mama to make anything. She looks so worn out that I wonder if she will have a breakdown because now she's working at a restaurant washing dishes. She goes to work at nine at night and comes home at seven in the morning.

She says to me with her eyes barely open, her shoulders bent over, and her breathing a slow gasp, *"I tired. Work very hard. I maybe quit Friday. Maybe next week, I work laundry. That better."* She and I both know Daddy insists that she find work because he needs help to pay the household bills.

While Mama collapses in her bed from exhaustion, I rummage through her clothes hung in her wooden valet closet, purchased long ago when she was a teacher in North Carolina. She has so many beautiful clothes; the one I like best is a dark navy, almost black, nylon dress with a taffeta satin slip attached underneath it. She looks so pretty in it that I think I will look pretty in it, too. Maybe she can alter it, and I can wear that dress for my speaking job. I'm not sure she will agree to cut up this dress—after all, she does look magnificent in it. I am taken aback when she says, *"You want dress? Yes, I fix dress,"* and in a few days, she begins to cut down the dress for me.

Now the momentous day is upon me. I put on my mother's dress, which fits perfectly, and rush to school to prepare for my speaking assignment. When I enter the sunlit auditorium, I notice the room is brighter than usual, perhaps because the ceiling lights are turned on and the room appears more brilliant than ever. I can see the dress I am wearing more closely now, almost for the first time. It appears out-of-date and worn out, and it is clearly a dress for an older woman. I feel awkward. I can't go back home now. Besides, what else do I have to wear? Under my breath, I nervously mutter my lines, rehearsing them just as I had been doing for days on end. But I can't get it out of my mind that I am wearing such a shabby dress.

At the appointed time, the teacher summons me to walk on the stage and make the first introduction. I look out and see the youngsters with their parents waiting . . . all staring at me, and I suddenly forget everything I am supposed to say. All I can think of is the tired old-fashioned dress they see on me, and I feel so very self-conscious. I start to say my first sentence, and then hesitate, forgetting the words. I quickly skip the next few lines because I just can't remember them; I pause again, and wait a few moments, which feels like an eternity. I start again, repeating the words I had just uttered. Finally, my memory comes back, and I am able to finish the rest of my lines. At last, the program ends. What a relief! No one, not even the teachers, compliments me on my speaking ability, so I instinctively know I did a lousy job.

I come home that evening, dragging at the heels and looking forlorn. I hang Mama's dress back in her closet, even though she has cut it down for me. Maybe she can uncut it.

I figure out one thing: What looks good on her does not look good on me.

Aw shucks!

JUST BEFORE Thanksgiving, I enter our dingy bathroom, a tiny square space six feet by six feet, with the bathtub situated underneath the window. The toilet is adjacent to the tub. A mere inch or two separates the tub from the toilet from the washbasin. Squeezed in between that washbasin and the wall is a white cabinet, six feet tall by two feet wide, which holds our aspirin, hair curlers, lipstick, Daddy's shaving mug and long-handled razor, and even the straightening comb Mama uses to take the kink out of our hair. Over the basin is a nine-by-eleven-inch mirror hanging beneath a naked lightbulb. I stand over the basin to stare at the mirror to style my hair.

Today I am sitting on the toilet seat with my underwear pulled down to my ankles when I see a dried-up purplish color stain on the crotch of my panties. What is this? Do I need to change panties? Maybe I need to wash myself more there, because I don't know where this stain came from. The next day it disappears. I tell no one, preferring to believe that it was my vigorous cleaning in that spot that caused this to happen. I forget about it. Another four or five weeks later, the stain on my panties appears crimson red. I am shocked at the sight of the blood. I don't know what to think or what to do; something is terribly wrong. I conclude that I'll shrivel up and die. I'm infected with a horrible disease. That's it. I have a disease, and I'll have to tell Mama sooner or later that I have a sickness, perhaps the plague, maybe even the bubonic plague, which caused many a person to die on a ship in a story I saw on television.

After days of deliberating, I muster the courage to tell my mother of my terminal condition, that I am dying.

"Mama, I have blood here," pointing to my vagina.

"Oh," she says, understanding immediately. "That's," and she signs the letter "a" on her cheek.

"What's that?" I mimic the sign. I might not die after all.

"That's menstruation," she said. "I not spell right, every girl have—mean you not pregnant."

"Oh," I said, sighing, not knowing what to make of this.

"You have 'apple' every month."

"Is it like an apple?" I ask, trying to understand the logic between the sign "a" and the sign apple.

"No. It blood every month. Mean you not pregnant."

"But you know you are not pregnant? How body tell you?"

"Body know."

I sigh and, feeling hopeless, decide to just let it go. At least, there's a little hope since apparently I am not going to die after all.

The next month, I see the blood again and show the panty to Mama.

"Apple come. You get rag (from) old white sheet." She says, *"I do (at) North Carolina School."*

So I tear a small rag from a clean old white sheet, carefully fold it, and place it in between my legs inside my panties. I attach a safety pin there, and at the end of day, I throw away the rag.

Weeks turn into another month, and my routine during those "period" days becomes the same: more study, study, study; more pretend smiles, trying to be nice despite my achiness. A few weeks later, it is the "apple time" again. I dutifully roll up a rag and insert it inside my panties. Only this time, I can't find a safety pin.

"Hurry, Maxine. . . . Hurry, you late (for) school."

So I abandon the project of looking for a pin and beeline it to school.

Am I making a big mistake, even attempting to hold the rag without a safety pin? As I go from class to class, I'm afraid to walk, feeling the cloth loosening up, wiggling in and out of the secure spot. I raise my hand and ask different teachers if I may be excused to the girls' room; there I adjust my rag, and after doing that, I feel secure walking carefully from one class to another.

It is later in the morning, around eleven o'clock. I am so weary. I can feel the pad loosening and slipping from its now less-than-secure spot between my legs. I climb the stairs in a queue with the other girls to go from one floor to another. I notice the walls are freshly painted a bright yellow, as I try to walk up the stairs in tiny steps to hold the cloth in place. Oh, God, will I make it? Terror. Sweat. The thought of going up one more flight of stairs hamstrings me, and that's when I move aside on a step allowing the girls to pass me so I can be last in line. I take more steps to reach a swinging door, slowly walk to reach still another flight of stairs, up a few steps, and then it happens, the rolled-up cloth slips out just as I am turning the corner on a landing to go up another set of steps. I bend over quickly to grab it, and stuff it in my book bag and glance around to see if anyone is watching. Several girls see me. I want to die. No, not die, just disappear into thin air, and just no longer be there. This can't be happening to me, not to Maxine, to the person who so desperately wants everyone to see that she really can be acceptable.

I go to the bathroom to wash my hands, throw the rag in the trash, go to the cafeteria, take out my lunch, and sit in the area designated for my class. I utter to the girl next to me that I had a bloody nose and was wiping my nose with a cloth when I dropped it on the stairs. She gives me a blank stare and says nothing. She is one of the students who saw me pick up the bloody rag. She nods her head and continues to eat her sandwich. I don't think she believes me. Did she? Does she know I am lying? How many other people know? She is the type to gossip and giggle with the other girls about what happened to me. God, please help me to evaporate into thin air.

As I am eating my sandwich, I am deep in thought, remembering a philosophy book I read stressing that humiliation builds character. I decide that that author is telling a lie. All humiliation has done for me is bring hurt and shame.

That evening, I go to the drugstore directly across the street from Don's Grocery at the corner of Sixty-First and Dix to ask the friendly female clerk what to do about menstruation. She looks at me with a smile and says, "Well, you're going to have to buy Kotex pads," and she points to where they are. I tell her I don't have enough money with me to buy a box of pads, and besides, I don't know how to use them. This dear friendly clerk looks at me so kindly and says, "Here honey, I'll give you a box with the belt to go with it and you can pay me later. Okay?" I am so happy, I head straight to the candy counter, where there are loads of penny candies, from Tootsie Rolls and Mary Janes to bubble gum and hard balls. I stand at the counter, telling the friendly clerk my choices and spend only five cents. She again smiles at me.

Now that I have change left from my quarter, I walk around the store and spot the magazine rack with romance stories lined up on it. I pick the magazine that has a torrid photo of a man and woman kissing on its cover, and buy it for twenty cents. I go home to read the magazine printed on cheap dime-store paper. The first story is about a young girl who meets a boy in a grocery store and he follows her home. She wants nothing to do with him at first, then he finally woos her by kissing her, and then they go and get married.

It's the last story in the magazine that really catches my attention. Yes, it is a love story, but this author describes everything in detail, unlike the other writer who uses broad general language to tell a story. In this one, the man meets the woman at a party. He tells her she is beautiful, and she tells him he is handsome; she invites him to her apartment, where they have sex. Naturally, the woman gets pregnant, and they must run to the justice of the peace to be married. Then they decide to move to another town to avoid the gossip that she was pregnant before they were married. They live happily ever after.

I am momentarily shocked by the graphic description of the sexual act. So that's how they do it. Why doesn't Mama tell me these things? Maybe she doesn't know. Wait a minute, she has us three kids,; she must know something. I am bewildered. Once again, I am the last to know. It just isn't fair.

15

The Notebook

"But I don't give up trying . . . trying to fit in, somehow."

It is an unbearably hot day, typical for Washington, D.C., with such intolerably high humidity that clothes stick to my body and perspiration rolls under my arms and down my back. School will be closing before long. The dense and stagnant air in my seventh-grade classroom refuses to move, making the air too heavy to even make a breeze.

I sit on the hard wooden seat attached to my desk, tired and wanting to go home. But it is far from time to go. I have to suffer through Miss Meyers's prattling voice as she teaches mathematics in the front of the class; she also supervises us in homeroom, which means I'll have to endure her even further. She is a gray-haired, cocoa-colored spinster with a big butt. Her clothes are nondescript, except they do not fit her properly. Her pear-shaped body has rejected the off-the-rack garment; the top half of the dress droops too loosely around her neck and shoulders, while the bottom half is much too tight, so tight that the material becomes warped as it extends as far as it will go to accommodate her hips. The stretched material hugs the stays of her girdle, revealing the telltale signs of an old-fashioned halter reining it all in. She has buck-teeth, making her lisp more pronounced as she sucks her teeth while whispering through her thin lips. She speaks in a light creaky voice, like a grasshopper's legs creaking to make broken chirpy sounds.

It is early afternoon. Miss Meyers is sitting at her desk peering through her rimmed spectacles, correcting papers, and occasionally cautioning us to cease talking and finish our assignments. That's when I see a student give a green notebook to another girl sitting two desks ahead of me. After thumbing through it, that girl turns around, giving it to the girl sitting behind her, who also takes time to read it. Afterward, she gives it to the girl sitting next to her. Then that girl reaches across the aisle and gives it to still another student. I wonder what the notebook contains and wait for it to come to me, but it is passed to everyone except me. When it finally comes to the student ahead of me, I tap her on the shoulder, "Could I see that please?" She glances at the girl next to her as if asking for permission, and receives a noncommittal response; she hesitates, shrugs her shoulders, and gives me the notebook.

I grab the book, flip through the pages and see at the top of the page the name of an obviously popular girl in our class. Below her name are individual comments by other students: "very pretty"; "She really knows how to dress." Another wrote "cute." Still another wrote the word "nice."

That's when I realize that this is a book of opinions, a gauging of each person's distinctive attributes. All the names have pleasant enough descriptions; I finally reach my name: "Stinko"; "Hot breath"; "Why doesn't she brush her teeth?"; "She stinks"; "Her breath is awful." The comments continue on and on, endlessly. My body freezes. I hold my breath as I stare at each comment, some written in blue or black or even green ink. I want to vanish, to evaporate into thin air. Then I put my head down on my folded arms on the desk, and begin to snivel. My whimpering becomes a wailing, which eventually becomes a fit of loud crying. No one says a word, not even Miss Meyers. As I continue my wailing, my bawling becomes louder and louder until reaching a crescendo that even cracks my ears. I keep my head down on the desk on top of my folded arms; I can never face the world again.

Everyone ignores me; Miss Meyers pays no attention. As far as I know, she never looks up, until finally, after about twenty minutes, she says, "Maxine, you're going to have to stop that crying." But I can't stop. I feel my chest heaving, my breathing interrupted by sobbing. When I try to muffle my crying, my sounds become moans, as I am consumed by the humiliation, the devastation, and the complete and total embarrassment of it all. Why didn't someone tell me? Was this the reason no one has liked me for all these years? I want to scream!

Finally, the hour ends as the students retreat to the cafeteria. I am the last to leave, and my flood of tears abruptly ends with an occasional whimper. Miss Meyers is standing there by the classroom door, apparently waiting for an explanation. I am amazed she did not throw me out of the room earlier. I take a deep breath and divulge that I saw the notebook and what was written after my name. She nods her head and says, "Well, you're going to have to stop all that crying."

Somehow, I get through the day.

I drag my body home and head straight to the bathroom to stare at my teeth in a magnifying mirror. Why does my breath stink? I brush my teeth every day. It must be because we use toothpowder, I rationalize. I put a towel over my mouth to smell the stench that others must smell. It doesn't work. The only odor is stale musty air.

That's when I have flashbacks of my friend Fola Carr, who sits next to me in homeroom class. She snickered, slightly embarrassed, when Cassandra, who was sitting directly in front of her, turned around and, reaching over her, said to me, "Here, Maxine, take a cough drop; you need a cough drop. Take two or three." I didn't understand their snickering. Now it all makes sense, especially the time when Alice Joyner, a friendly short girl whose head is a tad too big for her petite body, was walking home with me and started talking about someone who had underarm odor.

"I think it's because she only uses deodorant under part of her arm," she said. And then went on to say, "Why, I bet someone with bad breath only brushes their teeth in the front and doesn't brush the back of their mouth."

"Uh-huh," I say, dismissing her words as idle chatter. Now I know what she was trying to tell me.

I CONTINUE to stare pensively in the mirror, waiting for Mama to come home from her new job working in a laundry. When she finally arrives, I ignore her obvious weariness; I sign to her in obvious distress, "They laugh me in school. They say I bad breath. They not like me."

She then sniffs my breath, and in her usual way of trying to avoid hurt, she signs, *"It smells little bad, not very bad."*

Has she no sense of smell? Can't she smell things the way Daddy can? Does she have any idea of the humiliation I feel? Does she know I have no friends at all now? Does she know I want to die?

"You brush your teeth more toothpowder," she signs with a sigh, clearly worn out from work, and now my anxiety fatigues her even more.

"You not understand," I sign, tears flowing down my face. "I need toothpaste. Toothpowder not any good. Students say mouth stink."

"Toothpowder good; I use many many years school. Use more toothpowder," she says defensively. She looks so weary as she repeats, *"I use school."*

I go back to the bathroom, resume staring at the mirror, looking to see if something foreign, an unknown growth on my tongue, might be the cause of my misery. There has to be an explanation! Maybe I didn't brush the back of my teeth as thoroughly as I should, just as Alice suggested.

That's when I see them—the beads of pus on my tonsils. It could mean only one thing: that my tonsils are infected. Yes, now I remember. I had overheard our doctor, Dr. Randolph, admonishing my mother that I should have my tonsils taken out.

"Maxine must have her tonsils removed," he said, as he writes a note to her, which my mother promptly shows to me.

"What are tonsils?" I ask. That's when he explains they are round balls at the back of the tongue in the throat.

Dr. Randolph is a black doctor whose medical practice is on the second floor of his home, about three blocks from our house on Sixty-First Street. He charges five dollars for office visits, a lot of money for us. It has to be a crisis for us to see him: a persistent fever that would not break; a deep cut that requires stitches; or a pain that will not respond to Mama's remedies. Mama takes care of us by treating almost every malady with freshly squeezed orange juice made from dozens of oranges and a tablespoon of cod liver oil in the morning. Each morning she stands by the kitchen sink with tablespoon in one hand and a bottle of cod liver oil in the other. Ignoring our protests, she forces the spoon in our mouths, convinced that we are protected from any potential ailments lurking about to attack us. There is no orange juice to wash the nastiness down, since juice is given to us only when we are sick.

We do not see the inside of a hospital. To avoid going there, we go to a neighboring clinic for inoculations required by our schools. The nearby hospital is Freedmen's Hospital, which has a god-awful reputation. Hearing people shake their heads with disgust whenever the subject of Freedmen's Hospital comes up.

"Lordy, you can go in Freedmen's Hospital a little sick and come out in a casket 'cuz they sure 'nough will kill yah." The perception is that because Freedmen's Hospital is in a Negro neighborhood and in close proximity to a prison surrounded by a twenty-foot, barbed-wire fence, there is little effort to cure "colored" patients living in the neighborhood. Hearing people say, "If the white man can't kill us, he'll put us in jail."

So we only go to Dr. Randolph who, after a few years, has increased his fee from five dollars to seven dollars, truly a hardship. Mama purchases Dr. Randolph's services on credit, paying him on the installment plan with two or three dollars now and three or four dollars in a month or two. "How much would it cost to have my tonsils taken out?" No, we don't have any hospitalization insurance, in fact, it has never occurred to us to buy any. When Dr. Randolph tells us it might cost at least fifty dollars, maybe even one hundred, we're stunned. That is just too much money for Daddy to pay. After all, he only makes sixty-five dollars a week. Besides, I reason, even if we get the money for the operation, I surely will die there in Freedmen's Hospital; I imagine myself in a casket being carried out and buried in our backyard.

A few days later, after visiting Dr. Randolph, I am in the bathroom, staring at my tonsils with a hand mirror, when suddenly a little white bean rolls down my tongue. I put it in my hand to bring up to my nose and sniff the little pea-size ball; the smell is horrendous. I hold the mirror closer to my mouth and then see little white dots on my tonsils. I can't believe it: my tonsils are rotten, full of infection, full of pus, full of stinking rotten mold that has become little white balls. I reach into the cabinet, retrieve a large hairpin, and begin plucking each little white bead from my tonsils until I remove all the foul-smelling beads, and then gargle with salt and water, a homemade remedy Mama makes for sore throats.

I perform this ritual morning and night. Little by little, the smell dissolves. The girls don't shun me as much.

Now that I know the reason they acted so mean and spiteful, I find solace in knowing I've found a solution to the problem. That's a feeling of satisfaction I never expected to have.

I STILL SO want to be liked by the other kids that it becomes a goal, a chore, and a job to pursue each day. I know I don't fit in. So the task before me is to attempt, as best I can, to do whatever is necessary to become likeable, from trying to impress others by getting outstanding grades in all my classes to earning money by babysitting to buy the latest fashionable clothes. It is as if I am trying to mold myself from a pile of dirt into a shapely statue made of clay.

I am in Miss Meyers's homeroom class when I hear the announcement that we are to go on a field trip for an entire week. "Class, we can all go to New York City and visit the Statue of Liberty, the Empire State Building, and several museums. We'll be staying at the Waldorf Astoria. The cost will be fifty dollars for the trip, and that will include your hotel, transportation, and meals. Isn't that wonderful?"

Stupefied, all I can think of is the sixty-five dollars a week my father makes. Well, maybe he has money hidden at work and he'll give me the money. After all, he always hits the numbers, I think to myself. That evening, I wait impatiently for him to come home. Finally he arrives.

"Daddy, my class goes New York. Cost is fifty dollars. Can I have fifty dollars?" I sign to him slowly, holding my breath.

"F-i-f-t-y d-o-l-l-a-r-s!" He looks at me as if I am deranged.

"I broke. Broke. Broke," he says with the side of his hand chopping against his neck. His signs are definite; I know there will be no money forthcoming from my father.

My mother has stopped working at the laundry because the heavy work is too much for her. She only made about thirty dollars a week anyway. Having no steady income, she shakes her head when I plead with her for the money. She is making aprons now, magnificent chef-like aprons with two decorative pockets in the front, some with heart-shaped pockets with a contrasting color on the belt. The aprons are so decorative that Mama raises her prices from three dollars and fifty cents to five dollars and sells them at church or to visitors who come to our house.

A family photo taken at Christmas in 1955 with Mama, Daddy, Barbara, and Maxine.

When Mama says with a forlorn expression that she is unable to give me the necessary money, I remain undaunted. Surely I can get the money from somewhere; after all, this is just another challenge. Maybe we can go to a nearby bank and borrow the money; there's one in Seat Pleasant, Maryland, only six blocks away, easy walking distance from our house.

"Mama, can we go to Seat Pleasant Bank and borrow money?" I ask.

Mama looks surprised, *"Bank lend money?"*

"Yes, we try."

So Mama and I walk to the bank. As I approach it, open the door, and see the customers and staff, I feel jittery. There is no one there who looks like us; everyone's complexion is so white, and they are dressed in fancy clothes, so starched, and so pressed, so fashionable and coordinated. I walk up to the gentleman who is sitting behind the desk.

"Yes, may I help you?" he looks harmless; surely, he will tell us what to do.

"Yes, my mother would like to make a loan. She's deaf."

"Well, yes," said the gentleman as he looks over at Mama. The fellow is cordial enough. I feel inspired; this is the right move. He beckons us to come with him.

"Here, let me get a chair for your mother. You can sit here." He quickly exits the scene and goes back to the counter near the door. Another gentleman suddenly appears and begins to ask us questions.

"Well now, I understand you want to take out a loan."

"Yes." I feel heartened.

He pulls out an application. "What's your name?" "This is my mother, Thomasina Childress."

"And your father's name?"

"Herbert Childress."

"What's your address?"

"5901 Clay Street, N.E."

"Do you own your own home?"

"Yes."

"What's your father's occupation?"

"He's a shoe repairman and he works for Sam's Shoe Repair."

"Well, is this loan going to be in his name?"

"No. It will be in my mother's name."

"Okay. And how much do you want to borrow?" he asks.

"Fifty dollars."

The man noticeably pauses, looks down at his notes, and sighs. That's when I wonder if I am asking for too much money.

"And what work does your mother do?" he asks.

"My mother makes and sells aprons," I answer unhesitatingly.

"I s-e-e." He begins to speak slower and in a lower tone. "We can't give loans to people who are self-employed," he said. "Did you say your father is a shoe repairman?"

"Yes."

"Who did you say is his employer?'

"Sam's Shoe Repair."

"And how long has he worked there?"

"I'm not sure." I turn to Mama and sign to her, asking her the question. She responds that Daddy must have worked there for more than fifteen years. Then I tell this to the loan officer.

He nods his head encouragingly. "If you want a loan, your father will have to come and sign for it."

I sign the man's words to Mama.

"No. Your daddy not sign loan. Tell man 'thank you.' We go."

I leave the bank frustrated. Now what am I to do? When Mama and I begin walking back home, down Clay Street from Sixty-First Street, we pass Mrs. Chandler's house. Then

I remember Mrs. Chandler, an elementary school teacher who recently moved into a newly built house diagonally across the street from us. I had befriended her when she introduced herself as our new neighbor and invited me to be a babysitter for her four-year-old daughter.

I wait until the next day to approach Mrs. Chandler at her house; when I knock on her screen door, she opens it with a welcoming greeting.

"Why, hello there, Maxine. It's so pleasant to see you." She glances over at the television set. "I am watching *The Guiding Light*; I can't believe they changed the actress who plays the main character." She sounds so disgusted as she glares, perplexed, at the TV.

"What do you mean?" I ask, wondering what in the world she is talking about. Clearly, she is upset about a soap opera.

She goes on to say, rather disgustedly, "This actress has been playing the part of the daughter for a long time, and now they have another actress playing the part. The woman before was a blonde; now they have this brunette doing it."

"Oh," I say, trying to feel sympathetic, but really concerned about how to ask her advice on what to do about my plight. "I'm here because I don't know what to do about a trip my class is taking to New York City."

"What trip?"

"The whole class is going to the Waldorf Astoria in New York City and staying there for a whole week," I say breathlessly, hoping she would see the glory of the trip as well as the urgency.

"Well, what's the problem, Maxine?"

"The trip costs fifty dollars. And my mother and father do not have the money. Do you think I should ask the principal to lend me the money, and then I can pay her back five dollars a week?"

"Well, I don't think you should ask her for the money. After all, Maxine, you really don't want to beg."

"Thank you for telling me what to do." And I return back to my house. I want to cry, but the hurt is too deep in my chest. In the back of my mind I had even hoped Mrs. Chandler might give me the money, but I figure she would have offered it to me if she could. Then I think about the phrase she used when she said "beg," and I decide I will have to give up my quest to go to the Waldorf Astoria.

The week of the trip, almost the entire class of thirty-five students goes to New York City. Only a girl whose last name is Murphy, memorable for her dirty thick braids with white specks of lint in it, and a boy, memorable for his drab clothes, and me, memorable for my bad breath—only the three of us do not go on that trip.

But I don't give up trying . . . trying to fit in, somehow.

16

From Happiness to Misery

"What's wrong with you? You can hear."

The year is 1956 and I am thirteen years old, promoted now to the eighth grade, "classification 8-6," a class for all girls who are deemed to be academically gifted, by virtue of their test scores and superior grades. I am determined to excel in my studies because in my mind, getting A's in all my classes is the only way I can show that I am equal to the other students and gain some recognition in the school. Since I don't have money to buy my lunch every day, wear fancy clothes, or even have many friends, I know that getting good grades is the only avenue I have to prove my worth. Besides, my parents place an extremely high value on the good grades I hope to receive.

I begin studying day and night. First, I come home at four in the afternoon, after school. I am usually so tired I need to take a nap in the afternoon, waking up in the early evening around seven to eat the dinner that Mama has prepared. I study for at least two or three hours, putting on a nightgown, going back to sleep around nine or ten. I say a short prayer to Jesus asking him to wake me up at three in the morning so that I can resume my studying until five. (It seems hard to believe, but it always works. I actually awaken at three in the morning.)

As my eyelids begin to close, I see all the signs of an approaching new day: dawn with its sunlight filtering in between the shades, the gradual lessening of the crickets' and whippoorwills' sounds, and the yapping of an occasional dog let out for the morning. I fall into a sound sleep even at five in the morning, and before I know it, Mama is calling me around 7:30 to get up. My mind wrestles with my body to get up and get going while still half asleep. I wash up and force myself to find something clean to wear. I scramble to get dressed, eat the grits and sausage waiting for me on a plate, and zip out the door so that I'll be on time for school.

Worn out, I drag myself from class to class, managing somehow to score A's and B's on tests. I memorize any information the teachers recite, and then, eagerly raising my hand in class, I verbally regurgitate the same information back to them. Toward the end of the day, I shuffle and drag my tired and weary brain and body back to my homeroom. Exhausted, I am barely able to stand up when I enter my homeroom to see my name along with one other student, Barbara Crumlin, on the blackboard. The two of us have earned the highest grades for the semester in that class: five A's and two B's. I instantly perk up, feeling a newfound surge of energy. Where did it come from—this new surge? Who knows, but it doesn't matter to me because I now realize my hard work is paying off.

I rush home to show Mama my report card. But rather than an ecstatic look on her face, there is a scowling and questioning look, as she stares at the card.

"What wrong?" I ask.

"*Why say B's?*" she looks at me quizzically.

"B's good," I say, rather exasperated.

"*B's not A's. What wrong you? You can hear, why you not all A's?*"

That's when I recognize that good is not good enough, it never will be; whatever I accomplish at school has to be perfect—after all, I can hear. Mama and even Daddy often parrot the expression *"You can hear"* around the house, which translates in their minds to mean there's no excuse for anything less than the best.

I CONTINUE to study diligently and become less self-conscious about bad breath. After all, every day I go in the bathroom, hold the mirror up close to my mouth, and pluck out the beads of infection from my tonsils. My breath no longer has that stench. Slowly, girls become my friends, and boys begin to seek me out.

"Hey you, pretty girl, what's your name?" a boy says to me as I am walking home after school. I pay no attention to him, preferring to look straight ahead and ignore him completely.

"So you won't speak, will ya? Well, if you think you're stuck-up, you should see my wall," he says.

I keep walking, yet I'm so amused by the boy's comment that I chuckle to myself, plus I am pleased that I am attracting young fellows.

When I arrive home, I am relieved that for once, I don't have any homework. I relax on the front porch, rocking back and forth on our white wrought-iron glider. Feeling the glider smoothly roll forward and backward makes me feel free as a bird. I see a group of youngsters walking along Clay Street, two tall young lads about my age and several younger children trailing behind them. One of the older boys spots me on the porch, stops right in front of the house, and hollers, "Hi ya."

I say hello, step down our porch steps, and walk on the sidewalk fifteen feet to the street and ask, "What's your name?" eyeing the six or seven kids all lingering behind the two older youngsters.

"I'm George Neal, and these are my brothers and sisters."

The other lad says, "My name is Junior. What's your name?"

"Maxine," I reply. I notice that George is much heavier and looks older than Junior, who has a younger-looking oval face, while George's face is round with pimples.

George pipes up and says, "We just moved down the street." He points beyond the trees to an area next to our house. "Can we come and visit you sometime?"

I am startled by the unexpected question and hesitate for a moment, "Well, yeah . . . sure. You can come up now if you want to—and sit with me on the porch."

"Okay," says George, who leads the pack of youngsters with him and follows me; they all crowd together on the glider; George and Junior stand up while I sit in a chair. Just then Mama opens the door and steps out on the porch, peers at the youngsters, and signs to me, *"Who children?"*

"They new people, they move here. They live there," I say to her, pointing over the trees.

"This is my mother. She's deaf and we use sign language" I introduce her to the family.

Mama smiles at the children as she turns and signs, *"Children sweet."* She stares at George and Junior and says, *"You don't know boys. Be careful, they fight you."*

"Boys not fight me. They friends."

She gives me a skeptical look and turns around and goes back in the house. Next, Shirley comes out the house and joins us on the porch.

"This is my sister, Shirley," I say, as she stands beside me.

That day begins a delightful friendship between the Neal children and me and my sisters, Shirley and Barbara. We would visit with each other and laugh and make fun of each other. They especially loved to tease me about the picture hanging in our living room of my mother in a fine blue suit, holding me in her arms when I am about a year old. They all giggle, making fun of me.

Thomasina held me in her arms for a professional studio photograph taken in 1944.

"Look at Maxine. Why her cheeks are so fat it looks like she's got apples in them. Ha. Ha. Ha." I feel a little humiliated but

My father posed separately at the same photo shoot. It was one of the few times Herbert was photographed without a mustache.

decide to laugh with them, and try to pick on George's pimples to retaliate. For all our jesting, there was no meanness or hurt feelings, just pure innocent childish fun.

One day George rings the doorbell, and when I answer the door, he hands me a note and runs away:

Deer Macseene,
I love you. Will you be my girlfreind.
George Neal

I read the note carefully and am amazed that my name is misspelled. And why can't he spell girlfriend right? So, I promptly write him a note back, knowing he will return to look for an answer. Sure enough, George comes to my house about an hour or two later, and I give him my note:

Dear George,
I must have time to think about what you asked me.
See me tomorrow.
Maxine

P.S. You misspelled my name and the word girlfriend
and the word dear.

I had just seen a movie on TV with Jane Powell, a singing blonde teenager who runs away with a gang of adolescents to an apple farm and sings about her love for one of the youngsters. She becomes angry with her intended beau and slams the door in his face. He looks devastated and begs all the more for her attention. For some reason, I think this is the way to treat a lovesick boy.

When George comes to pick up my answer, I hand him the note and tell him to go to the side of the house. When he appears, I pull up the blinds and tell him I still need time to think about it, then I let the blinds down with a bang!

George didn't respond for at least two days. I wonder if he is ever coming back, thinking maybe the movies don't have the perfect script after all. Then he comes again to the house with another note:

Dear Maxine,

I will meet you at the creek.

George Neal

My mother sees George's note lying conspicuously on the living room table and asks, *"Why you go to creek?"* I explain that we are going with his sisters and brothers to talk because I am mad at him. She tells me not to be mean to George and his sisters and brothers.

That Saturday, George and all his sisters and brothers come with Shirley and me as we walk a short distance behind the house to the creek. The kids begin to sing, "George has a girlfriend. George has a girlfriend." Then they say, "Let's see you two kiss."

George walks up to me and gives me a quick kiss on the lips. His lips feel rough and dry. This certainly isn't romantic, nothing like what happens in some of the movies I've watched on television, I think to myself.

A few weeks later, George comes by my home looking very gloomy, "We have to move. The man we rent from says there are too many children in the house. So my father found us another house to rent in Northwest Washington. Don't worry, I'll try to see you again." He starts to walk away with a hurt look, and then says, "By the way Maxine, you always act as if you are smarter than I am. You're not," with his head bowed in shame.

I think about that comment he made to me many times. Do I think I am smarter than he? Well, yes maybe. I must have hurt his feelings when I corrected his spelling, something that never occurred to me. This much I do know—my mother and father always want me to be smart, even around my very first boyfriend. No doubt about that!

ALTHOUGH MY social situation is gradually improving, things are not as good at home. Daddy is becoming more and more angry—at his job because he still only makes sixty-five dollars a week, and at us because we eat too much food.

Maybe he's mad at us because he has to work six days a week, and he's tired. Maybe he's mad at us because he still wants to sue the woman who brought the charges against him. Maybe he is sorry he doesn't have a male child, or worse yet, he's sorry he married Mama. Or, maybe he's mad at us because of his deafness. Once I saw him talking quite seriously to another deaf person after church at Shiloh Baptist, *"Many hearing people think deaf people no good. Many 'colored' people deaf can't find work. I know deaf (on) welfare. Not me. I never (on) welfare, never."*

I really don't know why he seems mad all the time. No more jokes or laughter the way it used to be. He keeps two six-packs of beer in the refrigerator now, and when he comes home from work, he becomes more intoxicated than ever. I see him gulping down gin and drinking beer afterward. Then he explodes at us: *"You eat too much. You eat too much. Bills, bills, bills. I broke. I broke,"* is his constant refrain.

On this particular Saturday night, Daddy is banging on the door. *"I've got pee,"* he signs when I open the door for him. I see from his wet pants he has already urinated on himself and is now peeing on the floor; urine is streaming down his leg, wetting his socks and shoes, even on the floor mat placed neatly near the door. He frowns at me, seething with furious rage.

"Daddy, you drunk," I sign wildly. I want him to disappear, to leave the house and never come back. I hate to admit it, but I think I want him to die.

"Get out! Get out! You not need live here. Sheen. Sheen," he is yelling to me, his voice screeching. He must have read my mind, since he clearly wants me to disappear too, or at least move out of the house.

"You drunk!" I say with disgust.

"Get out. All you get out! You all eat too much. I pay money food all time. You make me broke. Get out." He looks utterly miserable, much like a wretched dog snipping at gnats swirling around him. It is not the first time he has told me to leave, but usually I ignore his tirades.

But at that moment, I can feel his violence and know an explosion is about to occur. Mama feels the tension, too. She is completely frightened for me, *"Go hide. Your father maybe kill you."* For some reason, I am not afraid, simply because at the time, I don't believe he will kill me. I ask Mama if I can stay with her sister, Mary. (Mama always calls her sister "Mary," while I have always referred to her as "Aunt Babe".) Mama is taken aback at my suggestion, thinks about it for a moment, then says, *"Yes, you go there."*

I put some clothes in a brown bag and walk twenty blocks from our house to my Aunt Babe's house on Jay Street. She has married Willie Minor, moved in his house along with her sons from her first marriage: Joe, Clarence, Charles, and David. I am not sure she has enough room for me, but when she listens to me explain what happened at home, she makes Charles move into a room in the basement and gives me his bedroom. He grumbles, but nonetheless obeys his mother.

Weeks later, Mama visits Aunt Babe to tell me it is safe to come home. Daddy isn't angry with me anymore, and he hasn't been drinking either. When I arrive, I am filled with trepidation thinking of what Daddy will do when he sees me. But nothing of the sort occurs. He enters the living room after coming home from work and sees me sitting on the couch; he smiles *"Hi"* to me, as if the animosity between us never existed. And certainly there is no mention of throwing me out.

An air of tranquility now occupies the house when Daddy comes home. He is sober and truly enjoys teasing us. Once a horrific odor emanates from the bathroom, where he obviously has had a bowel movement, and the three of us, Shirley, Barbara, and I, all complain of the pungent smell.

"Daddy, you stink! You make whole house stink! Ugh!"

He grins a bewitching smile as he clearly enjoys making a snappy comeback, *"This not stink. This perfume. Ha. Ha. Ha."*

The pleasant atmosphere only lasts a few weeks, because he begins coming home drunk again, demanding that all of us move out. He doesn't want us there because we cost him too much money. His ranting starts all over again, especially when he sees me. He comes home from work, breathing hard, stinking of beer, and filling the living room with loathing.

"Get out. Get out." He says, livid with rage. My mother rushes into the room and stands between my father and me, while wildly signing for me to hurry to my bedroom. I am scared for her and stand firmly, watching her explain to him, *"Please, please leave Maxine alone. She child. Why you mad Maxine?"*

He turns to her, almost as if he has rehearsed his response. *"You pet Maxine. You make Maxine against me. Maxine support you, against me. I know. I see what you do."*

My mother responds, *"No. No. She child. Not know better."*

He glares at her and then at me, snorting his hatred of life itself. His body weaves back and forth as he is barely able to walk to the bathroom, where he slams the door, takes his three-foot leather strap from the hook attached to the door, and begins sliding his straight blade razor up and down the strap, attempting to sharpen it even more. I can hear the scraping sound of the razor and become frightened. I go to my bedroom and hide for hours behind the clothes in the closet. When I finally go to bed, I sleep sparingly, trying to listen for my father's approaching steps. During this time Shirley and Barbara hover in the corner of the bedroom, not even venturing to say a word, lest they irritate my father even more than I have.

The next day, I am relieved to wake up alive and hastily dress to go to school. I am in my social studies class, sitting next to Manny Brown. Manny and I exchange friendly words with each other once in a while, especially around test time when he looks on my answer sheet to copy my answers.

"What's the matter, Maxine? You look upset about something," he asks.

"Oh nothing." I don't know what to tell him, and I'm surprised at myself when I confide in him, "My father wants me to move out."

"He does? My goodness!" He pauses a moment, "You can stay at my house if you want. I'll ask my mother."

"Really?" I don't know how to respond to such an unexpectedly generous proposition. I sigh, "Okay, if your mother says it is all right." All of a sudden I feel lost, like a person wandering in a forest, trying to find my way. I want to cry.

Manny tells me the next day that his mother says I am welcome to come there. I tell Mama about staying at Manny's house, and she says she is worried Daddy will try to kill me. She tells me I can stay at Manny's house or her sister's house, as she is leaving it up to me. I choose to stay at Manny's, only because that would be an adventure, something novel; plus, I won't cause Charles to move from his bedroom. Mama admonishes me again, *"You need be same as Shirley and Barbara. They say nothing. They safe."*

Manny is a short round boy who is his parents' only child. Just as he said, his mother greets me with warmth and genuine friendliness. She tells me that Manny has agreed to let me sleep in his room, while he will sleep on a sofa bed, and I can stay in their home as long as I need to. She works in a laundry and says when school is out, I can get a job there for the summer. Manny's father has a very dark complexion, almost ebony; he is of medium height and build and works as a construction worker. When he comes home from work, he is covered with white cement dust on his kinky hair, face, hands, and all over his clothes.

I stay with Manny and his parents for almost three weeks. Finally, I return to my house one day after school to find that no one is home. There is an eerie emptiness there. Mama, with Shirley and Barbara, comes home just as it is getting dark. Mama has two bags of groceries she has purchased from Don's.

She looks tired, weary, and so forlorn. She says with a weak smile, *"I happy see you. You look fine. Your daddy want me find work. He say no money (for) food. I borrow money my father."*

Daddy comes home a couple of hours later. Appearing sober, he looks at me and says nothing. Later, I hear his angry voice arguing with Mama in the kitchen, and I guess he is telling her to get out. This time, I heed Mama's advice and stay in the bedroom to avoid any confrontation with the man.

After several days have passed, Mama asks me if I want to go away with her to work for the summer, as she has learned about a place in New Jersey where there are many jobs.

I tell her, "Yes, sure." She also asks my three cousins to come with us; they are Ruth's children: Martha, Bonnie, and Louise. Their mother, Ruth, Mama's sister, had died many years before. And my cousins want to earn money for the summer, too. In the meantime, Mama sends my sisters, Shirley and Barbara, to stay with Grandma in North Carolina.

So Daddy finally gets rid of us. And sadly, he is home alone.

17

Asbury Park

"Southern schools plan massive resistance to court-ordered integration."

I am fourteen years old, and the prospect of going to a strange faraway place to earn money seems like a fairy tale to me. I am anxious to leave Washington, D.C., with its dark cloud of hurts and pains hovering over me, from all the angst at home to the trials and tribulations at school. I ignore the headlines in the papers and all the buzz at school: from the pending civil rights act to be signed by President Eisenhower to the rumored gossip about Elvis Presley's alleged comment that "the only thing colored people can do for me is shine my shoes."

Frankly, I don't care about President Eisenhower, civil rights, or even Elvis Presley, for that matter. I just want freedom from all my troubles and hurts. As soon as school closes, my time is consumed with preparing to finally get out of D.C. at last. I wash my clothes in the wringer washing machine and then iron them to be packed in an old worn suitcase with a belt tied around it to secure it from bursting open.

A few days earlier, Mama had sent her nieces a postcard as to when they should come to our house. When Louise and Martha arrive in the morning, we all leave together, boarding the Greyhound bus, changing buses in Philadelphia to finally arrive in Asbury Park, New Jersey, in the late evening. As soon as we arrive, Mama hails a taxi and tells me to ask the cab driver where we can rent rooms. He tells us he has a friend who rents the upstairs rooms in her house; he asks if we want to go there. Mama says yes, so we go to a house on a residential street, not far from downtown where a gray-haired, caramel-complexioned, middle-aged lady rents us a bedroom with twin beds, charging us twenty dollars a week. The landlady tells the cab driver that she doesn't have additional rooms to accommodate my cousins, so he recommends a boardinghouse to them and drives off hurriedly.

Mama and I meet our new landlady, who takes us to an immaculate room, freshly wallpapered with tiny roses on it. She wishes us a good night's sleep, telling us she will see us in the morning. Mama and I sit on the twin beds facing each other; while I am full of excitement, she is obviously tired and worn out.

"I sleep. Look job tomorrow." She quickly disrobes, and without even unpacking her clothes, she slips into the bed and soon is snoring, while I, on the other hand, am so excited by the prospect of everything being so different and new and finding a job, I barely sleep at all. Besides, the incessant buzz from Mama's snoring is hardly an inducement to getting a good night's sleep. We awaken the next morning, and Mama unpacks the leftover fried chicken and fruit she prepared for our bus trip. We hungrily gobble down the food before dressing in our better clothes and descend down the stairs to be greeted by the landlady, who tells us of an employment office with a good reputation for placing people in jobs. She also tells us that tourists, especially from New York City, come here during the summer because Asbury is a boardwalk town where people flock to vacation for a reprieve from the summer heat.

"If you want to work, this is the place to be, right here in Asbury Park," she says to Mama and me. I sign all this to my mother, who nods her head quietly.

Mama and I follow the landlady's instructions for catching a bus and going to the recommended employment agency.

When we arrive, a friendly receptionist appears genuinely interested in us and gives us applications to fill out, which we hurriedly complete.

During the interview by the reception lady, I explain that my mother can't hear and that I will be using sign language. The receptionist is engrossed by our hands moving in the air, and while simultaneously looking down at Mama's application, she says, "Well, based on the wealth of experience your mother has, I have a job that is perfect for her, working as an assistant cook in a cafeteria. She can go there right now. I'll call them and tell them all about her. They'll tell me if she will work out. The pay is forty dollars a week." She now looks directly at my mother and begins to talk louder and exaggerates her words by moving her lips slowly to say, "But they might give you more if they like you. Do you want to apply for this?"

I sign this to Mama, who says, *"Yes, I want work."* She is stunned at how quickly she is able to get a job, and smiles gratefully.

The receptionist turns and looks at me, "Well what kind of experience do you have?

"I don't have any experience. I've only been a babysitter."

"How old are you?"

I lie, telling her I am sixteen.

"I have the perfect job for you, Maxine. It's work as a nanny."

"What's a nanny?"

"Oh that's nothing but a glorified babysitter. It's in Ocean Park; the pay is twenty dollars a week and you are asked to sleep in during the week. Can you do that?"

"Sure," I said, not really understanding what all that would entail.

She gives me the address, and Mama and I part, Mama to go to the job in the cafeteria, and I to go to the job in Ocean Park.

I travel on the bus a long way to a town some distance from Asbury Park and finally arrive at a house, which is a magnificent mansion, the most glorious I have ever seen. The job is to be a live-in nanny for two boys, ages four and six, and to occasionally replace the housekeeper on her days off.

The housekeeper is a young "colored" woman in her early thirties who has worked for the family for more than six months, cleaning the house, cooking meals for the family, and answering the telephone.

"You've got an easy job," she told me. "All you have to do is play with the boys and cook dinner when I take my days off."

"But I don't know how to cook," I say in alarm.

"Don't worry. I'll prepare everything for you before I go. All you have to do is heat up the food."

I wonder if she knows that I don't even know how to heat anything up. But true to her word, it is a sheer delight to care for the boys. The kids and I have such fun as we fast become playmates: singing the latest tunes, laughing at each other, and jumping up and down on their beds. Oh, how sweet is the merriment! Actually, we are playing so loudly, the lady of the house abruptly appears from no place and interrupts our good time, telling us to quiet the racket. Were we too rowdy, making excessive noise and disturbing everyone in the house? I don't know, but in less than a week, I am fired. I can only guess I was having too much fun, making too much noise to suit the tranquility of the household.

So it's a Friday afternoon, and my employer waits at the back door for me as I'm about to leave for my day off. She says rather coolly and calmly to me, "We realize, Maxine, we don't need a nanny to help our present housekeeper right now.

Thank you so much for your services." She says this to me as she hands me a little brown envelope, which has in it my first and last pay of eighteen dollars, reflecting a deduction for room and board.

I TRAVEL the local bus a long way to Mama's job at the cafeteria to tell her I don't have a job anymore. She says, *"All right. I ask boss (let) you work here."*

She goes to her boss to introduce me to her. Her boss, who manages the cafeteria, is a short petite woman with salt-and-pepper hair, a huge hooknose, and very thin lips painted with ruby red lipstick. She swishes when she walks up to me and seems genuinely eager, almost thrilled, to see me.

She smiles so admiringly at Mama and says, "Your mother is just wonderful. She understands me and I understand her. All I have to do is point to things and she understands so quickly. Why, once I had to write her a note, she caught on, just like that!" Her words sound as if she thought Mama was not only deaf, but also dumb and illiterate. I want to tell her Mama was once a teacher, but decide to leave well enough alone.

Mama waits a moment and then tells me to tell her boss that I don't have a job and will she please hire me. And the lady says they happen to have an opening in the cafeteria for a silver girl, paying twenty-five dollars a week. The silver girl rolls the silver, placing fork, knife, and spoon in a napkin, and arranges the place settings on each of the tables. My job is to also help Mama clean fresh vegetables, prepare chicken salads, and assist in any way needed in the kitchen.

MAMA AND I each have one day off a week, using that time to haul our dirty clothes in a pillowcase to a laundromat, to wash, dry, and fold them, and lug them back to our room. Mama insists that we keep our things neatly in the bureau drawers, and to hide the money we earn. She suspects the landlady sneaks in our room and looks through our things during the day when we are at work. *"I know my things different place I leave morning."* I know instinctively that Mama is correct, since she has eyes like an eagle, spotting anything that might be even slightly out of place.

Once in a while we go down to the boardwalk, sit on the bench, and watch people walk up and down the boardwalk. The breeze blowing our way feels heavenly. I can't resist

During the summer of 1957, my mother and I went to work in Asbury Park. My mother sits on a bench on the boardwalk during a break from her job in the cafeteria.

taking off my shoes to walk in the sand along the shore. Mama cautions me to be careful, because there might be glass hidden in the sand. She is right! I find broken pieces of glass from Coke bottles and drinking glasses that could have easily cut my feet. I bring back the pieces of glass to show her; I laugh to myself when I see her "I-told-you-so" expression.

When we return to our rooms, we each take a good hot bath in the claw-foot tub. And the next day we go to the cafeteria refreshed, ready for work.

Every week Mama sends a letter to her mother with five dollars in it for the care of Shirley and Barbara. She encloses a brief note written on tablet paper asking how they are and saying that she hopes to see them soon. Grandma writes back that she received the money and the girls are fine.

One time, Mama sends an ivory-colored post card to Daddy, letting him know we are fine and will be home after Labor Day. He never responds, but then again, Mama has not given him a return address either.

Now it's the Fourth of July, and the tourist season has officially opened. Crowds of people pop in almost every day. Mama is extremely busy cleaning fruits and vegetables, mixing tuna fish salad, and making a variety of salads, from fruit platters to lettuce-and-tomato bowls. Three new busboys have been hired to wait on the hungry patrons.

That's when I meet Jesse Lewis, one of the busboys, originally from Sarasota, Florida, who is saving money for college. His male cohorts call him Lewis, and all of them are between eighteen and twenty years old. He is not much taller than I, is an extremely meticulous dresser, and has the whitest teeth I have ever seen. He owns an old Ford, which he keeps in mint condition.

I hesitate when he asks me out for a date because he seems so confident, suave, and knowledgeable, whereas I feel

awkward and clumsy. It is one of the few times when I hesitate
to volunteer any information about myself, afraid of being
misunderstood, preferring to be quiet. He did ask me how old
I am, and I answer, "a true lady never tells her age." He throws
back his head and laughs.

"Well, do you know how to drive?"

"No."

"Well, I'll just teach ya."

And so he does. He shows me where the "drive" and
"reverse" gears are behind the steering wheel, the lever signaling
the driver's intention to turn left or right, and the brakes and
accelerator on the car floor. Then he drives out to a highway
and insists that I slide behind the steering wheel.

I am tickled to see how a driver's use of signals lets other
drivers know their intention, either to make a left or right turn.

"It's like drivers are communicating with each other. That's
amazing," I say.

"Yeah, okay," he says, unimpressed.

I remain silent as usual, hardly ever engaging in conversation with him. It is so intimidating to be with a person who is
as cool and well spoken as he. He must enjoy knowing more
than I do, since he calls me his little "dumb one." I am not so
dumb, I think to myself, as to let your wandering hand go up
my thigh. Lewis says repeatedly that my frequent removal of his
hand from my lap to his lap is giving him a headache. I laugh.

Mama is worried about my going out with someone older,
and insists I come home by nine, since I have to be at work at
seven in the morning.

*"Be careful, you (go out) with man more old (than) you. You
know (what) man want."* (By this time, I have figured out the
"facts of life," having read romance magazines and listened to
girls tell how a man and a woman "do it.")

So whenever I go out to eat or see a movie with Lewis, I imagine Mama sitting on my shoulder watching me. Lewis and I rarely kiss each other, and little by little, his interest in me dwindles. My guess is that he wanted to be with someone who wouldn't move his hand away all the time.

Other than the occasional date with Lewis, I do little else that summer, except work. My take-home pay is twenty-two dollars a week. I pay the landlady the ten dollars each Friday for my share of the rent, leaving me twelve dollars. I have to pay bus fare to and from work, as well as buy evening meals. The cafeteria does not serve breakfast, but they do give me a free meal at lunchtime. Once in a while, I buy a blouse or skirt on what little money I am able to save. When I purchase anything like that, I have no money left to save. After nine weeks, I have barely saved fifty dollars.

Just before Labor Day weekend, our cousins come to our rented room one day and leave a note for Mama saying that they have decided to leave Asbury Park before Labor Day Monday. They want to go back to Baltimore to get ready for school.

Finally, the magic day—Labor Day—arrives, and the tourist season ends. The owner and chef sob; Mama's boss actually begins to blubber, telling us she will truly miss us. Finally, they all bid us farewell, with the owner putting an extra ten dollars in our pay envelopes. The busboys are hanging around to leave the next day; I give Lewis my address in D.C. He promises to write after he returns to Sarasota.

After Mama and I pack our bags, we catch a cab to the Greyhound bus station, and as we board the bus, Mama turns around and waves good-bye to Asbury Park. She mouths the words:

"Bye, bye Asbury. Thank you for work."

WHEN WE arrive in Washington, we hail a cab for home. When Daddy opens the door, he is glowing with joy, and it is clear to me that he is genuinely glad to see us, hugging Mama tightly several times. He turns to me and embraces me with a long hug. I detect an odor of stale beer. But he is so happy to see us, and we to see him, that I ignore the smell and forget the heated argument he had with me before Mama and I left for Asbury Park. I remember his incessant complaining and fuming that Mama had turned me against him, that I argue with him too much, and, worse yet, that I, with Shirley and Barbara, eat too much, costing him a fortune to support us.

Anyway, he is glad to see us, and at that moment, that was all that counted.

During my first week home, I receive a letter from Lewis and a second one two weeks later. In both letters, he uses the salutation "My little dumb one." Sick and tired of that greeting, I grab a red pen and begin circling any and all grammatical errors or misspelled words in his two letters. Then I write, "Who is dumb?" at the bottom of the letterhead. He never writes me again. I wonder why.

I TURN fifteen years old and am in the tenth grade. I study Latin, geometry, and biology. I also take a course in music appreciation with Mr. Walters, a very light, almost white-complexioned teacher who also teaches social studies on occasion. While he teaches the class to understand and value music as an art form, he talks extensively about the current news of the day, mostly about race relations. Mr. Walters talks about Paul Robeson, an actor with a magnificent bass voice and the outrageous discrimination he suffered at the hands of the U.S. government, as well as such topics as the death of W. C. Handy, a blues composer considered the Father of the Blues, and the life of William Grant Still, a composer whose works included opera, jazz, and classical genres. (I had never heard of William

Grant Still and am amazed that his musical works include five symphonies, four ballets, and nine operas.)

Sometimes, Mr. Walters talks about himself and the various experiences he has had. "I tell you, class, I noticed when I went to a music conference with my wife that the white people were very nice to us. We were the only Negroes there. Now, I remember I went to another conference last year, where there were about ten Negroes. Well, the whites weren't as nice to us Negroes at that particular conference. You want to know why? Because there were more of us. I've figured out that white people can accept one or two Negroes in their midst but not more than three."

I wonder how anybody can tell that Mr. Walters is a Negro and how white people can discriminate against him. But I give up thinking about what happens to Negroes—I need to worry about how I am going to earn money. As the school year comes to an end, I am anxious to return to Asbury Park to find work so I can buy my wardrobe for the coming school year. I am very self-conscious about the clothes I wear, and I long to have the latest fashions like other girls wear, but don't have the money to buy them. Mama says I can go back to Asbury Park, but she is not going with me.

"You big girl. You (be) careful." She wants me to go because the constant bickering between Daddy and me will temporarily come to a halt. For once the house will be silent, absent of the noise from our arguing.

It is rare for Daddy to come home sober now. He drinks more and more gin, becomes nastier, and uses malicious language to describe his feelings toward us: *"You (all) pigs. I hate you, you no good."* Shirley and Barbara never confront him; they prefer to hide somewhere in the house. Mama ignores him and continues her sewing.

One evening he is so drunk when he comes home from work that he starts shaking his fists in rage and threatening me for no reason. I'm afraid he's going to attack me. I grab an empty beer bottle and swing it, hitting him on his head. The bottle shatters into tiny pieces, glass flying everywhere. Daddy is dazed. I think he is going to come after me, but instead, he goes to his room and lies in a stupor on the bed. The next day, there are tiny wounds all over his face, neck, and head where the glass has cut him. I can't believe I am the cause of these injuries, but the evidence of my fear and bitterness is clear. I don't like Daddy.

So, I am happy to seek refuge in Asbury Park. Finally, the beginning of summer arrives, and Mama makes me a finely tailored pinstriped taupe suit to wear as traveling attire. I look older than I am, very professional, much like a career lady.

Mama and I ride the D.C. city bus downtown to the Greyhound station, where she gives me a five-dollar bill and five one-dollar bills and tells me to be careful. I tuck the money in my purse, board the bus, suitcase in hand, and wave to Mama through the window as we pull away. I miss her already and feel alone, but try to push back that nagging feeling by concentrating on the money I'll make when I work in Asbury. I think to myself that in a few hours, I'll be arriving in Philadelphia to change to another bus heading for Asbury Park, New Jersey.

As I begin to relax and enjoy the bus ride, I hear the driver suddenly say, "Folks we have to make an emergency stop. Don't be alarmed, but there's smoke coming from the engine." The other passengers begin to grumble as the driver stops at a coffee shop only a short distance away. He makes a call to the main office and another bus arrives about an hour later. At last, it feels like smooth sailing again when we arrive in Philadelphia, but alas! The connecting bus for Asbury just left fifteen minutes earlier. "The next bus for Asbury won't come in until tomorrow morning at nine o'clock," says the ticket clerk, who suggests, "Maybe you can stay at a hotel for the night."

Oh my goodness! What am I to do? I know I don't have enough money for a hotel. I sigh and look around at the hard wooden benches and feel utterly miserable at the prospect of sleeping on one of them all night. Just then, a rather short "colored" man with an obvious limp, (one leg shorter than the other), walks up to me and says, "I know where there is a hotel you can stay at. It isn't much money either."

I look at him cautiously, but he looks harmless and I sense that he can be trusted. "Well," I ask, "how much is it?"

"Oh, I don't know. Maybe five or six dollars, something like that."

I look over at the hard and uninviting wooden benches again and conclude that anything would be better than sleeping on one of them.

"Okay," I say.

"All right then, just follow me. I know a short cut." I pick up my suitcase and follow him as he limps out the door. By this time, night has come, as he hobbles along the side of the bus station building, with me close behind. He cuts over two blocks and then leads me down a dark alley. That's the first time it occurs to me that I may have made a mistake in my naiveté and won't be safe. After all, Mama did tell me to be careful, and following this strange little man does not feel very sensible. But I can't turn around now. I'll see where this goes.

Finally, we arrive at a run-down derelict brick building with a blinking sign over the door spelling the word "Hotel," except that the lightbulb behind the letters "t" and "e" are blown out, making the sign spell "Ho—l." I wonder what kind of place this is as the fellow takes me inside to a woman waiting placidly behind a counter.

"Yes, can I help you?" she says politely, in a bored tone.

"Yes, I'd like a room, please."

She stares at me and looks over at the crippled man and asks him, "By the hour or by the night?"

Now, why would anyone want to stay in a room for just one hour, I think. I reply, "By the night. For tonight, please."

She then looks at me, "That will be six dollars."

Both the woman behind the counter and the man standing beside me stare intently at my purse as I rummage through it, pull out the money Mama gave me, peeling off a wrinkled five-dollar bill and a one-dollar bill, and give the money to the woman. They look at each other; the woman finally hands me a key, telling me that my room is number 309 on the third floor. "You can go up on the elevator round the corner, or you can go up the stairs next to it. I recommend you walk up 'cuz the elevator has been acting up lately."

I lug my suitcase up the stairs to the room, where the paint on the walls is peeling; the dirty sheer curtains are whooshing toward me from the night breezes coming through the window; and the air reeks of a pungent smell akin to urine. I put down my suitcase, bolt the door, and put a chair under the doorknob for extra security. I don't want to change my clothes, but neither do I want to wrinkle the beautiful suit Mama made me. I decide to change into a nightgown and just lie on the bed. I refuse to sleep, but weariness and tension overtake me, and I finally doze off as the morning sun begins to peek through the dirty and dusty window. I don't know what time it is. I jump up, quickly change into the suit, rush out the door, exit the hotel, and practically run all the way back to the Greyhound station. When I arrive, I see it is only six o'clock in the morning. Even though the bus for Asbury does not leave for another three hours, that's still too much time for me to spend in that hotel.

I FINALLY arrive at Asbury Park and go directly to the house where Mama and I stayed the previous summer. She just happens to have a room with a single bed, and aren't I lucky that she has this one left? She asks why I didn't write her to let her know I was coming; I have to confess that I had long ago lost her address.

The next morning, wearing my tailored suit, I go to the same employment agency where Mama and I were given employment referrals the year before, only to see a different receptionist this time. She gives me a cordial welcome and an application for employment; as soon as I complete it, she says she has the perfect job for me, working for Murray's Bed and Breakfast in Ocean Park as a housekeeper/maid.

When I go there, Kitty and John Murray interview me, and say they would like to try me out for a week before deciding to hire me permanently. The job entails cleaning the eight rooms where guests stay for at least a week and the dining room where they eat their home-cooked meals. My other duties are to help Mrs. Murray serve breakfast and dinner, wash dishes, and keep the kitchen, living room, and stairway tidy. I start to work the next day, and one week later I pass the probation period and am hired permanently.

Mrs. Murray is about sixty years old, extremely short, four foot eight or nine, extremely round with a substantial bosom. She is very pigeon-toed and wears black open-toed hospital shoes to accommodate her crooked toes. She is never seen without an apron wrapped around her waist and is considered a fabulous cook. That is her job, to be the full-time chef— planning and cooking meals for the guests.

Her husband, John, is only a few inches taller than his wife. He works full-time for the New York Department of Labor as an employment specialist, interviewing candidates for different jobs. He is also an accountant, keeping all the financial records for the family enterprise, especially those required by the Internal Revenue Service. Although, it is clear that he is considered the "brains" of the outfit, he is no match for the feisty and energetic Kitty Murray, who seems to enjoy complaining to her husband.

When Mrs. Murray is lonely, she talks to me, telling me about her many miscarriages and how depressed she is that she does not have "even one child." "Oh well," she says, "at least I have nieces." She loves to ask me personal questions. I tell her my parents are deaf. She wants to know how we talk with each other and is fascinated with the fact that my two sisters and I have normal hearing. She is amazed that my parents are self-sufficient and not on public assistance. I tolerate her naiveté, and wonder why she is so elated when I tell her that my grandfather was a Cherokee Indian. She is so delighted that she tells a frequent guest, Robert Murphy, an attorney, "Maxine is part Indian. Imagine that! That's why she has such high cheekbones."

It seems she wants to minimize the fact that I am Black, and she glamorizes any Indian heritage I might have.

Perhaps my subdued reaction to Mrs. Murray's statement about my race is due to my growing awareness of my color, since unlike Washington, D.C., with its majority of Black residents, Ocean Park is a town comprised of almost all white people. Certainly, all the guests at the Murray's Bed and Breakfast are white. In fact, I never see a Black person come to the house, not even to deliver goods.

I've been paying attention to the headlines regarding race relations blazing in the newspapers and on the television evening news: "Southern schools' massive resistance to integration orders from the Supreme Court," or the "First major march on Washington led by black leaders of the day," speaking of Ralph Bunche, Jackie Robinson, Roy Wilkins, A. Phillip Randolph, and Coretta Scott King, among others. Martin Luther King was unable to attend, as he was recovering from a near-fatal stabbing.

Whatever the logic behind my thinking, I'm becoming prouder and more aware of my black heritage. So much so, that when I meet a young, short, dark-complexioned black man in Asbury Park who wants to take me to the movies, I tell him he has to come to Ocean Park to pick me up. I insist he must come to the front door, not the back door, at exactly five in the afternoon, when I leave the job.

On the appointed day, the young man, following my instructions, comes to the front door and rings the doorbell. The chimes ring. Mrs. Murray and I are in the kitchen; she goes to answer the door. When she returns to the kitchen, she looks as if she is in shock, as her face is pale, almost colorless.

"Maxine, there's a man looking for you," she says uncomfortably.

"Oh, that's my date. We're going to the movies here in Ocean Park. Did you invite him in?"

"Uh, yes. He's standing in the living room."

I smile, knowing she would never leave him on the porch because too many neighbors and passersby would see a black man standing there. I rush to get my sweater, and off I go to the movies, feeling somehow that I have changed a tiny piece of the world by actually seeing a black man come to the front door, not the accustomed back door. Once more, I do not lose my job. Thank God!

The day after Labor Day, I leave Murray's Bed and Breakfast, all the white people in Ocean Park and Asbury Park, and board the Greyhound bus back to Washington, D.C. I feel a little ashamed that I have not written one postcard or letter, not even to Mama. I think she will forgive me because this time, I have saved one hundred twenty-five dollars!

I can't wait to go to Lerner's Department Store and buy brand new clothes. And yes, now I will have a telephone installed in our house.

18

When Tempers Flare

"Daddy's praying. Is this the same man who almost killed me yesterday?"

Today I must go to Daddy's job, so I catch the bus on Dix Street and ride downtown to Daddy's workplace. I show up unexpectedly at the shoe shop to ask for money. When I arrive, I walk to the back of the shop and watch him closely to see if he has been drinking. If his face is red or if the aroma about him gives off the smell of beer, I know to say hello to him, turn around, and leave.

"Daddy, I need five dollars to go on a trip for school." He stares at me and shakes his head.

"I broke, broke, broke." So I just stand there, refusing to leave. About five minutes later he stares at me and asks me, *"What money for?"*

"I need money for school."

Then he turns his head to find Sam, his boss, working on a pair of shoes only a few feet away. *"Sam, give-me five dollars,"* he says.

Then Sam flips through a wad of dollar bills and yanks out a five, pulls out a pocket notebook, and records the amount to be debited from Daddy's pay. He gives it to Daddy, who, in turn, gives the money to me. I realize it is quitting time and the shop will be closing momentarily. Maybe Daddy and I can go home together. I patiently wait for Daddy to finish work for the day, and we begin to walk from there to the bus stop, about three blocks away.

Daddy strolls, while I do a peppy quick trot. Although I am now sixteen years old, my steps are still shorter than his, making it necessary to walk faster to keep up with his deliberately slow pace.

His shoulders sway. I think Daddy sees himself as "Mr. Gentleman," or "Mr. Cool," never rattled, never flustered, always dignified, and always appearing self-assured, at least in public.

"Walk slow. Why you hurry? Take it easy." He spells each letter with a slight pause, almost as if there is a period after each letter *"T-a-k-e I-t E-a-s-y. Stop run. Walk slow. Why you hurry all time? T-a-k-e It E-a-s-y."* He repeats his frequently used phrase to me.

We stroll, ever so slowly, to the bus stop, and now I restrain my pace, to keep it at the same unhurried rhythm as his. We ride the city bus marked "X2 Seat Pleasant" headed back to our home on the outskirts of Washington, D.C., often called the "boon-docks" because of its proximity to the Maryland boundary.

Here, again, Daddy shows himself to be a gentleman, most considerate, especially to all ladies and unless they prove them-selves otherwise to him, every female is a lady. Daddy always makes it a point to extend his hand under my elbow to help me up on the bus. Standing behind me, he taps me on the shoulder and motions me to a seat. I slide onto the seat, and he sits on the side closest to the aisle of the bus, so he can exit the bus first. He chastised me the first time we rode together for walk-ing in front of him.

"I walk first," he said.

When we arrive at our stop, he meanders down the aisle, and I follow. He walks to the front of the bus, steps down to the street, and pirouettes around to extend his hand upward and guide my hand, to help me as I take the two steps down to the ground.

It is as if he were Sir Lancelot, a chivalrous knight, holding his hand upward to assist me. I feel as if I am the bewitching beautiful princess from far-off never-never land. After disembarking, I join him, taking an occasional glance at the passengers staring at us through the boxlike bus windows, and I imagine their envy. See me with this wonderful considerate man who treats me as if I am the most magnificent princess in the world. This is the Daddy I remember loving so.

I think sometimes he has that calm exterior because he thinks he's cool. He told me that while growing up at the Overlea School, the kids thought he was Edward G. Robinson. I didn't see the resemblance until I saw a high school picture of him standing there in his shoe repair apron. I can see the likeness initially, especially the dark shock of hair and the thick eyebrows, maybe even the proud straight nose. But that's where it ends. Edward G. Robinson's lips are thick and wide. Dad's mouth is small, like the curve in Santa Claus's mouth. His upper lip is practically a line, his lower lip just a tad fuller. I remember asking him years ago how he kisses Mama, since her lips are full like mine.

"How you kiss Mama?" I asked.

His eyes would twinkle as he repeated his old refrain, *"My secret."*

He never talks much about his feelings to me or about his experiences growing up. Almost everything I learn about his life, from his birth to his marriage, I learn from Mama. He reveals everything to her, and she in turn tells me; she describes his moods, especially his darker moods when he is angry or drunk.

Once when I was twelve years old, Daddy took the family to the Overlea School for a reunion. That's when I heard more things about him as a former student: he was extremely diligent in all his subjects, had a quick wit and sense of humor, and occasionally demonstrated an explosive temper.

Mama says he was quite a lover, and women told her about their relationships with him, past and present. At least the deaf women do.

"Deaf people bold," she tells me. *"They say everything."*

At boastful moments, he told her about women who pursued him when he was single and even after he married her. Mama says nothing, even though she is terribly hurt, she nods her head. When he has had a few beers, he continues to brag that sometimes he couldn't help himself; women just throw themselves at him. He even boasts that he can always tell by looking at a woman's legs if she is still a virgin. Maybe he can.

I AM IN the midst of my teenage years, and I am utterly miserable and depressed. I don't know when it started, my despondency and unhappiness about being at home when I develop an attitude, almost a presumption, that I am an equal to my parents. My self-esteem is at its lowest point in my life. Maybe it is emotional fatigue from all my troubles at school: my resolve to cope with unfriendly students while trying to prove my worth to them by being an outstanding student earning A's in most of my classes. I suppose going away to work alone at age fifteen for the entire summer in New Jersey has something to do with it. After all, I had to support myself, pay the rent, buy my food, and pay bills as any adult, even though I am still a teenager.

I don't know when I changed from an obedient, careful, thoughtful child to being outspoken, candid, and even confrontational. It seems as if I grew almost overnight from four feet seven to five feet five, the way a squirt of water shoots up from just a little bubble to become a tall water fountain. All I know is that I changed almost instantly. I find myself standing up to anyone who challenges my perception of what is right or wrong—"justice," I call it. Perhaps I am unknowingly reacting to all the civil rights news constantly in the headlines and the angry talk I hear among black people on the street. Maybe it is because I can hear and my parents can't, and their reliance on me as their ears and mouthpiece has made me older than my years. It could be that I am just plain headstrong and stubborn—that's what Mama says, that I am just plain hardheaded.

But whatever the reason, Daddy and I seem to be embroiled in constant conflict: fussing, arguing, and his frequent temper tantrums. Many times I am clearly the one at fault. Once Daddy said, *"Come Maxine, I want you tell man he (do) bad job fix car."* He sees me shrug my shoulders and make a down-in-the-mouth expression that instantly tells him that I don't feel like interpreting. I don't want another confrontation with a hearing person. I am too exhausted from having been awake from midnight until three in the morning studying.

Daddy reads the lack of enthusiasm on my face, denounces me, and says I am no good. That is his favorite sign—a letter "n" along with the letter "g," flicked quickly, is the abbreviation for "no good."

Then he begins to swear, *"Mong Fong, Mong Fong."*

I ignore his obscenities. After that, I begin to sulk, because I have so much on my mind: having to do homework, especially geometry and Latin; studying for comprehensive tests; picking out clothes to wear for school; and trying to earn money from babysitting and doing housework. And now Daddy wants me to stop everything I am doing to immediately do something for him. That's when he accuses Mama of being a poor mother, since she can't teach me to respect him as my father; after all he is the boss in the house. *"She not respect me. You teach her obey you, not me. You no good mother, you."*

I am fifteen years old, and my resentment of him is growing almost daily: his swearing, his yelling, his screeching, and his accusing me of always being in the wrong. Almost every day, when he cannot find a misplaced item, he accuses me of being a thief, and I vehemently deny his accusation.

"No! I did not steal anything. No! I am not lying. You drunk." My signs are wild, flying in the air. I see him seething, gritting his teeth, and making angry, growling sounds. Barbara and Shirley, sensing the growing firestorm, do what they usually do and retreat from the heat of the moment, slipping away to the bedroom.

Mama, however, continues to be my protector. When we are fussing, she immediately jumps in between us, and that's when he lunges to hit me. He pushes and shoves Mama instead, who pleads with us, *"Please, please stop. I tired. Please stop."* Her voice and her signs all convey pain and agony, so much so that Daddy relaxes his arms and glares at her.

I go to the bedroom and Mama follows me. *"Maxine, I tell you, he wants kill you. Maxine, please why you fuss? Keep your mouth shut. Maxine, you hardheaded. He drunk, he kill you. He big man, more strong than you, he fight you, he stay alive. You child, you die. Maxine, I see him sharpen razor on strap, he come night (and) kill you when you sleep. My Lord! My Lord, I pray you. Help my girl!"*

"Why don't we leave?" I insist, signing to her. "He try keep us all scared. I not believe he try kill me." Perhaps it is my imagination, but with all our arguing, he has never actually hit me. He usually seeks out my mother, and then the actual jostling and shoving takes place, with Mama caught in the middle.

Sometimes after being caught up in a struggle, she complains of chest pains, and her face is swollen with puffed layers of skin under her eyes. She complains of aching arms from the pushing and shoving. Mama says I don't have sense enough to shut up; that I always have to answer him back.

"You hardheaded. Keep mouth shut." She is in perpetual fear that he is going to try to kill me. She makes the signs again and again that he is sharpening his knives and razor blades on his leather strap for the right moment to slay me. I don't quite believe her, believing instead that her fears are feeding her imagination.

Daddy is coming home later and later from work, more and more toward ten in the evening, instead of the usual seven. He arrives home and enters his room momentarily before going to the kitchen to get something to eat. Most of the time I am in the kitchen, sitting at the kitchen table doing my homework or, if I am too exhausted, napping in the bedroom preparing to get up to study.

On one particular evening, the doorbell lights flash on and off persistently, reflecting someone's impatience. Then there is a banging on the door, repeatedly and loudly. I look through the square glass rectangles in the door and see that it is Daddy. When I open the door, I can see that his round face, ordinarily beige, is a darker shade of fire engine red. His lips are tightly pulled in. A deep penetrating scowl masks his face; his breathing is audibly labored. He stinks of a sour pungent smell, an odor akin to a baby's vomit, and one that I long ago have come to recognize as day-old beer. The stench of countless cans of beer seems to penetrate his skin, invade his clothes, and attach itself to each strand of stringy, matted hair.

"I wait for you open door! I bang, bang. Can't you hear?" he signs.

I say nothing; I turn around and go back into the kitchen to get some water, when he begins to scream his obscenities.

"Sheen! Sheen! Where dinner?"

Sighing, I point to the one piece of fried chicken left on the stove, the chicken back.

"Sheen, I don't want chicken back!"

Uncharacteristically, I feel embarrassed for him, because after all, who wants to eat the back of the chicken?

He grabs the chicken and hurls it toward the kitchen cabinets.

"You drunk! You no-good drunk!" My hands yell the words uncontrollably; I turn to leave the kitchen. Something whizzes by my ear, a fraction of an inch by my face. It makes a rushing sound as it sails by me, hitting the wall so powerfully that an immense cavity is carved out in the wall. I look down and see the missile: a thirty-two-ounce can of peaches, now dented from the impact of hitting that wall.

I swirl around and stare at him; I imagine my skull crushed, looking at the gaping hole. Daddy has hurled the can directly at my head. I turn to look at him again, say nothing, and walk out of the kitchen to retreat to the bedroom. Mama is right! He just might kill me.

ARE MY EYES deceiving me? Tonight, he is on his knees in his bedroom, his back to the door where I am standing. The bed sits parallel to the wall. He is saying his prayers kneeling beside it, as he faces the window. Is this the same man who almost killed me yesterday? I sniff the air and conclude that he has not been drinking.

His hands are folded together, signing: *"Our father who art in heaven . . ."*

With his head bent forward, he cups with his hands the word "our" from one side of the chest to another; then he makes the universal sign for "father," with the thumb at the forehead. I stand there in the doorway watching a giant of a man praying. I still can't believe my eyes. He is wearing his old gray khaki pants, and his white T-shirt. His feet are bare except for the socks. His hair is long and curls midway down the back of his neck, emphasizing a round protruding lump at the base of his neck, just above his shoulder, a lump the size of a Ping-Pong ball. He has never given me an explanation as to what the lump is or how it came to be. I continue to stare at his back, thinking maybe his praying is somehow tied to the weekly prayers that he and Mama say at church every Sunday. Most of the time, Daddy doesn't drink on Sundays, so that we can faithfully attend Shiloh Baptist Church.

I step away from the door so Daddy won't see me.

A FEW WEEKS LATER, on a Saturday evening around eight, the doorbell light flickers on and off. I go to the door and see that it is Grindaddy, Mama's father.

"Hiya, Grindaddy."

"Hi, Maxine. How ya doin'?"

"Okay, you looking for Mama?"

"Yeah, where is she?"

"Mama and Daddy took Shirley and Barbara and went to see some friends of theirs. They'll be back in a little while. But I have to go, or I'll be late."

"Well, you go on. I'll wait here for your mother and father."

Grindaddy, is about sixty years old now, and comes around the house sporadically, sometimes to get something to eat, other times to ask Mama to make alterations on his clothes. On rare occasions he borrows money from Daddy. Once in a while, he will spend the night, sleeping on the sofa. He still works as a bricklayer, and he usually comes to the house when he is in between jobs. Sometimes it is months and months before we see him, and then only for a brief time.

He has never learned to sign to his daughter in all these years, preferring to gesture, write notes, or ask me to interpret for him.

Anyway, I leave him sitting on the living room sofa, since I have a babysitting job for the Glovers at 8:15 p.m. They want me to care for their four-year-old son, Kenneth, and their baby girl, only a few months old. I walk briskly to their second-floor apartment, just two blocks away on Clay Street between Sixtieth and Sixty-First, and am warmly welcomed by Mrs. Glover, who explains that she has already put the baby to bed. She picks up the phone to call for a taxi.

"The baby has already had her milk and should stay asleep for the next three or four hours. Please put Kenneth to bed in the next hour. Let him watch television if he wants to, or read him some stories. The books are on the table there. And, oh yes, there is some cake in the fridge, help yourself." She hesitates for a moment and says, "I am going to a nightclub to hear my husband play the saxophone. I'll be back in a couple of hours. Okay?"

"Sure," I say to her. She picks up her purse, and just then the taxi toots its horn, announcing its presence. She quickly exits the apartment. I look around the living room and decide to watch television with Kenneth, who is sitting cross-legged on the floor only a foot from the television.

"Don't sit so close to the television, you'll go blind," I caution the little fellow. But he ignores me and doesn't move. About an hour later, he falls asleep on the floor; I pick him up, carry him to his bed, and remove his play clothes to dress him in his pajamas. Once he is in the bed, I walk to the nearby crib to check on the baby, who is sound asleep.

"Good," I think to myself, this will be an easy night. I'll eat some cake and watch television. After another hour, I doze off, only to be awakened by the key turning in the door. I instantly stand up to straighten my skirt and try to appear alert. Mrs. Glover comes in and asks, "How was everything?"

"Just fine. The baby stayed asleep, just as you said she would. I put Kenneth to bed about an hour ago."

"Well, that's just fine, Maxine. Here's five dollars for you. Is that all right?"

"Oh yes," I exclaim, knowing that was much more than the two dollars she usually gives me.

"Maxine, my husband has to play until two in the morning, and I was too tired to stay at the club that long. One of the band members brought me home in his fancy Thunderbird convertible. He's waiting outside to take you home, too. I don't want you walking home this late at night."

"Oh, thank you." I pick up my little purse and run outside to the waiting car. With its top down, the car is breathtakingly beautiful, with its shiny black veneer, brilliant chrome handles, and smooth gray leather seats. I slide onto the passenger seat, feeling as if I were a princess. "This is what it is like to be rich," I say to myself.

"Where to?" asks the young band player.

"Just down the street."

As he takes off, I can feel the cool breeze in my face, in my hair. He drives the two blocks to my house and makes a U-turn, since my house is on the opposite side of the street.

"I'll wait here for you until you go in. Okay?"

"Thanks a lot."

I hop out and run the few steps on the front sidewalk, walk up the steps, and ring the doorbell light. Grindaddy answers the door and glares at the car.

"Where you been all this time?"

"Oh, I told you, I had to go babysitting," I remark rather blithely.

"What you doin' comin' home with that man?"

"What man? Oh, you mean the man who brought me home. He just gave me a ride."

Grindaddy explodes, "You'se nothin' but a dirty slut."

"What . . . what you say?" I am caught off guard, shocked that he would say something so absurd. "What do you mean? I told you I've been babysitting."

"Babysittin', my ass. I saw you with dat man in dat fancy car."

"I don't know what you're thinking. Look here, here's the money I earned." I pull out the five dollars Mrs. Glover gave me and thrust it in his face.

He gasps when he sees the money, and shouts, "Why, you filthy slut. You ain't no good. Dat's what you are, a no-good slut. I'm gonna beat the tar off you." He pulls his belt from his pants and whirls the belt buckle, hitting me on my upper arm. I wince. The pain is excruciating. He jerks the belt back to strike me again. I grab the end of the belt and we both tumble to the floor, wrestling with each other, pulling, tugging, and yanking on the belt.

"Let go of the belt!" he shrieks.

"No, you'll hit me again."

"I ain't gonna hit you no more. Let go of the belt."

I slowly release my grip off the belt, waiting to see if he is going to renege on his promise. I am breathing heavily, panting. Hot sweat is rolling down my face and neck, mingling with the blood on my arm where he struck me with his belt buckle.

Just then Mama and Daddy walk through the front door. I rush to tell them Grindaddy has been fighting me, and I show them my wounded arm.

"Grindaddy not believe me I babysit. I show him money, but he not believe."

My mother stares at him. Furious, she signs, *"I know Maxine babysit. I know people live near here."*

Interpreting for her, I say her exact words, "My mother says she knows that I babysit. She knows the people who live near here."

Grindaddy first looks at her, then at me. He says, "I'm leavin'." He walks out the door without so much as an apology, past my father, who is still stunned by what he has seen. Daddy says nothing.

I go to the bathroom to wipe my wound in alcohol, which makes it sting painfully. Mama follows me and beckons me to come to her room. She explains, *"In North Carolina, when Ruth, my sister, (go) with man, my father catch her. Beat her same he beat you. He beat Ruth hard. He not know Ruth pregnant, now lose baby. He wrong for beat Ruth. Ruth mad at him, she cut very long hair, more pretty (than) my hair, and it never grow again."*

Mama, forlorn, sits on the edge of the bed. I tell her I am tired, turn around, and go to bed myself.

LIFE can be hard.

19

Theodore Beamon

"This is the happiest day in my whole life."

The year is 1959, and I am sixteen years old. I am volunteering to help Mrs. Hughes in the library to check books in and out. It is near the end of May, and I am a tenth-grade sophomore, having learned my way around Spingarn High School (It is named for Joel Elias Spingarn, founder and president of the National Association for the Advancement of Colored People.) The school is a maze with pompous seniors who feel superior to everyone and everything, but in this instance, they are happy to be on their way to graduation. I'm in awe of their elite status. The only reason I am friends with several seniors is that my cousin is Clarence Gillis, Aunt Babe's son, a senior who is considered by the ladies to be so good-looking he is a 'dream.' The girls actually swoon when I mention his name. I convince them that he is indeed my blood relative, a fact that initially creates doubt in their minds since we don't look alike.

Claiming Clarence as my cousin is not enough to gain favor with other students, however. An opportunity comes when I discover Clarence has been nominated for King of Spingarn's Coronation Ball. I take on the job as his unofficial manager by promoting him as a brilliant, handsome senior who would lend esteem to the title of King. I fulfill my unsanctioned obligation for his election by putting posters and flyers everywhere and telling everyone who will listen that there is not a boy in the school equal to Clarence Gillis in any way.

And of course, Clarence wins.

Buoyed by this success, I begin volunteering for extracurricular activities: Thespians, Latin Club, library activities. Today I am volunteering to work in the library, and as I stand behind the counter, sorting the books according to classification, a fellow walks up to me.

"You're Maxine, aren't you?"

"Yes. What's your name?"

"Theodore Beamon," he replies, appearing ever so serious.

"May I help you?" I ask, while looking to see if he has books to return. He is neatly dressed, wearing a light-blue plaid shirt with a gray jacket over it. His hair is cut short, emphasizing his long eyelashes, keen nose, and very full lips; his complexion is medium tan, slightly browner than I, and he is about six feet tall.

"Are you going to the prom with anyone?" he asks.

"No," I say very slowly, wondering why in the world he is asking me that.

"Well, will you go with me?" he inquires with a hint of uncertainty in his voice.

I stare at him, muttering skeptically, "You want to take me to the prom?"

"Yes," his eyes are fixed on mine.

"Okay," I say with absolutely no hesitation or reservation.

He gives me a slow ear-to-ear grin.

"I'll pick you up at eight on prom night, in three weeks. Oh, call me Teddy."

He pivots around, and as he heads out the library door, I yell, "Wait, you need my address."

"Oh, yeah," he says as he reaches in his jacket for a pencil and walks back to the counter to grab a piece of scrap paper.

"My address is 5901 Clay Street, N.E. It's near Seat Pleasant, Maryland."

He looks at me, smiles as he writes the address down, and then zooms out the door.

I wonder what made him ask me; I don't even know him. I hadn't seen him around school at all. Maybe he has seen me somewhere and I never noticed him. After all, I am so bogged down in my studies, I hardly notice or mingle with anyone. Anyway, for some reason, I instinctively trust him; he is so forthright; his clothes are neat; and he has nice eyes and nice teeth.

Delirious with glee, I rush home to tell Mama I am going to the prom with a senior, even though I am just in the tenth grade, and I will need a new dress. She gives me an apprehensive look. I know she has been working from sunup to sundown lately, making clothes for men and women customers at home. She was already exhausted, but needed the money to pay bills.

"We buy dress . . . Sears . . . credit. I not make dress, no time."

I sigh when she mentions Sears, because it was only four or five months ago when we tried to purchase several items of clothing from them. I recall it vividly. With apprehension, Mama and I put the items on the counter and tell the saleslady we are purchasing these items on credit, when she asks for our account number. Mama, as usual, fumbles through her purse, pulling out scraps of paper, mostly odds and ends, when she finally locates her wallet. After that, she begins rifling through it, pulling out a Social Security card, the appointment card for her next clinic appointment, more notes and cards, postal stamps, and at last, she finds the card bearing the Sears account number neatly printed in her handwriting. She hands it to the saleslady, who then picks up the black wall telephone attached to a white pole beside the counter and calls a mysterious authority. After keeping us in suspense for at least ten minutes, she turns to us and shakes her head, "I'm so sorry. But your purchase is declined."

I tell Mama what the sales clerk is saying, and Mama nods her head. I expect her to have a dejected expression, because I really feel as though the world is against us; but instead, she politely turns around and walks away.

"I understand . . . not pay last month," she says.

NOW ONCE AGAIN, we are at Sears, at the mercy of the mysterious authority that dictates whether we can purchase an item or not. I enter the store with Mama, having some trepidation. Will we get credit approval? My Lord, this is the only way for me to buy a dress for the prom, so I ask Mama a second time if she has made a payment on the Sears bill.

"Finish," she replies, almost annoyed that I would ask such a silly question.

I have serious reservations, but I'm willing to take the risk and go through the agonizing wait for approval again, anything to go to this prom and boast to Clarence that I am going to his prom, too.

First, I must pick out a dress, and I select one made of sheer nylon with fuchsia roses imprinted in the material and a rose-colored taut taffeta slip attached underneath. After trying it on, I parade before Mama, to have her further inspect the dress and ultimately approve it. She eyes it, first peering at the collar and sleeves, then taking the hem of the dress and turning it inside out to examine it, and also checking the inner seam, making certain that the seam allowance is a generous one and not a thin loose stitch. She asks me to turn around to see how the dress looks from the rear. I twirl about. Mama slowly smiles favorably.

One more thing to do, and that's to see if Sears and Roebuck is inclined to give us credit once more. After putting the prized dress on the counter, a young blonde clerk greets us;

she is not the same person who denied us credit before. We explain that we would like this dress on credit; she rings up the accounting office, recites our name and account number to an enigmatic voice, and waits a tedious long two minutes before beginning to write on a paper the approval of the credit office. I am so elated, I become delirious with excitement as I tell Mama, "We have dress. Credit office says okay." Mama gives me a knowing smile.

I'm posing in a dress purchased on credit from Sears; I'd later wear it on Graduation Day.

On the night of the prom, I decide that the black pumps I had originally intended to wear don't look as glamorous as Mama's plastic see-through strapped heels. The glitzy open-toe and open-heel shoes, together with the matching purse, are made of colorless plastic and are a perfect match with my new dress. I ask Mama if I can wear her shoes; she nods her head to show that I can wear them, but cautions that they are a little too big for me, easily one size larger than my feet. I don't care. I'll wear them anyway, even though my feet will slide toward the front of the shoe, making it apparent that these shoes are too big for me.

Teddy is to pick me up in a car at eight. And I am ready at 7:30. When eight o'clock arrives and I don't see him, I think he is a bit tardy because he is taking extra time to purchase me a corsage. Soon it is 8:30, and there is no Teddy. I go outside, stand on the porch, looking to see if there is a car that may have lost its way. I feel mist in the air and realize it is beginning to drizzle. I go back inside and see the clock ticking to nine, and by then, I feel jilted. No Teddy. Now I realize that going to the prom was too good to be true. Dusk has turned into a dark night, and I conclude he is not coming. I rush to the bedroom, thrust myself on the bed, and sob that my whole world has come to an end. It is around 9:15 when Mama comes in the room, calls out my name, and says there is a boy at the door. I can't believe it. All is not lost after all.

It is Teddy at the door, in a splendid tuxedo and cummerbund, looking very apologetic. He explains that the driver of the car had to pick up two other couples. Since I live so far out, I was the last to be picked up.

"Oh, that's okay," I say, trying to sound as if I was not concerned at all. We get in the car. Teddy has to sit in the front seat by the door with two other passengers, and I have to squeeze in the back seat with two other girls. The driver whisks us away to Spingarn High School gymnasium, where Teddy and I join the other students dancing to a live band. I see Clarence dancing with his lovely date; he waltzes over to us, and he leans over to greet me warmly. I've never been so happy.

"Hiya, Maxine. Hiya, Teddy. Havin' a good time?"

Teddy grins, "Yep. Things are going great."

Theodore "Teddy" Beamon invited me to Spingarn's prom on June 17, 1959. I was fifteen; Teddy was eighteen.

I look at my cousin, and I want to tell him that this is the happiest day in my whole life. I'll tell him another time.

TEDDY STARTS coming to our house so regularly that he becomes a fixture. When he visits, he either gestures to Mama and Daddy or he grabs a plain sheet of paper to write them, printing in uniform, clear-cut letters, so much so that they are impressed with him right away. Daddy writes down jokes for him, and Teddy truly enjoys them; Teddy chats and laughs with Shirley and Barbara; and he does anything around the house that Mama wants him to do, like hanging up curtains or cutting the grass. He is fast becoming a pseudo son to my parents and a brother to my sisters and me. Even though I'm known as "Teddy's girlfriend," I am really more a sister, in that our relationship is chaste, innocent, and naïve. But at the same time, we are companions, going to an occasional party together or to a special event like the Ice Capades, which is Teddy's favorite show.

Only once did our relationship begin to waver from being buddies to a relationship that could have become a torrid affair. That's when Teddy comes to my house after we went to an Ice Capades show in nearby Maryland. We are standing on the front porch in the dark and chatting about how the show was exhilarating with dancers gliding to music on the ice.

"It was so beautiful Teddy, I've never seen anything like it. This is the first time I've seen a show like this," I say admiringly.

Teddy grins, pleased to introduce me to something so novel and different, and especially delighted that he secured tickets for front row seats where we practically sat on the ice rink itself. I could feel cool air coming from the ice. The dancers had appeared from nowhere, whirling and twirling, pirouetting in circles. They were a sight to behold. I could feel tiny flakes of ice splash in my face when they slid and spun around; I heard the skidding sound of ice skates when the dancers put on their brakes. I was mesmerized when the young men swung ladies high in the air, so high that they seemed to be flying. I couldn't believe my eyes, watching this paradise on ice. When it all comes to an end, I am left breathless.

As we chat on the porch about this fabulous event, the night becomes pitch black. Teddy grabs me, kissing me passionately. I kiss him back and we are locked in a sizzling embrace when I feel a flash of electricity charge through my body. I am sure he feels it, too. Suddenly, the porch light comes on—a spotlight beaming in our faces. We abruptly stop in our tracks, as Mama yanks the door open and glares at the both of us. I hang my head in shame and Teddy abruptly says good night, dashing down the front steps. I know right then and there'll be no "loving stuff" around this house.

Teddy disappears for two days, but he reappears to tutor me in geometry. While Teddy is a whiz at mathematics, I consider anything with numbers to be a source of annoyance, and if left up to me, I would eliminate all mathematics courses, especially algebra, geometry, and calculus from the school's required courses for students. Whenever I struggle with geometry, Teddy volunteers to help me, saying, "Here, Maxine, here's a step-by-step way to solve this problem." He actually writes down each step, beginning with a number one beside the first instruction, then a number two beside the next step, and so on. I can't believe how easy he makes it.

When I grow tired of all his tutoring, I make frivolous comments to distract Teddy, hoping it will discourage him from trying to teach me to solve any more geometry problems. I say, "Look at my fingers, Teddy, they look like Oscar Mayer Sausage Links."

He laughs; his shoulders shake; undeterred, he says "Maxine, I love your hands; I love your fingers; I love your fingernails. Now let's finish this homework."

"I'm tired. I don't feel like finishing this stuff," I proclaim.

"Okay, when are you going to finish it, then?"

"I'll get up early tomorrow, maybe at three in the morning and work on it. That's if I can get up. I've been oversleeping lately and just can't get up the way I used to," I sigh.

"Well, I'll set my alarm and call you at three. Then you can have your homework ready for school. Okay?" He looks at me with such good intentions that I can't tell him I really want to sleep through the night.

I reply, "Yeah, that will help me a lot."

And sure enough, Teddy calls at exactly three in the morning.

It's a Saturday afternoon when Teddy comes by to take me to the movies. As we're walking to the bus stop, he mentions his two older sisters, one of whom is married to a swell guy. A little later Teddy talks about his younger brother, Benjamin, who has a flock of young girls after him. Teddy hopes these activities don't interfere with Benjamin's schoolwork.

"My mother is worried about him," Teddy says. "She's also worried about me."

"She's worried about you?"

"Yeah, she's always worried about me. I guess it's because I have paralysis in my arm."

"You have paralysis in your arm?" I repeat his phrase, actually surprised that I had not noticed any loss of movement in either arm.

"Yeah, it got twisted when I was being born. Look, I can't bring my arm up behind my neck or even brush my hair. See."

Showing me, he swings his left arm upward, but it bends slightly toward his head, instead of going straight upward. He continues, "That's why I lift weights, so I can grow strength in it."

"Oh, I see." I am unimpressed and don't see why it is a big deal to his mother. So I change the subject: "Didn't you say your brother-in-law will let you use his car sometime?"

Teddy seems surprised by my question, obviously having forgotten that he had mentioned it to me several weeks ago. He replies, "I'll ask him next week."

The following week on a Friday afternoon, Teddy calls and announces excitedly that his sister's husband will lend him his car and that we can actually drive to the movies, instead of taking the bus. There is such exhilaration in his voice that I tell him I must share the good news with my mother. I hang up and look for Mama.

Mama is in the kitchen, and I sign to her, *"Teddy says he borrow sister's husband car. We go movies tomorrow."*

"Good. Now you tell Teddy cut his lips," she says quite seriously. She slides her thumbnail along her bottom lip.

I make a frown, "I not understand. You want him cut his lips?" I copy her sign for "cut lips."

"Yes, he has big lips. Need go doctor. Doctor will cut his lips," she declares.

"You want Teddy have operation his lips?" I fingerspell the word "operation" to make certain I understand what she is saying, that she wants him to have surgery.

"Yes," she exclaims, her head bobbing up and down emphatically.

I am so amazed at her request that I think it is absurd. I decide it is so ludicrous and that I will never say anything like that to Teddy. My God! That would hurt his feelings something awful.

It is sometime later when I understand why Mama wanted Teddy to have this procedure done. It is because she is such a perfectionist when it comes to a person's appearance. Her perfection is reflected in her observations of what one should do to look better. For example, she makes comments such as these: *"Your father hair gray, need dye hair black"*; or *"Your father need shave beard, make look old"*; or *"Maxine, push front teeth together every day, must close gap"*; or *"Maxine, squeeze nose, make nose thin."* Her criticisms are endless. I just ignore them. And of course, I pay no attention to Mama's frequent comments about Teddy's lips. It is one of the few times when I refuse outright to do something she asks of me.

MANY MONTHS PASS, and I begin to see Teddy as a bit controlling, and on many occasions, we argue. Initially, I don't tell him that I feel frustrated and unhappy about our relationship. But he starts to guess that "something is up" when I begin going to dances at the Marine and Army bases on Saturday nights.

It began when Mary Arnold came to our house and asked me to accompany her to a dance at Fort Belvoir, Virginia. Mary Arnold is a hard of hearing albino, about twenty-eight years old, who wears eyeglasses with extremely thick lenses. She talks as clearly as any hearing person, but she also signs to deaf persons very smoothly and skillfully. She is quite overweight, with huge hips that bounce uncontrollably when she walks. She has a round face; blonde, nearly white hair; and a white moustache over her very full, naturally pink lips.

At first I am reluctant to go with her, but she pleads with me, telling me she needs me to interpret for her. That's nonsense, because even if she can't hear some words, she has superb lipreading skills, which makes it almost impossible for anyone to detect that she has even a minuscule hearing loss. I tell her

I am too young to go dancing on the base, but she insists, saying that no one will check my age. She flatters me by telling me how pretty I am and that no one will guess I am only a teenager. I succumb to her smooth talk and agree to meet her on Pennsylvania Avenue at eight the following Saturday night. Mama walks in the living room and sees Mary Arnold, who casually explains to her that she is asking me to go with her to a dance. Of course, she will look after me and make certain that I am safe. Mama says that is fine, but we are both to be careful.

That Saturday I dress in a white nylon blouse and navy blue skirt with white pumps. My hair is straightened into a curly pageboy hairdo. (I had washed and straightened my hair with a hot comb the night before. Then using curlers cut from a brown paper bag, I rolled up my hair to eventually create the curly hairdo.) Finally, I am dressed and catch the usual X2 bus to downtown and walk over to Pennsylvania Avenue, where I see Mary Arnold waiting for me on a corner, standing next to the parked bus marked "Fort Belvoir."

She is so delighted to see me, acknowledging that she was afraid I would not show up. I smile and let her know that I'm looking forward to the fun we will have. When we board the bus, I see another dozen or so ladies, wearing lovely attire for dancing, and I notice that all the ladies are much older than I am. The bus departs; in about twenty minutes, we arrive on the base to go to a building where there is a dimly lit large room with light oak wax flooring. Metal folding chairs hug the walls. In the center of the room is a square area, about thirty feet by thirty feet, clearly designated for dancing. Soldiers enter the room one by one, some in uniform, some in civilian clothes.

The jukebox is playing popular tunes. I sit on one of the chairs by the wall, next to Mary Arnold. One by one soldiers enter the hall, beginning to form a crowd. The music from the jukebox stops playing and a live band appears from out of nowhere to begin playing popular tunes. At first, only two or three couples walk to the floor to dance. Then almost like magic, the floor has dozens and dozens of couples dancing to the swing and sway of music from the Glenn Miller era. A young fellow in a uniform asks me to dance, and I begin to have fun jitterbugging to the fast beat tunes. I notice Mary Arnold is sitting by herself looking a bit gloomy. I ask the fellow I am dancing with if he would do me a favor and dance with her, and he obliges. I dance every song the entire evening, and thereafter I ask each fellow I dance with to please dance with Mary Arnold. Most of the soldiers indulge my request.

Before we know it, it is midnight and the evening has come to an end. Mary tells me she has never had so much fun; she is certain that I am her good luck charm, and she hopes I will come back with her the next week. We all board the bus, laughing and chatting about the good time we had. When the bus arrives downtown, the center of Washington is practically a ghost town. I bid Mary Arnold good-bye and walk the few blocks to catch the bus back to Seat Pleasant. It is almost an hour before the bus arrives, making it well after two in the morning before I get to my designated stop. I am terrified to walk the poorly lit street, so I trot quickly down Sixtieth and over to Fifty-Ninth and Clay Streets. I continually look behind me, hearing squeaks and weird sounds, but no one is there. I run terrified to my house, holding a key in my trembling hand to unlock the door and hastily scoot inside, only to hear sleeping sounds, which lets me know that I've come home unnoticed. Next time, I say to myself, I'll bring enough money to catch a cab.

The following Monday, Teddy comes by and asks what I did that Saturday. I tell him about the dance and how much fun I had. He sighs and appears so low-spirited, I hardly know what to do. But that doesn't stop me from going to the dances. I notice that the more I go to the dances, the less he comes around.

That June, Teddy graduates from Spingarn, and in the fall, he becomes a student at the Howard University School of Architecture. Before we know it, we decide to break up. I am sad; he is sadder still.

Teddy has abruptly stopped coming to visit us, and it is lonely without Teddy to make us laugh. So I decide, after a month's absence from the dances at the army base, that I will swing and sway on the dance floor again. That Friday evening, I dress in a pleasant two-piece outfit I had taken out of the layaway from Lerner's Department Store and ride the Fort Belvoir bus to the base. Oddly, I am the only passenger on the bus that evening, not realizing that this is a holiday weekend. When I arrive to a practically empty dance hall, I stroll to a round table with chairs and sit to listen to the jukebox music, expecting the room will fill up with soldiers soon and we'll be dancing to a live band.

Rock-n-roll music floats from the jukebox. But no live band appears. No soldiers either. I see a white fellow wearing civilian clothes passing by the table and ask him why there isn't a band tonight. He replies that it's a special holiday weekend, and most of the soldiers have left the base. "Hey, do you want something to drink?" he asks.

"Sure, I'd like a Coke," I answer.

The soldier walks across the empty dance floor to the bar located in the far end of the room and brings back two tall glasses of Coca-Cola.

"Mind if I join you? My name's Jack."

"My name's Maxine. You can sit here," I quickly reach over to remove my jacket and purse from the chair next to me. When he sits down, he begins to talk about his family in San Diego, California. "It's too far for me to travel there and be back by Monday," he says. "Besides, my kid brother isn't home from his school where he stays. He's deaf. He's sixteen years old. I sure hope to see him this summer."

I couldn't believe my ears. "My mother and father are deaf, too."

"*R-e-a-l-l-y*. Do you know sign language?"

"Sure I do."

"I don't," he says apologetically. He sighs. "Mostly my brother knows what I am saying to him anyhow. I just point to things and he understands me. Well, sometimes he doesn't, but it doesn't matter, we figure it out sooner or later." He pauses a moment, "So you know sign language, huh? Do you sign to your folks all the time?"

"All the time," I reply.

"No kiddin'." Suddenly, the music has stopped and he looks across the room, "Come on, let's pick out some songs from the jukebox and dance."

We walk over to a huge jukebox and push buttons next to songs with a lively beat: Chuck Berry's "Johnny B. Goode"; Little Richard's "Good Golly Miss Molly"; and Bobby Freeman's "Do You Want to Dance?" There are so many songs, I become delirious with glee especially since money was not required to put in the machine. I pick more: "Splish Splash"; "Chantilly Lace"; "Rockin Robin"; "Willie and the Hand Jive"; "What'd I Say"; "Handyman"; "Charlie Brown."

Then Jack begins to push buttons, too. He selects even more lively tunes and we dance the jitterbug to one song after another. We whirl and twirl as we spin our bodies, dancing

to the beat, laughing uncontrollably because it's sheer fun
to rock-n-roll. Finally the jukebox music stops; I notice the
army bus in front of the building is waiting to take me back to
downtown D.C. Jack walks with me as I am leaving the dance
hall. I suddenly have a idea.

"Would you like to come to our deaf church in D.C.?"
I ask.

"Come to church?"

"Yeah, it's a deaf church. Aw, come on. You'll meet a lot of nice
people there. It's Shiloh Baptist Church at Ninth and P Streets,
N.W. Meet me there at 6:45. Church starts at 7:00 sharp."

"O.K. I'll meet you there." He is smiling broadly.

Jack is there, promptly at 6:45, wearing his uniform and
standing on the corner waiting for me. I take his arm as we
enter the church, which no longer have deaf services in a dingy
little room, but rather in a large, brightly lit room renovated
with oak pews. I am amazed at the changes since it's been a year
or two since I was last here. Several deaf people come over to
greet me, telling me they hadn't seen me in a long time. I introduce each person to Jack, who appears a little nervous and shy.

"Let's sit here," I suggest, pointing to a pew in the center
of the room. I decide not to sing in sign language this time,
but instead concentrate on the hearing minister's sermon being
interpreted by a person I don't know.

After service, Jack walks me to the bus stop as I will head
home while he goes back to the base.

"Thank you Maxine. I really had a nice time." He stands
with me until the bus comes, and says, "I'll call you, O.K.?"

"O.K."

The next day, I must stop by Daddy's shoe shop to ask for
$5.00. As soon as I enter the shop, I can see his face is filled
with fury. I sniff the air, but it is clear he has not been drinking.

"You shame me," he signs wildly.

"What? What you say?" I don't know why he is so angry.

"You bring white man church."

Astonished, I say, "He nice man. He soldier. I bring him see deaf church."

"Awful. Awful. Why you bring white man?"

"His brother deaf. I think maybe man enjoy church."

"No. No. You stop. Never see white man again. Understand. Never."

"Alright," I sigh because it is useless to try to talk to him. My father's stance is rigid, undoubtedly molded by the flames of racial hatred often thrust upon young people who dared to socialize across the color line. He is mindful of the many laws, especially in the South, which prohibit interracial marriages and the punitive jail sentences inflicted on couples who defy the law to marry.

I rush out of the shop to catch the bus home and wonder how Daddy knows about the church service. After all, I was just there yesterday; then I realize I forgot to ask for the five dollars. "This aggravation is not worth it. No more white boys for me," I murmur to myself. Sadly, that's the end of that.

20

Let It Go

*"Now I understand how this godless creature terrified kids
in the neighborhood."*

It is the late winter of 1960, and I am seventeen years old. I am
at home, preparing for another school day. I sigh, telling myself
I must find the energy from somewhere to go to school one
more day. I am suffering from the winter blues, as I feel listless,
tired, and apathetic about everything. I have never ignored or
neglected my homework, but this time I can appreciate Rhett's
poignant comment to Scarlett O'Hara as he walks out the door
in *Gone with the Wind*: "Frankly, my dear, I don't give a damn."
That's how I feel about school, teachers, and even my own family. But somehow I stumble through the routine of putting on
clothes for school—a kelly green dress embossed with a black
print design. It has long sleeves, a Peter Pan collar, and pleats
around the waist. I don't wear it often, but it is the only thing
I have that isn't dirty. Thank goodness, I have white socks that
are clean, which I put on with a pair of loafers. I say good-bye
to Mama, and instead of running to catch the X2 bus, I lei-
surely walk to the bus stop, not caring if I make the bus or not.
Unfortunately, the bus is on time, and it zips me to school,
even though I am not in a hurry.

I go to my homeroom, then go to my first-period class,
German II. Dr. Woods, my German teacher, returns our test
papers, commenting that there weren't many high grades this
time. He glares at me as he hands me my test with the letter

"C" boldly written in red at the top of the test paper. I wonder if he can see from my facial expression that I just don't care.

Right then a female voice booms over the loudspeaker that there will be a special assembly meeting the next period in the auditorium. All students are required to attend. The bell rings, and Dr. Woods dismisses us, telling us to return to our homerooms and that our teacher will take us to the auditorium. I make my way back to the homeroom and join the other students as we form a line to go to the special assembly. I enter the auditorium from a side door and walk along the passageway behind the last row of seats, and see that the auditorium is already filled with people.

Just then I spot the backs of my parents' heads; they're sitting three rows from where I am standing. I can't believe my eyes—what are they doing here? I see from the back of the room that my father has on his taupe suit and Mama has on

In 1959, while attending Spingarn High School, I was an ardent student of both Latin and German languages. Mr. Woods, who loved to tell tales of his experiences in Germany, is standing by the blackboard. I am seated in the second row, farthest right.

one of her fancy hats. The principal of the school, Dr. Williams, walks out on the stage to announce, "This is a special program to induct new members into the National Honor Society. The new members are unaware they are to be inducted today. When the honoree's name is called, please come forward to the stage and sit in these chairs."

One by one, each student's name is called, and there is thunderous applause as that person goes to the stage and sits in a chair. I notice that most of the girls are dressed in lavish outfits with stockings and high-heel shoes. There is one boy in a navy blue suit. Then my name is called, and I am amazed and a little astonished as I walk up to the stage. I am the only one wearing bobby socks and loafers. I don't know whether to be excited or embarrassed. The principal asks us to stand and raise our hands to take an oath to honor the rules and regulations of the National Honor Society. We all agree to do so. The audience goes wild with applause, and we are now dismissed to join our families. I rush off the stage and greet my parents, who are so deliriously happy they radiate exuberance, so much so that I am dazzled by their joyfulness. I ask Mama how she knew about the program. She quickly hands me a letter from the office of Spingarn High School informing her that Maxine Childress has met the qualifications to be in the National Honor Society. It gives the date when the program for inducting honorees will take place, and the letter goes on to say they are requesting each parent withhold this information, as they would like to surprise each student. That's when it becomes obvious to me that Mama and Daddy were the only parents to oblige their request, since I am the only one who is not dressed up. It feels so great to see my parents full of pride that for once, I'm not critical of my clothes or myself.

Daddy pulls out his Kodak Brownie camera and begins taking pictures of me on this honorable day; I haven't seen him or Mama this full of joy and happiness in a long time.

IT IS NOW springtime. On this particular day, it is eight in the morning, and I am wearily getting dressed for school after spending most of the night tackling homework and studying for this morning's test. I am relieved that I had the foresight yesterday to pick out the clothes to wear for today, because now I am rushing to wash up, fix my hair, and put on my clothes

Photo of me taken months after I was inducted in the Honor Society.

to leave by 8:30, all this in only a half hour. I am determined to wake up earlier from this day forward, a resolution I make frequently, but rarely keep. Glancing at the clock, I think maybe I can leave at 8:32, since that allows me eight minutes to catch the bus at 8:40 and be at school by 9:00.

"Oh goodness, it's already 8:34. I've really got to run," I say to myself. As I rush out the front door onto the porch, fresh balmy air and brilliant sunshine unexpectedly greet me, instantly lifting my spirits and reinforcing my confidence that all will be well today. "Things can't go badly on a morning this beautiful," I say out loud, as it is a classic spring day for Washington, D.C. I recall the newspaper announcing when the cherry blossoms are expected to bloom at their peak. I smell the faint sweet aroma of flowers in the air, and wonder if the smell of cherry blossoms can travel from the National Mall all the way to the suburbs.

I dash down Fifty-Ninth Street, realizing that I have less than two or three minutes to make that left turn onto Fifty-Eighth and Dix Streets. Annoyed, the thought comes to me once again that it is my misfortune that I live in between Sixtieth and Fifty-Eighth and must run from Fifty-Ninth to Fifty-Eighth to catch the bus. So I sprint down Fifty-Ninth, out of breath, and as I round the corner, I look back to see if the bus is coming, and sigh in relief that it is yet to head my way. I begin to slow down to a trot.

In the distance, there is a man already at the bus stop, and as I approach him, I see his lurid grinning face. His pants are undone and the zipper is open and his penis is hanging out. A flash of blood rushes to my face. Shocked, I do an abrupt about face and run as fast as I can toward Sixtieth Street, never turning to see if he is following me. My heart is pounding as if it is going to leap from my chest. Breathless, I am near collapsing as the bus appears at the Sixtieth Street stop, and I dash aboard, panting. My hand is shaking so badly that I have trouble putting the bus token in the meter. I finally do so, taking the nearest seat behind the driver. The bus approaches Fifty-Eighth Street, where I had originally seen the man, but he is gone. Finally, the bus arrives at school, but I can't stop the feeling of panic.

Should I tell anyone about this? What should I do? Maybe I should go to Daddy's shop and tell him, but then I remember I have a crucial national exam this afternoon, and I need to focus on that. What to do? What to do? I finally decide that I need advice, and I seek out Mrs. Hughes, the Spingarn High School librarian who has been so kind to me. I approach Mrs. Hughes in the library and tell her I have to talk about something extremely important; she takes me to her office in the rear of the library.

I carefully and slowly describe the events this morning, together with the horrible story of my father's arrest seven years earlier for the very same crime. As I describe the fellow, I can see how my father could have been mistaken for him. He is not as light-complexioned as my Daddy, more my complexion, a light honey brown. I couldn't tell if his hair was kinky or straight, because it is cut short, but I do remember it as salt and pepper, similar to Daddy's hair.

I tell all of this to Mrs. Hughes, wondering aloud whether I should tell the police. She sighs, and walks to the window; the sun streams through it, exposing the dust on the sill. While staring out, with her back toward me, she says slowly, "Well, Maxine, if you go to the police, you know they will dig up the entire court case about your father. Also, because you are his daughter and you have witnessed this horrible man, you must anticipate that they may not believe you. This could be quite a mess. Yes, quite a mess. Maybe you should let it go. If this sick man is exposing himself as you say, someone will report it. Maybe you should leave this alone."

Leaving her office, I wonder whether, if I do as Mrs. Hughes suggests, I will be abandoning my responsibility to tell someone in authority. Shouldn't I do something about what has happened to me? After all, the man has to be caught. Now I fully understand how this godless creature has terrified others in the neighborhood, especially the girl whose mother brought charges against my father. I become fearful of what Daddy might do. If I tell him, will he explode? Will he go into a tirade? Will we have to go through the whole court thing again? I walk out of the library burdened by the weight of my troubles, very weary, and afraid of making the wrong decision.

By the end of the day, I feel relief, because I have finally decided to take Mrs. Hughes's advice to leave this all behind me. I make up my mind to never tell anyone, not even Mama or Daddy. That's when I remember Aunt Arnell's firm words of advice from so long ago, "Let it go. Let it go." And so I do.

IT IS NOW JUNE 1961. Excitement is in the air because I am graduating from Spingarn High School. A photographer has come to take pictures in the school gymnasium of the graduating honor society students. He positions six students around me on a bleacher.

Several days later when Daddy comes home from work, he calls for me as soon as he walks in the living room. He has two shopping bags, one in each hand, and a folded newspaper tucked under his arm; he puts both bags on the floor. I glimpse at the shopping bags, see a watermelon in one bag, look over at the other bag full of steamed crabs giving off a potent odor.

Daddy says, *"I buy watermelon. You love watermelon. Watermelon for you."* He looks so proud of himself, so very pleased, as he picks up the bags by their handles, brings them to the kitchen, puts them on the table, and still keeps the newspaper under his arm. Then he takes the paper, hands it to me, watching intently for my reaction. I unfold the paper and there is the very same photograph of us students on the front page of the *Afro-American* newspaper. The caption below the photo says, "Honor Society Students graduate from Springarn High School,"and list each of our names. I am flabbergasted, but vanity prevails, because I admit that I look lovely, and yes, I just love the photo since I dominate the picture by being in the center!

I look at Daddy who signs, *"Deaf people bring paper (to) my work. Shoeshine man bring paper. Sam bring paper. Many people bring paper about you."* He is beaming with delight as he pulls the watermelon out of the bag, and immediately slices it in four quarters. He looks at me, then at the watermelon on the table and says, *"You eat watermelon, You eat middle,"* pointing to the heart of the melon, knowing it is the part I love and usually grab before anyone else beats me to it. (I had heard that black people are associated with eating lots of watermelon. If white people believe such a silly notion, then they are stupid because watermelon is just too delicious— more delicious than chocolate candy!)

"Where Mama?" Daddy asks.

"I don't know. Mama, Shirley, and Barbara not home."

"Alright. You eat watermelon. I eat crabs all myself," he signs cheerfully and with such glee, it is astonishing to see him so happy.

As he stands beside the table, getting ready to sit down, he gives me a warm look. That's when I see for the first time his expression of love mingled with pride and awe. Not only are his eyes full of sweet admiration, but he also seems to have grown taller, his shoulders straighter, and his face brighter. I wonder why he is showing me such affection. Maybe he feels he has credibility with his friends because my photo is on the front page of the *Afro-American*; maybe he feels extraordinary pride—a feeling he hasn't known for a while—restoring his belief in me; just maybe this is his only way of showing how much he cares.

I don't remember Daddy ever saying *"I love you"* to me, but on this particular day there is not a hint of our quarrelsome past. It is clear he has let go of the harmful bickering, fussing, fighting that happened in yesteryear.

No. Daddy doesn't have to say I love you because he just does.

Epilogue

Our home was the epicenter of comings and goings of African American deaf folk, and it was not unusual for unannounced visits from deaf out-of-towners, local residents, and even deaf students. In fact, the first African American student to graduate from Gallaudet University was Andrew Foster who was close friends with our family. His brother, Edward Foster, rented a room from us and his photo is in the background on page 154. Andrew delighted in eating dinner with us, accompanying us to Shiloh Baptist Church, and particularly, teaching me technical signs he learned from his studies.

It was during these many social gatherings that my mother would boast about everything: her experience as a teacher of the deaf; her most recently sewn outfits; her travels here and there; her religion as a Jehovah's Witness and so on and so on. But there was one particular topic that was the source of her incredible pride: her children and grandchildren's accomplishments. Once I told her, "Mama, you brag too much about us. People fall asleep because you talk long time, bored, while you brag and brag."

She responded with such innocence: *"That all right. If people asleep (while) I talk, I touch them on shoulder, wake them up, then I talk more."*

My mother's longtime aspiration to significantly improve her English language skills was steadily realized over the years,

Thomasina Childress at age ninety-five. This is an award-winning photo taken by Nikki Brown, Thomasina's granddaughter.

principally because of her intense study of the Holy Bible as a Jehovah's Witness for more than fifty-five years.[1] My dear sweet Mama died on March 31, 2011, at the age of ninety-six.

My dear father died suddenly and unexpectedly in 1968. He was fifty-five years old. We are not sure of the exact cause of death, whether from a heart attack or stroke, or from a blow to the head from behind, while walking to a bus stop after work. It continues to be a mystery to me. He, in his own way, was a

---

1. The Jehovah's Witnesses began to provide local interpreters for the deaf sometime in the 1970s, and they began holding national conventions for deaf people in the 1980s.

loving, caring man with a marvelous sense of humor. My only regret concerning him is that he lived in a time when alcoholic treatment programs and facilities that focus on the needs of deaf people did not exist, as they do today. The fact that there is, even today, a high incidence of alcoholism among Native Americans certainly contributed to Daddy's problems.

I guess I would say to Mama and Daddy if they were here, "Well done!" So in their honor, I will list the accomplishments of their children and grandchildren. And by the way, Mama, I'll continue your legacy of boasting about your children, grandchildren, and great-grandchildren!

My sister, Shirley Childress Saxton, is a prominent international interpreter for the deaf in the group Sweet Honey in the Rock. She has traveled all over the world, from Japan to Turkey, from the United Kingdom to Sweden, bringing entertainment and joy to both hearing and deaf audiences alike. Her younger son, Deon Johnson, is an accomplished accountant; her older son, Reginald, is a highly distinguished noncommissioned officer in the U.S. Marines.

My youngest sister, Barbara, now Dr. Khaula Murtadha, is Vice Chancellor at Indiana University–Purdue University Indianapolis (IUPUI). She is nationally recognized for her expertise in education, and she successfully mentored the first deaf PhD candidate at IUPUI a few years ago. She has seven children: Abdul-Khaliq Murtadha, actor; Adam Murtadha, entrepreneur; Abdul-Haleem Young, computer scientist; Yusuf Young, educator/teacher; Ahmed Young, attorney; Usama Young, professional football player in the National Football League; and Thomasina, an honors student at IUPUI.

All three of us are working in one way or another with individuals in the deaf community. In 1972, when I was an interpreter at the University of Massachusetts, I, along with other citizens living in New England, founded the Connecticut River Valley Interpreters for the Deaf, with the goal of providing services to those who needed these services in Massachusetts, Connecticut, New Hampshire, Vermont, Rhode Island, and Maine. The organization is probably defunct now, but I do remember we were among the first to develop a code of rules and regulations establishing a Massachusetts registry of interpreters for the deaf. I was one of the first to be evaluated by a panel of expert interpreters and am relieved to tell you I passed their rigid examination. Currently, I am a retired professor and local politician in Rochester, New York, where I initiated the requirement that all city council meetings be interpreted for deaf citizens. Unfortunately, since very few deaf and hard of hearing persons attended the meetings, we now make interpreters available when someone requests them. I married James Brown, an attorney, and we have three children: Dr. Scot Brown, a professor; Dr. Nikki Brown, a professor and photographer; and Kimberly Brown, an actress and social activist.

If you are wondering what happened to the important people in my life, read the following accounts, as I list names chronologically according to the year of their death:

In the year 1954, Ruth Brown Wagoner, my mother's sister, died in childbirth at the age of thirty-seven. The baby was a breech birth; Ruth died from loss of blood. I was eleven years old. Her sudden death was a huge shock to her family, and it was many decades before they were able to recover from her loss. When Ruth died, she left her husband Orether.

Theodore (Teddy) Beamon, the fellow who took me to my first prom and who was a beloved friend to my family, died in October 1965 in the Vietnam War. His name is permanently engraved on the Vietnam Veterans Memorial Wall in Washington, D.C. The last time I saw Teddy was in 1964 before he joined the army. He will always be remembered for the unconditional love he gave to his family, to my family and my relatives, and, of course, to me.

My grandmother, Martha Nero Brown, stayed in the same house described in this book until her death in the spring of 1968, at around age seventy-three. She was an extraordinary woman: accomplished singer and pianist; talented dressmaker; and a most able farmer. Back in 1961 she wrote to my mother when I turned eighteen, asking for me to come and visit her in Rockwell, North Carolina. That's when my loving grandmother gave me $218—all in one-dollar bills—to use toward my college education.

Clarence Brown, my grandfather ("Grindaddy"), died in 1978, after battling prostate cancer and becoming too exhausted to continue fighting any longer. He will always be remembered as a family man who hopped a freight train to Washington, D.C. to find work and eventually send for three of his four daughters. He was known for his extraordinary mason/bricklaying skills, which he used to build many houses, including our home and his own Baptist church. A self-educated man, he owned a cleaners; fish market; and a construction company where he had an phenomenal capacity to calibrate the exact number of bricks and mortar necessary to build a house with his own hands. He, like my grandmother, loved music, especially music from marching bands like John Phillip Sousa.

My aunt Della Brown Handy, my mother's sister, stayed in Concord, North Carolina, all her life, and died in 2007 at the age of ninety. My mother, age ninety-two, and I were able to visit her in a nursing home a few months before Della died in Concord. What a magnificent reunion! They had not seen each other for at least a decade. (This trip was a minor miracle, since my mother was born before the state of South Carolina issued birth certificates, and we had to wade through many layers of bureaucracy to obtain a photo identification card for my mother to fly there.)

Mary Magdalene Minor, my favorite "Aunt Babe," the sister closest to my mother and my mother's best friend, died in a car accident in Tucson, Arizona, in December 2010, at the age of ninety. She lived in Washington, D.C., for many years before she moved to Tucson for health reasons; she lived there for sixteen years. Mary had a powerful story of her own to tell: her violent trials and tribulations from living with an alcoholic husband, Joe Gillis; her subsequent divorce, her challenges in trying to raise four boys amidst poverty; and her eventual marriage to Willie Minor for more than twenty years. When she was struggling to raise her sons, she was extremely fortunate to secure secretarial work in a Washington, D.C., government bureau. The highlights of her life were her four sons, her faith as a Jehovah's Witness for sixty years, and her longtime career as a civil servant.

**Creativity, courage, and wisdom are the legacy
my forebears left to me.**

— Maxine Childress Brown

Thomasina Childress making the ASL sign for "I love you."